the Secrets of St. Anthony's Creek

and other MOVING MOUNTAIN WATERS

a Flyfisher's Manual

written and illustrated
by
Mike Rahtz

Frank Amato
PORTLAND

to
MORKER

WHEREVER
YOU ARE

ADVOCATION

THOSE WHO WOULD DEBASE, AND IN SO DOING ATTEMPT TO REDUCE TO THEIR LEVEL THE PEERLESS SPORT OF FLY FISHING, ARE MOST FOND OF MAKING TWO OBSERVATIONS. FIRST THAT "FLYFISHERS TEND TOWARD SNOBBISHNESS" AND THEN THAT "THEY DON'T CATCH MUCH". TO THE UNINITIATED THE FIRST OBSERVATION IS LIKELY ALLURING. IT IS THE SECOND THAT IS TOO OFTEN AN EFFECTIVE DETERRENT. TRULY IT DOESN'T SEEM THAT A WAD OF FEATHERS AND FUR, ATTACHED TO A HOOK BY THREAD AND FINGERNAIL POLISH, IS LIKELY TO LURE EVEN THE MOST PRIMITIVE ICHTHYOID.

NOW, AFTER OVER A SCORE OF YEARS IN THE PURSUIT OF FISH WITH FLIES, I AM PREPARED TO STATE UNRESERVEDLY THAT WHILE THERE IS SOME TRUTH IN THE FIRST OBSERVATION, THE SECOND IS A PESTILENT PREVARICATION. NO DOUBT PROMULGATED AND PERPETUATED BY THE PERNICIOUS PROPRIETORS OF WORM FARMS AND AUTO-WRECKING YARDS. I WILL FURTHER STATE THAT ANY FLYFISHER WILLING TO USE WHATEVER CONCOCTION OF HACKLES AND HAIR IS CALLED FOR BY CIRCUMSTANCES, AND TO USE THEM IN WAYS NOT TOO INCONSISTENT WITH THOSE PRESCRIBED IN THIS MANUAL, CAN EXPECT TO OUTFISH HIS OR HER FELLOWS IN THE BAIT-N-BRAC BUNCH.

I URGE YOU TO READ THIS MANUAL STRAIGHT THROUGH THE FIRST TIME, DO NOT MARK THE MARGINS OR UNDERLINE OR HIGHLIGHT OR WHATEVER IS YOUR WAY. THIS IS NOT A FORMIDABLE UNDERTAKING FOR THE TEXT INCLUDES OVER 250 ILLUSTRATIONS.
ONCE YOU HAVE THE OVERVIEW THAT THIS WILL GIVE, GO BACK AND TREAT IT LIKE A TEXT BOOK. YOU WILL LEARN MORE, AND MORE QUICKLY, IN THIS WAY.
(PAY HEED, YOUR HUMBLE SCRIBE HAS A MASTERS IN PSYCHOLOGY.)

THROUGHOUT THIS MANUAL YOU WILL FIND THAT THE TECHNICAL ACCURACY OF ILLUSTRATIONS HAS BEEN COMPROMISED BECAUSE THE AUTHOR IS AN UNREPENTANT CARTOONIST. EVEN SO, THE REPRESENTATIONS YOU'LL FIND HEREIN ARE MUCH MORE ACCURATE THAN IN MOST CARTOONS.

© 2010 by Mike Ratz

All inquiries should be addressed to:
Frank Amato Publications, Inc.
P.O. Box 82112
Portland, Oregon 97282
www.amatobooks.com
(503) 653-8108

SB ISBN-13: 978-1-57188-466-4   SB UPC: 0-66066-00306-8

Printed in Singapore

1 3 5 7 9 10 8 6 4 2

TABLE OF CONTENTS

UTFITTING

IS THE BUSYNESS OF SPENDING MORE THAN YOU DARE ADMIT TO YOUR SPOUSE TO PURCHASE THE GEAR NECESSARY TO CONVINCE YOURSELF THAT YOU'RE SINCERE ABOUT TAKING UP FLY FISHING.

THE **ROD** SHOULD BEND RATHER LIKE THAT SHOWN ABOVE, PROGRESSIVELY TOWARD THE TIP. TOO MUCH BEND IN THE MIDDLE WILL TAKE THE SNAP OUT OF YOUR CAST. THE PREFERRED CONSTRUCTION MATERIALS ARE EITHER GRAPHITE OR SPLIT BAMBOO (YOU CAN PROBABLY BUY TEN GOOD GRAPHITE RODS FOR THE PRICE OF ONE SPLIT BAMBOO). ROD LENGTH SHOULD NOT BE LESS THAN 8 1/2 FEET, 9 FEET WILL SERVE YOU BETTER. THE RECOMMENDED LINE WEIGHT IS PRINTED ON THE ROD DOWN NEAR THE HANDLE, WE'LL GET TO THIS AFTER A BRIEF DISSERTATION ON REELS.

REELS ARE EITHER OF THE __AUTOMATIC__ OR THE __SINGLE ACTION__ PERSUASION.

THE __AUTOMATIC__ HAS A SPRING WHICH IS WOUND UP AS YOU PULL OUT LINE. WHEN YOU PUSH A BUTTON OR PULL A LEVER (EACH REEL HAS IT'S OWN WAY) THE SPRING UNLOADS PULLING THE LINE BACK IN. FELLER UP ON SWAUGER CREEK WAS VERY FOND OF HIS AUTOMATIC, THOUGH WHEN ASKED IF HAVING TO TAKE IT APART TO GET THE SAND OUT DIDN'T SOMETIMES RUIN HIS DAY HE SAID "NO PROBLEM, I ALWAYS CARRY A SINGLE ACTION FOR BACKUP".

THE __SINGLE ACTION__ IS SIMPLER, MORE DEPENDABLE, AFFORDS BETTER CONTROL, IS MORE FUN AND—MORE EXPENSIVE. MOST SINGLE ACTIONS CAN BE EASILY CONVERTED FOR LEFT HANDERS. THEY ARE THE CHOICE OF THE GREAT MAJORITY OF FLY FISHERS.
THE REEL SHOULD BE DESIGNED TO HOLD ABOUT 100 YARDS (OR MORE) OF BACKING. THIS IS A LINE OF ABOUT 20 POUND TEST THAT IS TIED TO THE SPOOL OF THE REEL AND WOUND ON BEFORE THE FLY LINE (SEE THE CHAPTER ON RIGGING).

BACKING SERVES TWO FUNCTIONS: FIRST IF A FISH MANAGES TO PULL OUT ALL YOUR FLY LINE THE BACKING WILL KEEP YOU CONNECTED, NEXT IT INCREASES THE DIAMETER OF THE BASE BELOW THE FLY LINE SO THAT EACH TURN OF THE REEL BRINGS IN MORE LINE.

AND THEN THERE IS THE MATTER OF CHANGING SPOOLS, WHICH YOU CAN ONLY DO WITH A SINGLE ACTION. THE SPOOL IS THE CENTER OF THE REEL AROUND WHICH YOU WIND THE LINE. IT IS REMOVABLE, AND THEREFORE EXCHANGEABLE.
INDULGE ME IN THIS—YOU'RE FISHING A STREAM USING FLOATING LINE (THIS IS ALMOST ALWAYS THE CORRECT LINE ON MOVING WATER, EVEN WHEN YOU'RE USING SUBSURFACE FLIES) WHEN YOU COME UPON A BEAVER POND. YOU STAY WELL BACK FROM THE POND AND OBSERVE, AND YOU SEE NO SIGN OF SURFACE FEEDING. YOU KNOW THERE ARE MORE AND BIGGER FISH IN THERE BUT YOU HAVE TO GO DEEP TO GET THEM. THE BEST ANSWER IS TO CHANGE FROM FLOATING TO SINKING LINE AND IF YOU HAVE AN EXTRA SPOOL IN ONE OF THOSE VEST POCKETS WHICH FITS YOUR REEL AND IS ALREADY RIGGED (BACKING, SINKING FLY LINE, LEADER AND TIPPET) THEN YOU CAN MAKE THE CHANGE IN A MINUTE.

FLY LINE

FLY LINE: WHEN I WAS QUITE YOUNG MY FAVORITE TV SHOW WAS "WATCH MR. WIZARD" (A SCIENCE SHOW FOR KIDS) AND I RECALL THE TIME MR. WIZARD DEMONSTRATED THAT YOU CAN FLOAT STEEL ON WATER. HE VERY CAREFULLY PLACED A RAZOR BLADE ON THE SURFACE FILM, FLAT SIDE DOWN, AND IT FLOATED. WHEN HE MOVED IT JUST BELOW THE SURFACE FILM IT WENT DOWN AS STEEL SHOULD. WHEN YOU LAY YOUR FLY UPON THE WATER IT WILL "FLOAT" AS LONG AS THE HACKLE AND THE TAIL REMAIN ABOVE THE SURFACE FILM, WHEN THEY BREAK THROUGH THE FLY WILL GO DOWN. NOW THE PROBLEM IS, HOW DO YOU CAST SOMETHING SO LIGHT AND DELICATE THAT IT WILL HOLD ABOVE THE SURFACE FILM WHEN IT IS TOO LIGHT TO BE CAST? YOU DON'T, INSTEAD YOU USE A WEIGHTED LINE, YOU DON'T CAST THE FLY, INSTEAD YOU CAST THE LINE AND THE FLY FOLLOWS ALONG BEHIND. AS THE PROFICIENT ARCHER FLIES WITH HIS ARROW, YOU FLY WITH YOUR LINE.

KEEP YOUR MIND ON THE LINE

IT MAY HAVE OCCURRED TO YOU THAT IF THIS STUFF IS SO IMPORTANT THERE MUST BE SOME SORT OF COMPLICATION. UNFORTUNATELY THIS IS TRUE, ONE MAJOR MANUFACTURER OF FLY LINES BOASTS THAT THEY MAKE OVER 300 DIFFERENT TYPES! THE FOLLOWING DISCUSSION WILL BE RESTRICTED TO THE LINE TYPES MOST OFTEN USED IN THE MOUNTAINS.

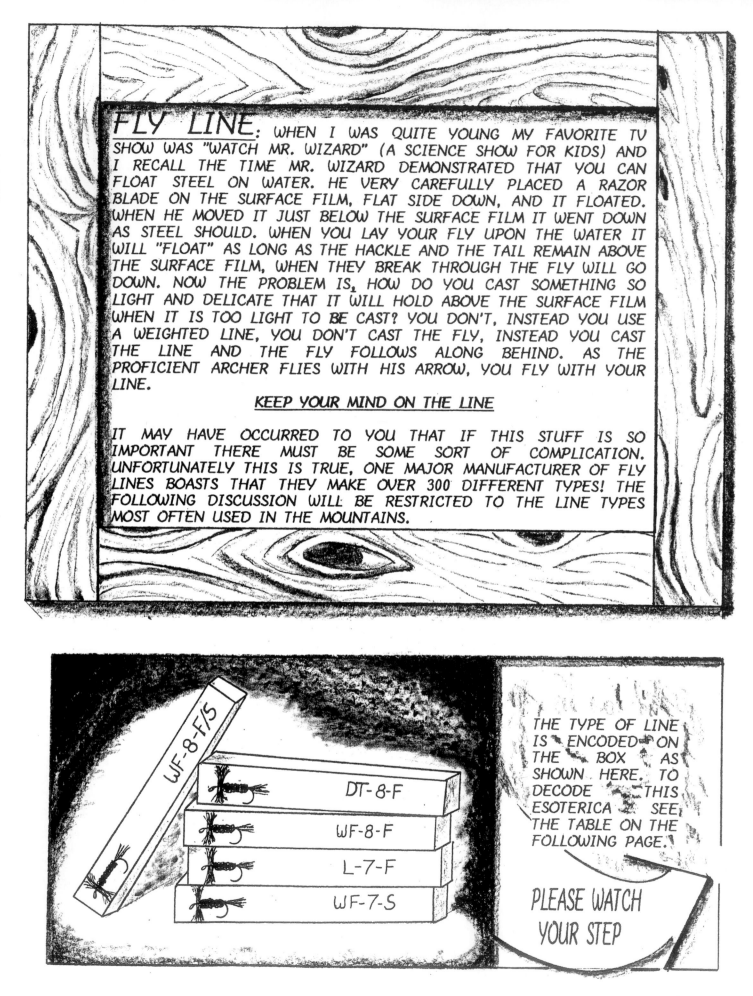

WF-8-F/S

DT-8-F

WF-8-F

L-7-F

WF-7-S

THE TYPE OF LINE IS ENCODED ON THE BOX AS SHOWN HERE. TO DECODE THIS ESOTERICA SEE THE TABLE ON THE FOLLOWING PAGE.

PLEASE WATCH YOUR STEP

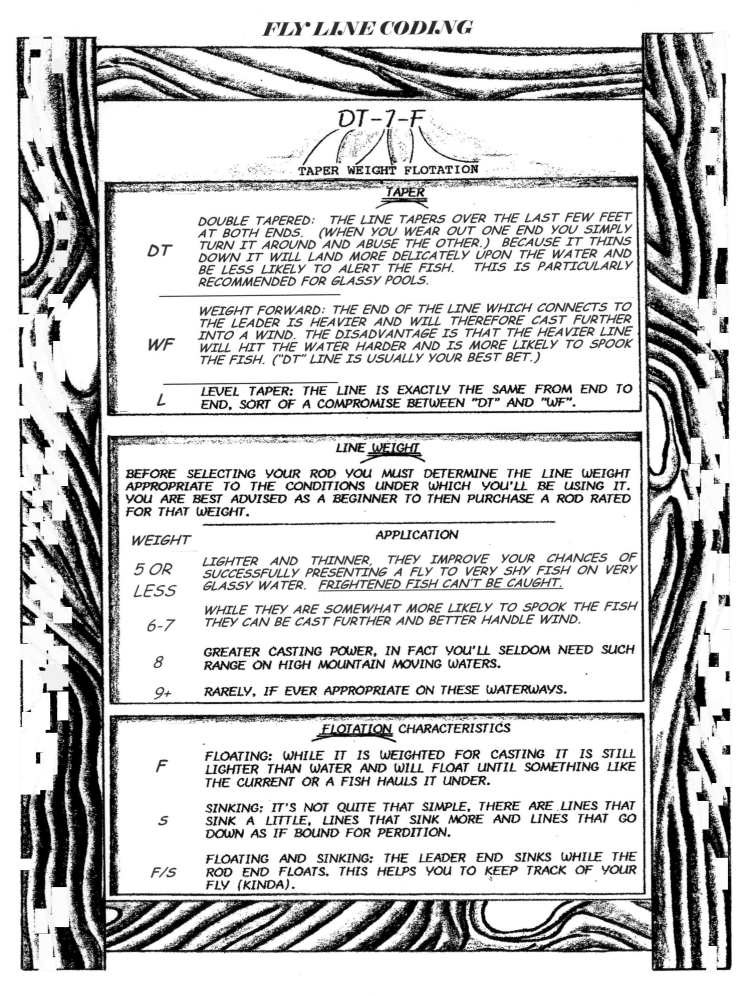

DT-7-F
TAPER WEIGHT FLOTATION

TAPER

DT   DOUBLE TAPERED: THE LINE TAPERS OVER THE LAST FEW FEET AT BOTH ENDS. (WHEN YOU WEAR OUT ONE END YOU SIMPLY TURN IT AROUND AND ABUSE THE OTHER.) BECAUSE IT THINS DOWN IT WILL LAND MORE DELICATELY UPON THE WATER AND BE LESS LIKELY TO ALERT THE FISH. THIS IS PARTICULARLY RECOMMENDED FOR GLASSY POOLS.

WF   WEIGHT FORWARD: THE END OF THE LINE WHICH CONNECTS TO THE LEADER IS HEAVIER AND WILL THEREFORE CAST FURTHER INTO A WIND. THE DISADVANTAGE IS THAT THE HEAVIER LINE WILL HIT THE WATER HARDER AND IS MORE LIKELY TO SPOOK THE FISH. ("DT" LINE IS USUALLY YOUR BEST BET.)

L   LEVEL TAPER: THE LINE IS EXACTLY THE SAME FROM END TO END, SORT OF A COMPROMISE BETWEEN "DT" AND "WF".

LINE WEIGHT

BEFORE SELECTING YOUR ROD YOU MUST DETERMINE THE LINE WEIGHT APPROPRIATE TO THE CONDITIONS UNDER WHICH YOU'LL BE USING IT. YOU ARE BEST ADVISED AS A BEGINNER TO THEN PURCHASE A ROD RATED FOR THAT WEIGHT.

WEIGHT	APPLICATION
5 OR LESS	LIGHTER AND THINNER, THEY IMPROVE YOUR CHANCES OF SUCCESSFULLY PRESENTING A FLY TO VERY SHY FISH ON VERY GLASSY WATER. <u>FRIGHTENED FISH CAN'T BE CAUGHT.</u>
6-7	WHILE THEY ARE SOMEWHAT MORE LIKELY TO SPOOK THE FISH THEY CAN BE CAST FURTHER AND BETTER HANDLE WIND.
8	GREATER CASTING POWER, IN FACT YOU'LL SELDOM NEED SUCH RANGE ON HIGH MOUNTAIN MOVING WATERS.
9+	RARELY, IF EVER APPROPRIATE ON THESE WATERWAYS.

FLOTATION CHARACTERISTICS

F   FLOATING: WHILE IT IS WEIGHTED FOR CASTING IT IS STILL LIGHTER THAN WATER AND WILL FLOAT UNTIL SOMETHING LIKE THE CURRENT OR A FISH HAULS IT UNDER.

S   SINKING: IT'S NOT QUITE THAT SIMPLE, THERE ARE LINES THAT SINK A LITTLE, LINES THAT SINK MORE AND LINES THAT GO DOWN AS IF BOUND FOR PERDITION.

F/S   FLOATING AND SINKING: THE LEADER END SINKS WHILE THE ROD END FLOATS. THIS HELPS YOU TO KEEP TRACK OF YOUR FLY (KINDA).

NEXT IN LINE THE **TAPERED LEADER:** YOUR FLY LINE IS RATHER THICK AND IS WEIGHTED SO THAT IT CAN BE CAST, BUT IF THE FLY WAS TIED TO THAT FEW FISH WOULD BE FOOLISH ENOUGH TO TAKE IT. IT IS NECESSARY TO TRANSFER THE CASTING POWER OF THE BULKY LINE TO SOMETHING SO LIGHT AND TRANSLUCENT THAT THE FISH WON'T DETECT IT (USUALLY). THIS IS THE FUNCTION OF THE TAPERED LEADER. IT IS OF TRANSLUCENT MONOFILAMENT, USUALLY AROUND .020 INCHES THICK AT THE BUTT AND TAPERS TO A THINNESS WHICH IS DESCRIBED BY IT'S "X" RATING. (PLEASE NOTE THE TABLE SO LABORIOUSLY ASSEMBLED FOR YOUR EDIFICATION.)

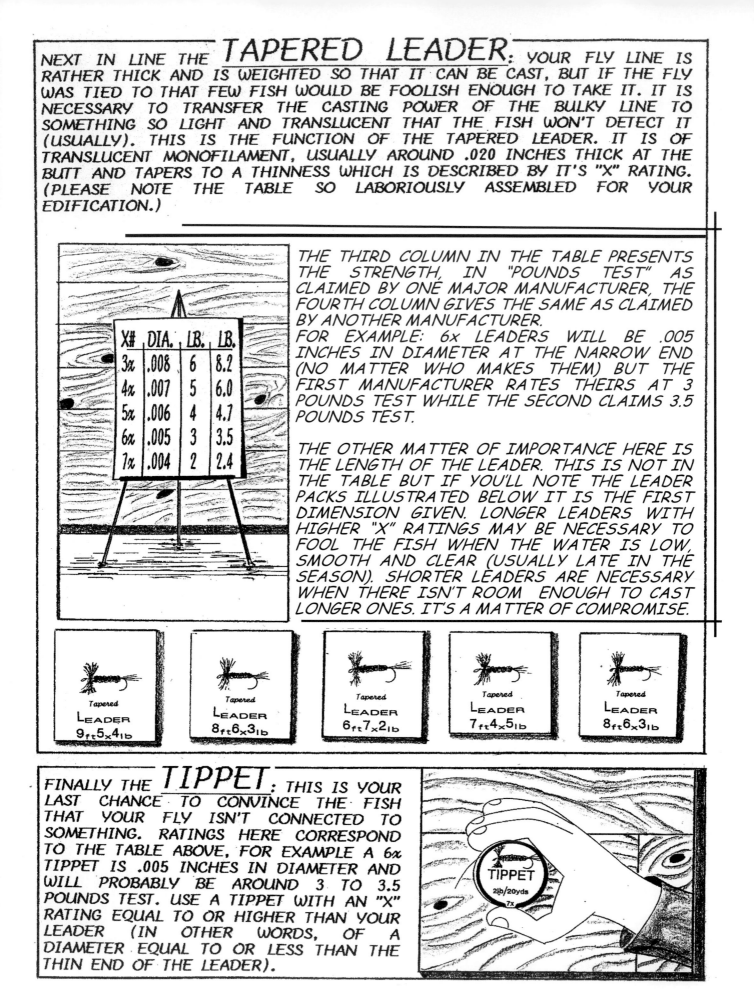

X#	DIA.	LB.	LB.
3x	.008	6	8.2
4x	.007	5	6.0
5x	.006	4	4.7
6x	.005	3	3.5
7x	.004	2	2.4

THE THIRD COLUMN IN THE TABLE PRESENTS THE STRENGTH, IN "POUNDS TEST" AS CLAIMED BY ONE MAJOR MANUFACTURER, THE FOURTH COLUMN GIVES THE SAME AS CLAIMED BY ANOTHER MANUFACTURER.

FOR EXAMPLE: 6x LEADERS WILL BE .005 INCHES IN DIAMETER AT THE NARROW END (NO MATTER WHO MAKES THEM) BUT THE FIRST MANUFACTURER RATES THEIRS AT 3 POUNDS TEST WHILE THE SECOND CLAIMS 3.5 POUNDS TEST.

THE OTHER MATTER OF IMPORTANCE HERE IS THE LENGTH OF THE LEADER. THIS IS NOT IN THE TABLE BUT IF YOU'LL NOTE THE LEADER PACKS ILLUSTRATED BELOW IT IS THE FIRST DIMENSION GIVEN. LONGER LEADERS WITH HIGHER "X" RATINGS MAY BE NECESSARY TO FOOL THE FISH WHEN THE WATER IS LOW, SMOOTH AND CLEAR (USUALLY LATE IN THE SEASON). SHORTER LEADERS ARE NECESSARY WHEN THERE ISN'T ROOM ENOUGH TO CAST LONGER ONES. IT'S A MATTER OF COMPROMISE.

Tapered LEADER 9ft 5x 4lb

Tapered LEADER 8ft 6x 3lb

Tapered LEADER 6ft 7x 2lb

Tapered LEADER 7ft 4x 5lb

Tapered LEADER 8ft 6x 3lb

FINALLY THE **TIPPET:** THIS IS YOUR LAST CHANCE TO CONVINCE THE FISH THAT YOUR FLY ISN'T CONNECTED TO SOMETHING. RATINGS HERE CORRESPOND TO THE TABLE ABOVE, FOR EXAMPLE A 6x TIPPET IS .005 INCHES IN DIAMETER AND WILL PROBABLY BE AROUND 3 TO 3.5 POUNDS TEST. USE A TIPPET WITH AN "X" RATING EQUAL TO OR HIGHER THAN YOUR LEADER (IN OTHER WORDS, OF A DIAMETER EQUAL TO OR LESS THAN THE THIN END OF THE LEADER).

TIPPET 2lb/20yds 7x

THE <u>UNIFORM</u>: WHILE IT'S COOLER IN THE MOUNTAINS THE AIR IS THINNER AND THE SUN CUTS THROUGH. A <u>HAT WITH A VISOR</u> IS STRONGLY RECOMMENDED.

THE GLARE OFF THE WATER ALSO GIVES TROUBLES, A PAIR OF <u>POLARIZED GLASSES</u> SHOULD GIVE ADEQUATE PROTECTION.

THEN THERE'S THE <u>VEST</u> TO STOW ALL YOUR GEAR. THERE ARE SO MANY POCKETS THAT EVEN THE POCKETS HAVE POCKETS. TROUBLE IS TRYING TO REMEMBER INTO WHICH POCKET YOU PUT WHATEVER YOU'RE LOOKING FOR. LOTS OF "D" RINGS TO HANG THINGS FROM TOO.

THE <u>CREEL</u> IS PRIMARILY OF HISTORICAL INTEREST. IT IS A NOSTALGIC ALTERNATIVE TO THE VEST. ONE MANUFACTURER ADVERTISES IT AS ". . . A DECORATIVE ADDITION TO YOUR LOG CABIN." GOOD IDEA.

THE WATER UP HERE RUNS COLD AND CLEAR, AND *COLD*, AND WATER DRAWS OFF BODY HEAT MUCH MORE QUICKLY THAN AIR AT THE SAME TEMPERATURE. IT'S AMAZING WHAT A VERY THIN LAYER OF WATER PROOF MATERIAL CAN DO TO ENHANCE COMFORT. TO THIS END THE FOLLOWING HAVE BEEN CREATED:

FIRST THE <u>HIP BOOTS</u>, WHILE LESS CUMBERSOME THEY'RE NOT USEFUL IN WATER MUCH MORE THAN KNEE DEEP. GET YOUR FLY CAUGHT IN A BUSH ACROSS THE POOL AND THE BOOTS MAY BE SWAMPED BEFORE YOU REACH IT.

THEN THE <u>WADERS</u>, THEY GET YOU IN DEEPER BUT FEEL CONFINING AND ON A HOT DAY CAN HAVE THE EFFECT OF A STEAM BATH. IF YOU USE THESE PLEASE WEAR A BELT. YOU CAN FALL INTO KNEE DEEP WATER AND FIND THAT THE CURRENT FILLS THEM LIKE A PARACHUTE, DRAGGING YOU HELPLESSLY DOWN STREAM. A PROPERLY AFFIXED BELT WILL SAVE YOU FROM SUCH EMBARRASSMENT, INDEED, PERHAPS SAVE YOUR LIFE!

<u>STOCKING WADERS</u> AFFORD A MORE COMFORTABLE FIT, MANY ARE MADE OF A "BREATHABLE" (SIC) MATERIAL SO THAT PERSPIRATION CAN EVAPORATE AND SOME ARE LINED FOR ADDED WARMTH. YOU MUST PROVIDE YOUR OWN BOOTS, THOUGH THERE ARE ALSO MODELS WITH PERMANENTLY ATTACHED BOOTS.

TRACTION:

IF YOU WERE TO POLL FLY-FISHERS YOU WOULD MOST LIKELY DISCOVER THAT THE THING THEY FIND MOST ANNOYING IN THE PRACTICE OF THIS SPORT IS SLIPPERY ROCKS. ANY ROCK BENEATH THE SURFACE WILL SOON BECOME COATED WITH ALGAE. IT'S NECESSARY, IT'S THE BOTTOM OF THE FISH'S FOOD CHAIN, BUT IT'S A (EXPLETIVE DELETED) PAIN IN THE NECK WHEN YOU'RE WADING. THERE IS NO CURE FOR THE PROBLEM BUT THERE ARE A FEW AMELIORATIVES. ONE IS FELT SOLES, YOU CAN BUY BOOTS THAT COME SO EQUIPPED OR BUY A KIT WITH TWO SOLES AND A GLUE THAT YOU'LL NEVER GET OFF YOUR FINGERS. THEN THERE ARE CLEATS, SOME WADERS COME EQUIPPED WITH THEM. YOU CAN ALSO GET "SANDALS", THEY GO ON OVER THE FEET OF YOUR WADERS AND HAVE A FELT OR CLEATED SOLE, I SAW SOME RECENTLY THAT LOOKED LIKE TIRE CHAINS.

A BIT MORE ON THE FLAT ROCK, DON'T YOU THINK?

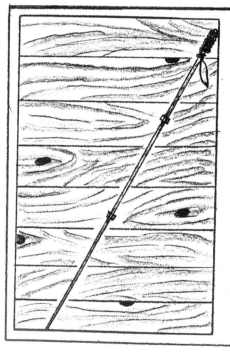

A ## WADING STAFF IS QUITE HANDY WHEN THE WATERWAY BECOMES WIDER AND DEEPER AND THE CURRENT GATHERS MOMENTUM. YOU MIGHT FIND AN OLD DEAD BRANCH BY THE RIVERSIDE BUT YOU CAN HARDLY COUNT ON IT. ON THE OTHER HAND YOU CAN BUY SUCH THINGS THAT EITHER FOLD OR TELESCOPE DOWN AND HANG FROM YOUR BELT SO THEY'RE NOT SO MUCH IN THE WAY WHEN NOT IN USE. I USE A LEG FROM A STURDY OLD CAMERA TRIPOD I FOUND IN A THRIFT STORE. EXTENDED IT'S 48 INCHES LONG, COLLAPSED IT'S 19. JUST ADD A STRAP TO GO ROUND YOUR WRIST WHEN IN USE AND TO HANG IT FROM YOUR BELT WHEN NOT, AND A HAND GRIP. COST ME ABOUT TWO DOLLARS AND I STILL HAVE THE OTHER TWO LEGS.

A ## LANDING NET WILL USUALLY MAKE CAPTURING THE PREY EASIER FOR YOU AND CONSIDERABLY INCREASE THE PROBABILITY THAT THE FISH WILL SURVIVE IF YOU CHOOSE TO RELEASE IT. THE NET'S RELATIVELY GREATER LENGTH WILL ACCOMMODATE THE FISH IF YOU USE IT PROPERLY (TO BE COVERED IN A LATER SECTION), WHILE THE LESSER WIDTH MAKES IT SIMPLER TO DRAG THROUGH HEAVY BRUSH. BESIDES, A FLY-FISHER WITHOUT A NET ALWAYS LOOKS LIKE HE FORGOT SOMETHING.

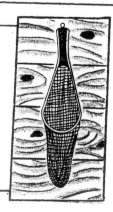

YOU MUST HAVE SOME WAY TO **REMAIN CONNECTED TO THE NET**. THERE ARE A NUMBER OF CONTRIVANCES THAT SUIT THIS PURPOSE, THE SIMPLEST IS AN ELASTIC CORD YOU LOOP THROUGH THE "D" RING ON THE BACK OF YOUR VEST (LOCATED BETWEEN THE SHOULDER BLADES), THEN CONNECT THE HOOK AT ITS END TO THE SCREW EYE ON YOUR NET HANDLE.

OR THERE IS WHAT IS CALLED A "RETRIEVER", IT HAS A CLIP ON THE BACK WHICH YOU ATTACH TO THAT VEST "D" RING, THEN AFFIX THE NET TO ITS HOOK. INSIDE THE THING THERE'S A CORD WOUND AROUND A SPRING LOADED SPOOL, WHEN YOU GRASP THE NET AND PULL IT OUT THE SPRING WINDS TIGHT, WHEN YOU RELEASE THE NET THE SPRING UNLOADS PULLING IT BACK TO ITS RESTING POSITION.
YOU WILL ALSO FIND A NUMBER OF QUICK RELEASE CLIPS ON THE MARKET.

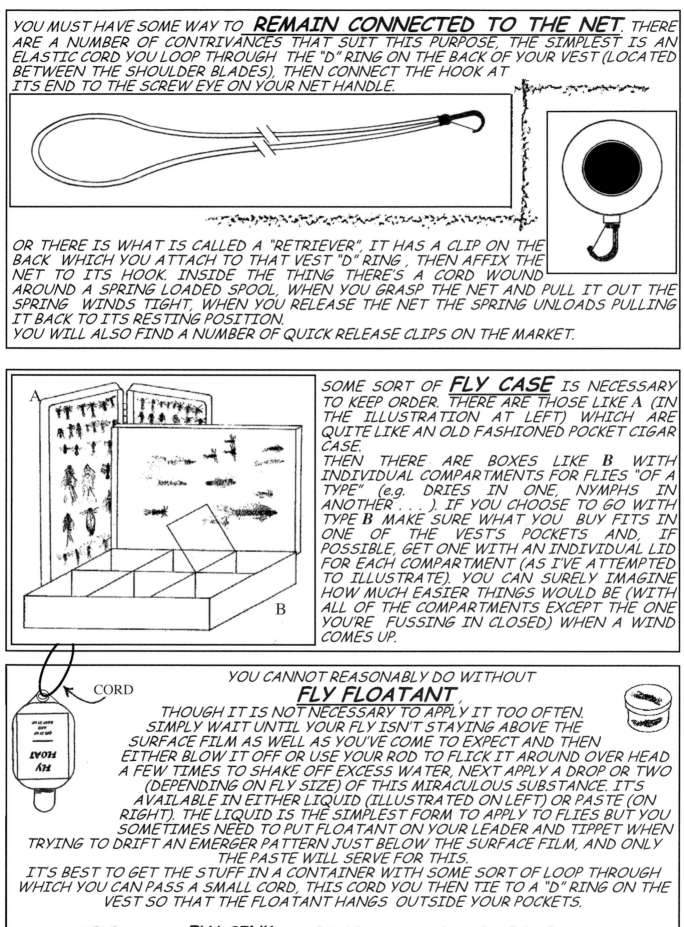

A

B

SOME SORT OF **FLY CASE** IS NECESSARY TO KEEP ORDER. THERE ARE THOSE LIKE **A** (IN THE ILLUSTRATION AT LEFT) WHICH ARE QUITE LIKE AN OLD FASHIONED POCKET CIGAR CASE.
THEN THERE ARE BOXES LIKE **B** WITH INDIVIDUAL COMPARTMENTS FOR FLIES "OF A TYPE" (e.g. DRIES IN ONE, NYMPHS IN ANOTHER . . .). IF YOU CHOOSE TO GO WITH TYPE **B** MAKE SURE WHAT YOU BUY FITS IN ONE OF THE VEST'S POCKETS AND, IF POSSIBLE, GET ONE WITH AN INDIVIDUAL LID FOR EACH COMPARTMENT (AS I'VE ATTEMPTED TO ILLUSTRATE). YOU CAN SURELY IMAGINE HOW MUCH EASIER THINGS WOULD BE (WITH ALL OF THE COMPARTMENTS EXCEPT THE ONE YOU'RE FUSSING IN CLOSED) WHEN A WIND COMES UP.

CORD

FLY FLOAT

YOU CANNOT REASONABLY DO WITHOUT
FLY FLOATANT,
THOUGH IT IS NOT NECESSARY TO APPLY IT TOO OFTEN.
SIMPLY WAIT UNTIL YOUR FLY ISN'T STAYING ABOVE THE
SURFACE FILM AS WELL AS YOU'VE COME TO EXPECT AND THEN
EITHER BLOW IT OFF OR USE YOUR ROD TO FLICK IT AROUND OVER HEAD
A FEW TIMES TO SHAKE OFF EXCESS WATER, NEXT APPLY A DROP OR TWO
(DEPENDING ON FLY SIZE) OF THIS MIRACULOUS SUBSTANCE. IT'S
AVAILABLE IN EITHER LIQUID (ILLUSTRATED ON LEFT) OR PASTE (ON
RIGHT). THE LIQUID IS THE SIMPLEST FORM TO APPLY TO FLIES BUT YOU
SOMETIMES NEED TO PUT FLOATANT ON YOUR LEADER AND TIPPET WHEN
TRYING TO DRIFT AN EMERGER PATTERN JUST BELOW THE SURFACE FILM, AND ONLY
THE PASTE WILL SERVE FOR THIS.
IT'S BEST TO GET THE STUFF IN A CONTAINER WITH SOME SORT OF LOOP THROUGH
WHICH YOU CAN PASS A SMALL CORD, THIS CORD YOU THEN TIE TO A "D" RING ON THE
VEST SO THAT THE FLOATANT HANGS OUTSIDE YOUR POCKETS.

THERE IS ALSO **FLY SINK** TO HELP GET YOUR SUBSURFACE FLIES DOWN.

A FEW **MISCELLANEOUS TOOLS**
ARE NECESSARY:

LIKE A SMALL PAIR OF NEEDLE NOSE PLIERS TO SMASH DOWN THE BARBS ON YOUR HOOKS (PLEASE) AND CRIMP ON SPLIT SHOTS. AND IF YOU DON'T SMASH THE BARBS YOU'LL LIKELY NEED THEM TO **RIP** THE HOOK FROM THE FISH'S MOUTH.

A SMALL PAIR OF SCISSORS IS USED TO TRIM THINGS SUCH AS "STRIKE INDICATORS". BOTH THE PLIERS AND SCISSORS SHOULD HAVE ROUNDED OR BLUNT ENDS SO THAT THEY DON'T PUNCH HOLES IN YOUR POCKETS.

TOENAIL CLIPPERS ARE USED TO CUT OFF FLIES YOU WANT TO CHANGE, TIPPETS THAT HAVE BECOME TOO SHORT, AND TO TRIM THE TAG END OF YOUR LINE AFTER YOU'VE TIED A NEW KNOT.

A SMALL SAFETY PIN IS USED TO CLEAN OUT THE JUNK WHICH SOMETIMES BLOCKS THE EYE OF YOUR HOOK. YOU CAN STORE THIS PINNED BENEATH A POCKET FLAP OR ATTACH IT, ALONG WITH THE TOENAIL CLIPPERS AND SCISSORS, TO A CORD WHICH IS HOOKED TO A "D" RING AND SLIP THE TOOLS IN A NEARBY POCKET. MAKES THEM EASIER TO FISH OUT WHEN NEEDED.

SPIKE

RING

A **STRINGER** IS (IN MY OPINION) THE BEST WAY TO BRING BACK THE ONES YOU KEEP. SOME FISHERS WHO USE CREELS CHOOSE TO STORE THEIR FISH THEREIN, THOSE WHO PREFER VESTS MAY USE THE VERY LARGE POCKET NORMALLY PROVIDED ON THE BACK OF THAT GARMENT, BUT EITHER WAY IS A MESSY BUSINESS.
TO USE THE STRINGER SIMPLY PASS THE SPIKE AT ITS ONE END IN AT THE FISH'S GILL, THEN ON UP THROUGH AND OUT THE MOUTH, NEXT PUT THE SPIKE THROUGH THE RING AT THE STRINGER'S OTHER END AND SLIP THE FISH DOWN TO THE BOTTOM. SUBSEQUENT FISH ARE ADDED BY PASSING THE SPIKE THROUGH THE GILL AND OUT THE MOUTH, WHEN THEY SLIDE DOWN TO THE FIRST FISH IT WILL HOLD THEM IN PLACE.

NOTE: THAT POCKET ON THE BACK OF THE VEST IS A GOOD PLACE TO CARRY A LIGHT WEIGHT RAIN JACKET WITH HOOD ON DAYS WHEN THUNDERSTORMS ARE A THREAT.

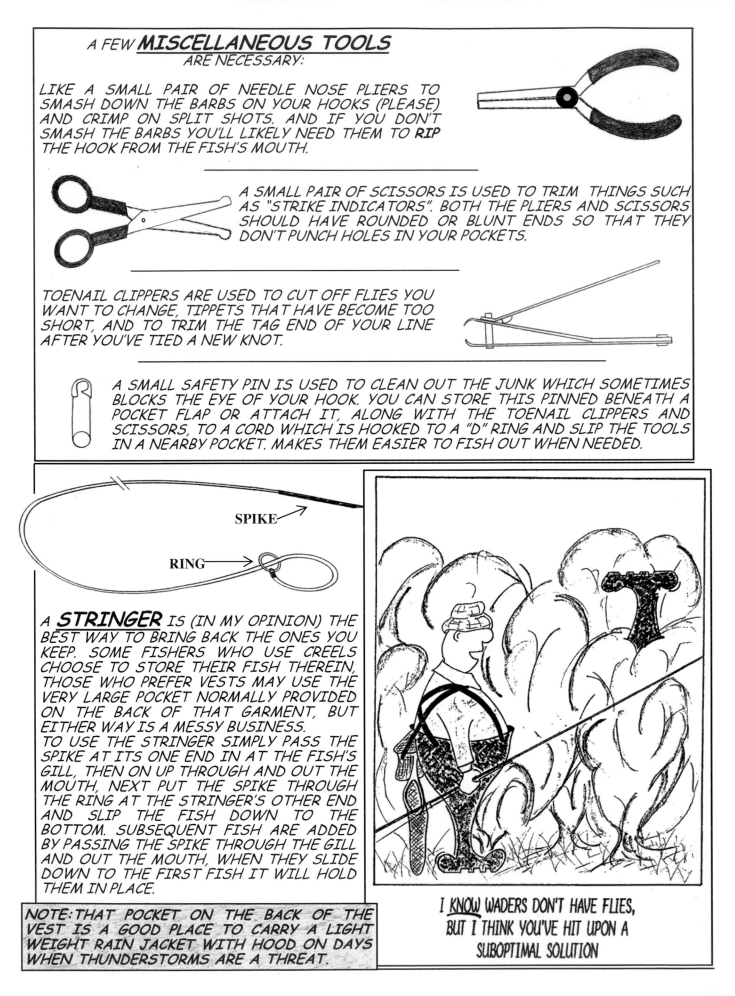

I <u>KNOW</u> WADERS DON'T HAVE FLIES, BUT I THINK YOU'VE HIT UPON A SUBOPTIMAL SOLUTION

A SHORT **POCKET KNIFE**
(BLADE AROUND 1 1/2 — 2 INCHES)
IS THE SIMPLEST AND SAFEST TOOL FOR
CLEANING (EVISCERATING) YOUR CATCH.
KEEP IT SHARP, DULL KNIVES ARE DANGEROUS.
('COURSE THEY SAY THAT ABOUT EMPTY GUNS TOO.)

A **FILLETING KNIFE**, WITH ITS LONG, NARROW AND THIN BLADE, IS WELL DESIGNED TO CREATE "BONELESS" FILLETS.

YOU SHOULD ALSO PURCHASE SOMETHING TO **CLEAN YOUR FLY LINE**. THERE ARE THOSE WHO DO IT EVERY DAY, AND THE REST OF US WHO ONLY DO IT UPON THE OCCASION OF THE FIRST FULL MOON FOLLOWING THE VERNAL EQUINOX. IT WOULD SEEM THAT A REASONABLE COMPROMISE WOULD BE TO CLEAN IT WHENEVER IT'S DIRTY ENOUGH AND IF IT'S NOT FLOATING AS WELL AS IT USE TO IT'S DIRTY ENOUGH.

A **PEN LIGHT** IS OF INESTIMABLE VALUE. YOU CAN CLICK IT ON AND HOLD IT BETWEEN YOUR TEETH SO THAT YOU HAVE BOTH HANDS FREE TO DO WHAT YOU MUST, LIKE TYING KNOTS IF YOU STAY UP LATE TO FISH A CADDIS FLY HATCH. IT WILL ALSO BE HANDY IN FINDING YOUR WAY BACK TO CAMP (TAKE IT OUT OF YOUR MOUTH NOW) AND THEN FINDING THE LANTERN AND MATCHES WHEN YOU GET THERE.

AN **AQUATIC THERMOMETER** IS SOMETIMES QUITE USEFUL IN FINDING FISH BECAUSE THEY ARE MOST ACTIVE WHEN WATER TEMPERATURES ARE IN THE UPPER FIFTIES OR LOWER SIXTIES.

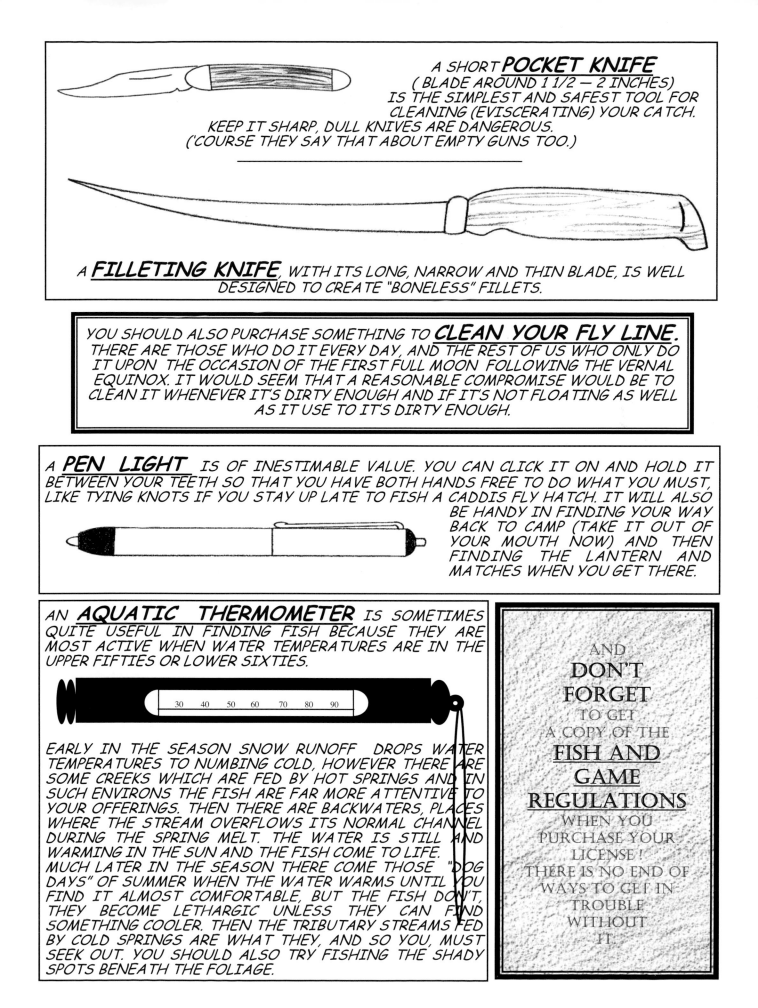

EARLY IN THE SEASON SNOW RUNOFF DROPS WATER TEMPERATURES TO NUMBING COLD, HOWEVER THERE ARE SOME CREEKS WHICH ARE FED BY HOT SPRINGS AND IN SUCH ENVIRONS THE FISH ARE FAR MORE ATTENTIVE TO YOUR OFFERINGS. THEN THERE ARE BACKWATERS, PLACES WHERE THE STREAM OVERFLOWS ITS NORMAL CHANNEL DURING THE SPRING MELT. THE WATER IS STILL AND WARMING IN THE SUN AND THE FISH COME TO LIFE. MUCH LATER IN THE SEASON THERE COME THOSE "DOG DAYS" OF SUMMER WHEN THE WATER WARMS UNTIL YOU FIND IT ALMOST COMFORTABLE, BUT THE FISH DON'T, THEY BECOME LETHARGIC UNLESS THEY CAN FIND SOMETHING COOLER. THEN THE TRIBUTARY STREAMS FED BY COLD SPRINGS ARE WHAT THEY, AND SO YOU, MUST SEEK OUT. YOU SHOULD ALSO TRY FISHING THE SHADY SPOTS BENEATH THE FOLIAGE.

AND
DON'T
FORGET
TO GET
A COPY OF THE
**FISH AND
GAME
REGULATIONS**
WHEN YOU
PURCHASE YOUR
LICENSE !
THERE IS NO END OF
WAYS TO GET IN
TROUBLE
WITHOUT
IT.

RIGGING

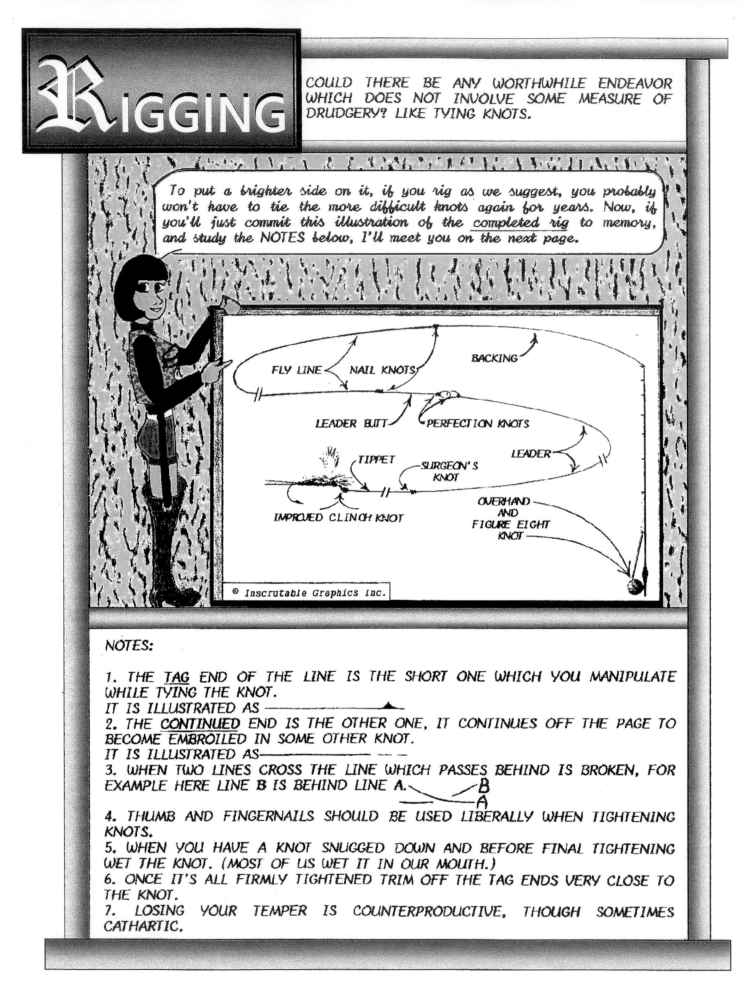

To put a brighter side on it, if you rig as we suggest, you probably won't have to tie the more difficult knots again for years. Now, if you'll just commit this illustration of the *completed rig* to memory, and study the NOTES below, I'll meet you on the next page.

© Inscrutable Graphics Inc.

NOTES:

1. THE **TAG** END OF THE LINE IS THE SHORT ONE WHICH YOU MANIPULATE WHILE TYING THE KNOT.
IT IS ILLUSTRATED AS ————————————
2. THE **CONTINUED** END IS THE OTHER ONE, IT CONTINUES OFF THE PAGE TO BECOME EMBROILED IN SOME OTHER KNOT.
IT IS ILLUSTRATED AS———————— — —
3. WHEN TWO LINES CROSS THE LINE WHICH PASSES BEHIND IS BROKEN, FOR EXAMPLE HERE LINE **B** IS BEHIND LINE **A**.
4. THUMB AND FINGERNAILS SHOULD BE USED LIBERALLY WHEN TIGHTENING KNOTS.
5. WHEN YOU HAVE A KNOT SNUGGED DOWN AND BEFORE FINAL TIGHTENING WET THE KNOT. (MOST OF US WET IT IN OUR MOUTH.)
6. ONCE IT'S ALL FIRMLY TIGHTENED TRIM OFF THE TAG ENDS VERY CLOSE TO THE KNOT.
7. LOSING YOUR TEMPER IS COUNTERPRODUCTIVE, THOUGH SOMETIMES CATHARTIC.

AND NOW TO THE KNOTS: Hopefully you've studied the material on the prior page for you're about to be tested there on—sorely tested. (It's an open book test.)

To begin, if you know how much backing to use with your reel (it should be stated in the instructions that came with the reel) then proceed as follows.

(If you don't know how much backing to use it's best to do it the hard way, it is by far the most precise. I'll describe that on the next page.

THE OVERHAND AND FIGURE EIGHT KNOTS: USED TO ATTACH BACKING TO REEL.

The spool must be in the reel and the reel on the rod, you may detach the upper part of the rod, it's just in the way.
Start by tying the backing around the hub of the spool with an overhand knot backed up with a figure eight knot.
Then reel in the prescribed amount of backing.
And next, proceed to the NAIL knot.

THE NAIL KNOT: TO CONNECT THE BACKING TO THE FLY LINE AND THE LEADER TO THE FLY LINE.

The knot was so named because originally something like a nail was used to hold open the loops allowing the line to be run back through. It's much easier to use a small tube. Last time I tied one I used about an inch and a quarter cut from the end of a small soda straw.

First overlap the tag end of the two lines about 5 inches. Place the tube near the end of the fly line. Then make 4 or 5 turns around the tube and lines with the tag end of the backing. Now push the tag end of the backing through the tube. Next slip the tube out and snug the knot down. Finally, wet the knot and tighten it very firmly. Tighten by pulling on both ends of the backing, don't pull the fly line.

IF YOU DON'T KNOW HOW MUCH BACKING TO USE, you can simply guess, but

there are reels that only require sixty yards, and then there are reels that need over three hundred!

If you're willing to go to some effort to insure that you get it right (this does improve performance) then we suggest the following:

1. Tie the fly line to the hub of the spool _backward_. That means if it's a DT line tie on either end, if it's a WF tie on the weighted end, if an F/S tie on the sinking end. (Tie it on loosely, it's temporary.)

2. Reel in the fly line and tie the backing to it with a nail knot. (Tie it very tightly, it's permanent.)

3. Reel in enough backing to fill the spool to within about three sixteenths of an inch of the top.

4. Cut the backing and then pull all of both lines off the spool. (Don't wrap it around something, just spread it around, it goes back on in the reverse direction.)

5. Tie the backing to the spool hub using the overhand and figure eight knots and reel the whole mess back in.

You are now ready (after a well deserved break) to tie on the leader.

OK, IT'S ALL OFF THE SPOOL, NOW GIMME THE OTHER END

AH — ARE YOU SURE THERE IS ONE?

TIE THE LEADER TO THE FLY LINE JUST AS YOU DID THE BACKING, THAT IS, YOU TIE THE LEADER **AROUND** THE FLY LINE USING THE NAIL KNOT.

THE LEADER BUTT is an _optional_ system which allows you to change

leaders without having to tie any knots when out on the stream and without having to cut off any of that all too short specialized end of your fly line.

| NAIL KNOT | PERFECTION KNOTS |
| FLY LINE | LEADER BUTT | LEADER |

We suggest that you tie on the leader without the leader butt and go try it out. If you later decide that you'd like to try the butt then simply cut the leader off about 12 inches beyond the fly line and tie a perfection knot (described on the next page) on the end.

To get connected pass the loop at the end of a leader (you can buy them with loops or tie your own) over the loop on the leader butt and then pull the entire leader through that butt loop, you've made an easily replaceable connection.

SEE "LEADER BUTT" IN THE CHAPTER ON **ANGLING TECHNIQUES** FOR MORE.

THE PERFECTION KNOT IS USED TO MAKE AN EASILY REMOVABLE CONNECTION BETWEEN LEADER BUTT AND LEADER.

This one is conceptually quite simple but dexterily (a word?) it's as easy as building a four story house of cards. (Using a ball point pen should reduce that problem.)

Follow me through:

1. First form a loop (A) about 1 inch in diameter, then a second, smaller loop (B) in front of A. Form both loops by pulling the tag end of the line behind the continued end.

2. Loop B will be the final product so make it the size you want (we suggest about 3/4 of an inch). Next pull the tag end of the line between the two loops with A behind and B in front.

3. Clamp the point labeled X (in drawing 2) between thumb and forefinger, then slip a pen through loop B catching the top under the pocket clip.

4. Let the pen dangle down behind your finger. Now pull down on the continued end of the line. This will pull loop A down until it disappears behind your thumb, pull it snug. Then pull the tag end down firmly. Release the line, wet it, and tighten by holding loop B and pulling alternately on the extended end and the tag end of the line.

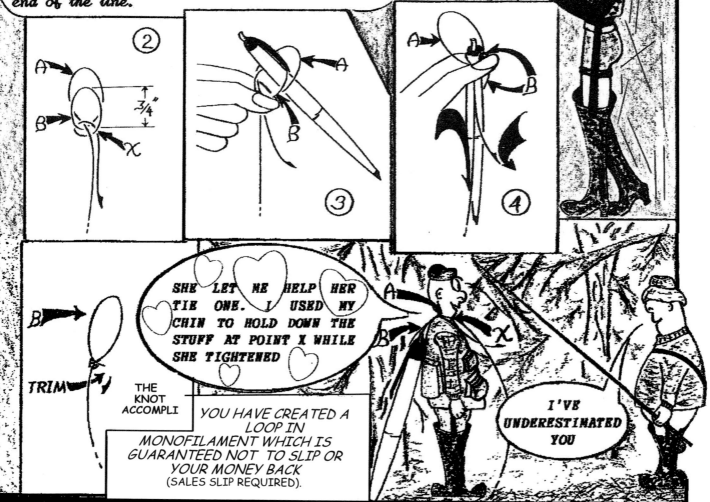

THE KNOT ACCOMPLI

YOU HAVE CREATED A LOOP IN MONOFILAMENT WHICH IS GUARANTEED NOT TO SLIP OR YOUR MONEY BACK (SALES SLIP REQUIRED).

SHE LET ME HELP HER TIE ONE. I USED MY CHIN TO HOLD DOWN THE STUFF AT POINT X WHILE SHE TIGHTENED

I'VE UNDERESTIMATED YOU

THE SURGEON'S KNOT CONNECTS THE LEADER TO THE TIPPET.

According to "The Official Boy Scout Handbook" this is not a "Surgeon's Knot" but a variation thereof called a "Fisherman's 'Surgeon' Knot".

To the tying :
1. Overlap the two lines about 6 inches.
2. Bring the continued end of the tippet along with the tag end of the leader over forming a large loop and pass those ends twice through that loop. Both times you must pull the entire continued end of the tippet through, but what the heck, it's only a couple feet long.
Snug it down, wet it, then tighten vigorously.

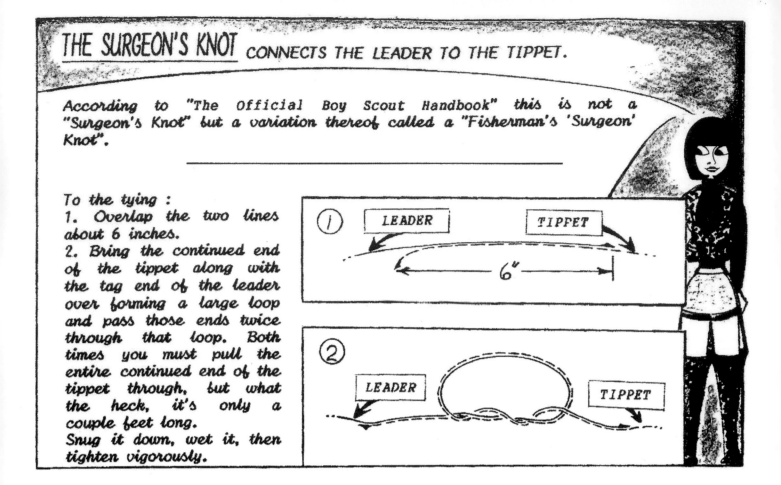

THE IMPROVED CLINCH KNOT HOLDS THE FLY ON THE TIPPET.

The last one and the one you'll tie most often. Fortunately it's also the one that's easier to tie than it looks. (Easier that is if you're not using 7 or 8x tippet, the light is good, your hands aren't numb, the wind isn't too high, the mosquitoes aren't vexing — you know, all that "great outdoors" stuff.)

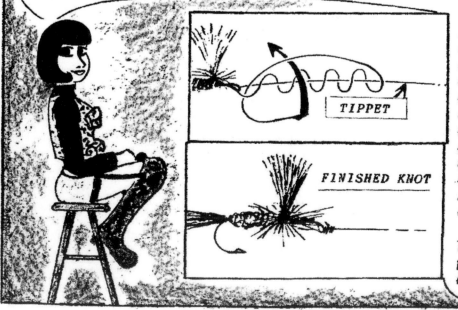

First pass the tippet through the hook eye, then wind the tag end around the continued end four or five times. Loop the tag end over and then put it through the small loop just in front of the hook eye, then put it through the larger loop. Pull it all down, wet it and tighten very firmly.

The finished knot should be pulled snugly against the hook eye.

THE SNARL: *ONE KNOT NO ONE WOULD TIE—ON PURPOSE, YET ONE WE ALL TIE—TO OFTEN.*

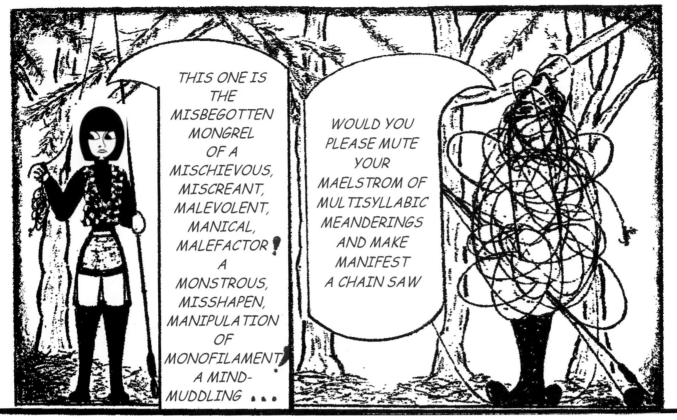

TO *UNTIE* THIS MESS: 1. CLIP OFF THE FLY.   THEN 2. STARTING AT THE FLY END OF THE TIPPET FOLLOW IT THROUGH SEVERAL CONVOLUTIONS OF THE KNOT, NOT TOO MANY OR YOU'LL LOSE YOUR PLACE.   3. FROM THAT POINT PULL THE TIPPET THROUGH.   4. REPEAT STEPS 2 AND 3 UNTIL FINISHED, OR UNTIL IT GETS TOO DARK.

CASTING

WHATEVER MAY BE YOUR PROWESS AS A CATCHER OF FISH IT WILL AVAIL YOU LITTLE, FOR IN THIS SPORT, BE IT RIGHT OR WRONG,

BY YOUR CAST THEY SHALL JUDGE YOU

The Overhead Cast

WHILE MASTERY OF THE OVERHEAD CAST IS SOMETHING OF A FEAT, THOSE OF US WHO HAVE NOT CAN TAKE HEART—I'VE SEEN A MONTANA GUIDE TEACH HALF A DOZEN NEW JERSEY NEOPHYTES TO CAST WELL ENOUGH TO START FISHING IN LESS THAN TEN MINUTES.

THE **GRIP**: TO BEGIN THE ROD IS HELD IN THE RIGHT HAND, THE LINE COMING DOWN THE ROD PASSES UNDER THE RIGHT INDEX FINGER WHICH IS USED TO SQUEEZE IT AGAINST THE ROD HANDLE TO ACT AS A DRAG AND A BRAKE. (IF THERE IS A DRAG ADJUSTMENT ON YOUR REEL BACK IT ALL THE WAY OFF). THE LINE THEN PASSES THROUGH A LOOP FORMED BY THE LEFT HAND AND ON TO THE REEL. (ALL INSTRUCTIONS ARE GIVEN FOR RIGHT HANDERS, IF YOU'RE LEFT HANDED SIMPLY HOLD THIS MANUAL UP TO A MIRROR TO READ.)*

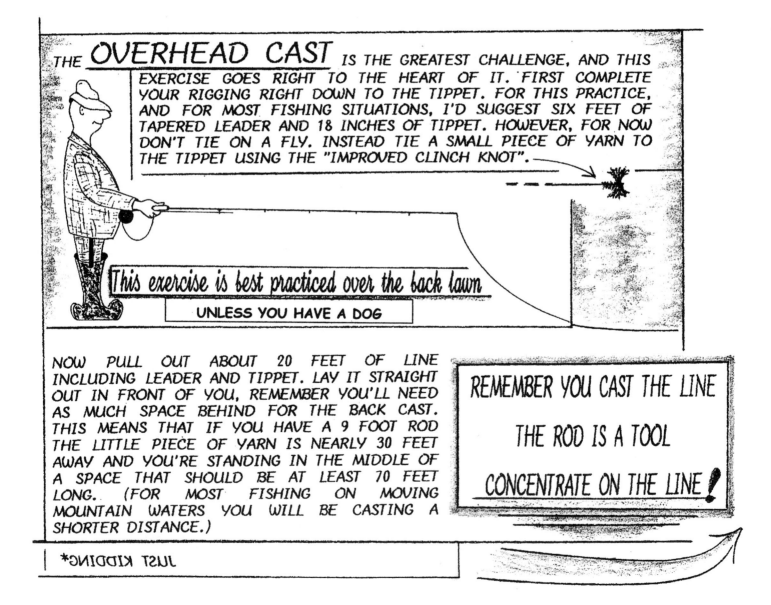

THE OVERHEAD CAST IS THE GREATEST CHALLENGE, AND THIS EXERCISE GOES RIGHT TO THE HEART OF IT. FIRST COMPLETE YOUR RIGGING RIGHT DOWN TO THE TIPPET. FOR THIS PRACTICE, AND FOR MOST FISHING SITUATIONS, I'D SUGGEST SIX FEET OF TAPERED LEADER AND 18 INCHES OF TIPPET. HOWEVER, FOR NOW DON'T TIE ON A FLY. INSTEAD TIE A SMALL PIECE OF YARN TO THE TIPPET USING THE "IMPROVED CLINCH KNOT".

This exercise is best practiced over the back lawn

UNLESS YOU HAVE A DOG

NOW PULL OUT ABOUT 20 FEET OF LINE INCLUDING LEADER AND TIPPET. LAY IT STRAIGHT OUT IN FRONT OF YOU, REMEMBER YOU'LL NEED AS MUCH SPACE BEHIND FOR THE BACK CAST. THIS MEANS THAT IF YOU HAVE A 9 FOOT ROD THE LITTLE PIECE OF YARN IS NEARLY 30 FEET AWAY AND YOU'RE STANDING IN THE MIDDLE OF A SPACE THAT SHOULD BE AT LEAST 70 FEET LONG. (FOR MOST FISHING ON MOVING MOUNTAIN WATERS YOU WILL BE CASTING A SHORTER DISTANCE.)

REMEMBER YOU CAST THE LINE

THE ROD IS A TOOL

CONCENTRATE ON THE LINE!

*JUST KIDDING

NOW LOCK YOUR RIGHT INDEX FINGER OVER THE FLY LINE, COMPRESSING IT AGAINST THE ROD HANDLE SO IT CAN'T SLIP. THEN <u>POWER</u> THE ROD BACK UNTIL IT'S 30 DEGREES BEHIND VERTICAL (THE 11 O'CLOCK POSITION). NEXT STOP IT SO ABRUPTLY THAT YOU MIGHT HAVE STRUCK A LOG THAT SOMEONE WAS HOLDING UP BEHIND YOU.

PLEASE SEE IN THE ILLUSTRATION WHAT'S HAPPENING, YOU NEED TO UNDERSTAND THIS. AS YOU POWERED THE ROD BACK THE ROD TIP FELL BEHIND, LARGELY BECAUSE OF DRAG THE WEIGHTED FLY LINE IMPOSED UPON IT. WHEN YOU STOPPED THE ROD <u>VERY ABRUPTLY</u> AT 11 O'CLOCK THE ROD TIP AND LINE CONTINUED BEYOND AND THEN THE ROD SNAPPED BACK, PULLING THE LINE WITH IT. IF YOU WERE VIGOROUS ENOUGH YOU SET A SHARP LOOP IN THE LINE.

NOW TURN YOUR HEAD (DON'T MOVE YOUR FEET) AND LOOK BEHIND. IF YOU USED ENOUGH POWER IN THE CAST AND STOPPED VERY FIRMLY THE LINE SHOULD STRAIGHTEN OUT BEHIND AT NEARLY ROD TIP HEIGHT AND BE CLOSE TO PARALLEL TO THE GROUND. WATCH THE LOOP UNFURL AND BEFORE THE LINE IS STRAIGHT (WITHIN A FEW INCHES) BEGIN THE FORWARD CAST. (DON'T LET THE LINE COMPLETELY STRAIGHTEN AND THEN BEGIN TO FALL.)

THE FORWARD CAST IS THE MIRROR IMAGE OF THE BACK CAST. PUT POWER INTO THE STROKE AND STOP FIRMLY WHEN THE ROD IS THIRTY DEGREES IN FRONT OF YOU (THE 1 O'CLOCK POSITION). WHEN THE LINE IS NEARLY STRAIGHT IN FRONT DO ANOTHER BACK CAST, THEN ANOTHER FORWARD. KEEP FLICKING THE THING BACK AND FORTH UNTIL YOU'RE TIRED, THEN TAKE A BREAK AND START AGAIN.

"LINE" includes Leader and Tippet.

ONE MORE THING BEFORE YOU START

LET YOUR ROD LEAN OUT A BIT WHEN CASTING.

NOW, GO OUT AND TRY IT A WHILE, IF YOU EXPERIENCE DIFFICULTIES DON'T LET IT DISCOURAGE YOU, WHEN YOU'VE SEEN WHAT'S GOING WRONG (FOR EXAMPLE THE LINE'S CRASHING INTO YOUR ROD AND ABRUPTLY ENDING THE CAST, THIS ONE'S A FAVORITE) COME BACK TO THE MANUAL AND START WORKING THROUGH THE NEXT FOUR PAGES BEGINNING WITH THE HEADING.

"CASTING CLINIC".

THIS SECTION IS DEVOTED TO DIAGNOSING, TREATING AND (ALMOST CERTAINLY) CURING WHAT AILS YOUR CAST.

YOU SHOULD LEARN THIS BUSINESS BY THE BOOK,
BUT WHEN YOU FEEL YOU'VE GAINED AN ADEQUATE DEGREE OF MASTERY OVER THE LINE YOU CAN BEGIN TO PERSONALIZE YOUR CAST.
INDEED YOU CAN LEARN TO DO ALL MANNER OF FANCY THINGS WITH THAT LINE
(NEVER MIND THAT MOST OF THEM ARE USELESS WHEN FISHING).

JUST AS WELL WARN YOU NOW, YOUR FLY GOES ALMOST AS FAR BEHIND ON THE BACK CAST AS IN FRONT ON THE FORE CAST AND THERE ARE LOTS OF THINGS BACK THERE TO GRAB YOUR HOOK. WHEN THIS HAPPENS YOUR CAST IS BROUGHT TO A SUDDEN AND UNSATISFACTORY CONCLUSION. YOU MUST LEARN TO

WATCH YOUR BACKSIDE*

SAD BUT TRUE YOUNG MAN, THEY ALSO EAT FISHING FLIES

RATZ, I WAS BORN TO FISH WORMS

*MY DEAR EDITOR HAS INFORMED ME THAT THE USE OF THE VERY WELL KNOWN COMIC STRIP CHARACTER HIDDEN BEHIND THE BLACK BOX WOULD BE A COPYRIGHT VIOLATION AND, AT THE WORST, I COULD BE DRAWN AND QUARTERED FOR SUCH MISCONDUCT. (I DO THINK SHE SOMETIMES TENDS TO EXAGGERATE.)

CASTING CLINIC

IF THE LINE ISN'T FLYING AROUND UP THERE AS YOU HOPED IT WOULD, TAKE HEART, FEW PEOPLE GET THE **HANG** OF THE OVERHEAD CAST ON THE FIRST TRY (I CERTAINLY DIDN'T). SO MUCH FOR COMMISERATION, NOW I CAN ONLY REPEAT WHAT YOU'VE ALREADY READ, THOUGH THIS TIME IN A SOMEWHAT DIFFERENT WAY AND WITH INCREASED EMPHASIS.

FIRST THEN, ARE YOUR LINE AND FLY FOLLOWING A COURSE SOMEWHAT LIKE THAT IN FIGURE A? THE LINE NEVER DROPPING MUCH BELOW THE HEIGHT OF THE ROD TIP WHEN IT'S AT 11 OR 1? IF SO, EXCELLENT, THOUGH THAT WOULD BE SOMEWHAT UNUSUAL FOR A FIRST ATTEMPT. MORE LIKELY YOUR RIG IS FOLLOWING A RATHER LAZY FIGURE 8 LIKE THAT IN ILLUSTRATION B.

IF THIS IS THE CASE IT IS BECAUSE:

A) YOU'RE NOT PUTTING ENOUGH **POWER** INTO YOUR CASTING STROKE. THINK OF THE ROD AS A FLY SWATTER — **WHACK** IT HOME! YOU CAN OVER WHACK, BUT GO AHEAD, THEN BACK OFF UNTIL YOU'RE USING THE MINIMUM AMOUNT OF FORCE TO GET IT RIGHT.

B) YOU'RE NOT STOPPING THE STROKE ABRUPTLY ENOUGH. REMEMBER THAT ILLUSTRATION? STOP THE ROD **SHARPLY** AND IT'S TIP WILL BEND OUT BEYOND AND THEN SNAP BACK. THIS IS **ESSENTIAL** IN SETTING A PROPER LOOP. REMEMBER THAT OTHER ILLUSTRATION? TWO FRIENDS HOLDING UP LOGS, ONE TO STOP THE ROD COLD AT 11 O'CLOCK, THE OTHER AT 1? KEEP ACCELERATING THE CASTING STROKE UNTIL YOU HIT THAT IMAGINARY LOG! DON'T GO BEYOND!

WITH THE LINE WAVING AROUND AS IN (B) IT MAY HIT THE SURFACE IN FRONT OF OR BEHIND YOU, ESPECIALLY IF YOU'RE STANDING WAIST DEEP IN A RIVER. WORSE, YOUR RIG MAY HIT THE ROD RESULTING IN A NASTY SNARL.

C) YOU ARE CONTINUING YOUR CASTING STROKE BEYOND 11 OR 1 O'CLOCK. IT SHOULD BE OBVIOUS THAT THIS RESULTS IN YOUR THROWING THE LINE AT THE SURFACE, AND YOUR FLY IS SURE TO FOLLOW. (IF YOU HAVEN'T YET LEARNED TO TELL TIME IT IS SUGGESTED THAT YOU DO SO BEFORE CONTINUING WITH THESE LESSONS.)

D) YOU'RE NOT TIMING THE BEGINNING OF THE NEXT STROKE CORRECTLY. THE LINE (THAT'S WEIGHTED FLY LINE, TAPERED LEADER AND TIPPET) MUST BE **STRETCHED OUT STRAIGHT** (OR AT LEAST NEARLY SO) BEFORE YOU THRUST THE ROD INTO THE NEXT STROKE. WAIT UNTIL THE COLORFUL FLY LINE IS STRAIGHT AND THEN SOME PART OF A SECOND (THIS VARIES WITH THE LENGTH OF YOUR LEADER AND TIPPET) BEFORE WHACKING YOUR ROD INTO THE NEXT STROKE.

E) SOME OR ALL OF THE ABOVE.

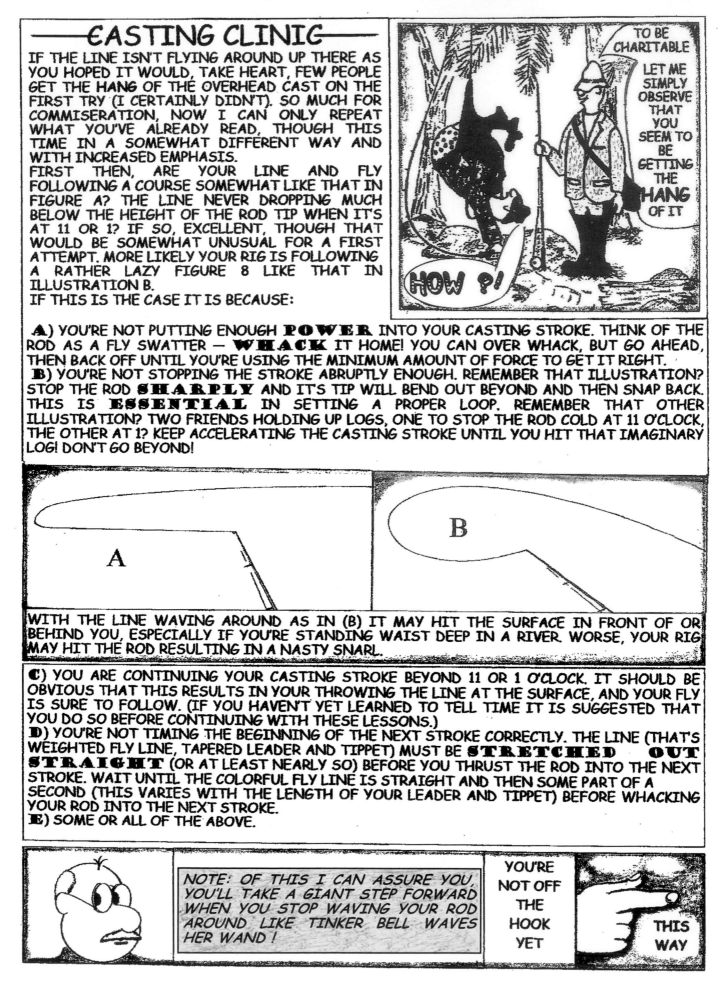

NOTE: OF THIS I CAN ASSURE YOU, YOU'LL TAKE A GIANT STEP FORWARD WHEN YOU STOP WAVING YOUR ROD AROUND LIKE TINKER BELL WAVES HER WAND!

YOU'RE NOT OFF THE HOOK YET

THIS WAY

CHECK THE TIPPET, IS THE LITTLE PIECE OF YARN STILL THERE? IF NOT AND IF YOU HAVEN'T HIT ANYTHING WITH IT THEN YOU HAVE ALMOST CERTAINLY **"CRACKED THE WHIP"**. THE PROBLEM IS IN YOUR TIMING, I WILL ILLUSTRATE:

IDEALY THINGS GO AS SHOWN IN ILLUSTRATION C, AS THE LOOP ROLLS OUT THE LINE BETWEEN THE "TURNOVER POINT" (SEE ILLUSTRATION) AND THE ROD TIP IS NOT MOVING WHILE THE LINE BETWEEN THE TURNOVER POINT AND THE FLY IS OUTWARD BOUND AT A CONSIDERABLE SPEED. WHEN THE LINE STRAIGHTENS COMPLETELY, (THE POSITION LABELED 2) IT IS SAID TO BE "LOADED" AND YOU FIRE THE NEXT CASTING STROKE. (IF YOU POSTPONE THAT STROKE THE LINE BEGINS TO FALL AND YOU ARE BACK TO CASTING LAZY EIGHTS.)

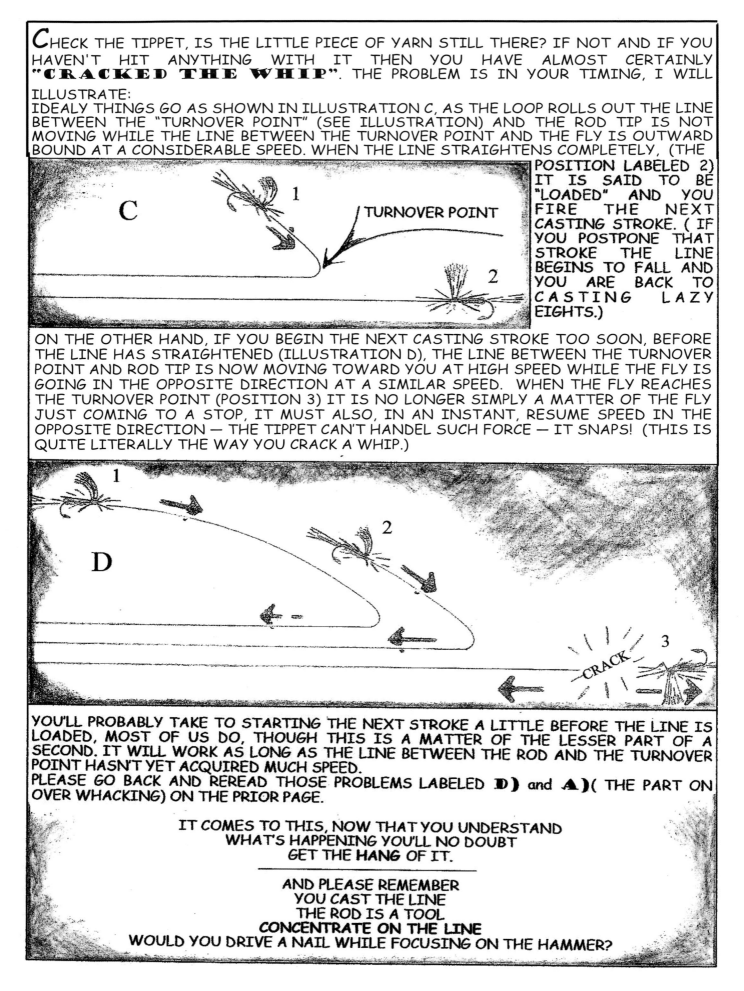

ON THE OTHER HAND, IF YOU BEGIN THE NEXT CASTING STROKE TOO SOON, BEFORE THE LINE HAS STRAIGHTENED (ILLUSTRATION D), THE LINE BETWEEN THE TURNOVER POINT AND ROD TIP IS NOW MOVING TOWARD YOU AT HIGH SPEED WHILE THE FLY IS GOING IN THE OPPOSITE DIRECTION AT A SIMILAR SPEED. WHEN THE FLY REACHES THE TURNOVER POINT (POSITION 3) IT IS NO LONGER SIMPLY A MATTER OF THE FLY JUST COMING TO A STOP, IT MUST ALSO, IN AN INSTANT, RESUME SPEED IN THE OPPOSITE DIRECTION — THE TIPPET CAN'T HANDEL SUCH FORCE — IT SNAPS! (THIS IS QUITE LITERALLY THE WAY YOU CRACK A WHIP.)

YOU'LL PROBABLY TAKE TO STARTING THE NEXT STROKE A LITTLE BEFORE THE LINE IS LOADED, MOST OF US DO, THOUGH THIS IS A MATTER OF THE LESSER PART OF A SECOND. IT WILL WORK AS LONG AS THE LINE BETWEEN THE ROD AND THE TURNOVER POINT HASN'T YET ACQUIRED MUCH SPEED.

PLEASE GO BACK AND REREAD THOSE PROBLEMS LABELED **D)** and **A)**(THE PART ON OVER WHACKING) ON THE PRIOR PAGE.

IT COMES TO THIS, NOW THAT YOU UNDERSTAND
WHAT'S HAPPENING YOU'LL NO DOUBT
GET THE **HANG** OF IT.

AND PLEASE REMEMBER
YOU CAST THE LINE
THE ROD IS A TOOL
CONCENTRATE ON THE LINE
WOULD YOU DRIVE A NAIL WHILE FOCUSING ON THE HAMMER?

EXAMINE THE TIPPET CLOSELY, DO YOU FIND ONE OR MORE VERY SMALL KNOTS? THESE ARE CALLED **"WIND KNOTS"**, NOT BECAUSE THE WIND CAUSES THEM BUT BECAUSE CASTING INTO A WIND OFTEN CAUSES <u>YOU</u> TO CAUSE THEM. YET IN YOUR BACKYARD PRACTICE THERE MAY HAVE BEEN NO WIND. YOU CAUSED THOSE KNOTS BY PUSHING THE ROD FORWARD AS ONE MIGHT NATURALLY FEEL COMPELLED TO DO WHEN CASTING SOMETHING INTO A HEAD WIND (SEE **G**, THIRD ILLUSTRATION BELOW).

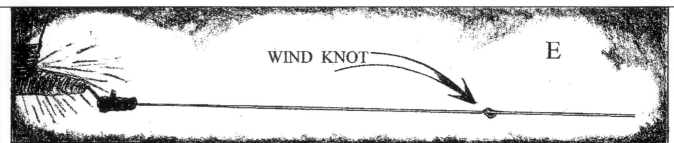

WIND KNOT

E

DRAWING **F** SHOWS THE PROPER FINISHING POSITION FOR A CASTING STROKE, YOUR SHOULDER HARDLY MOVED AND YOUR UPPER ARM IS NEARLY WHERE IT WAS WHEN YOU STARTED THE STROKE. THE CAST HAS BEEN POWERED FROM THE ELBOW AND ONLY THE FOREARM HAS MOVED.

BUT YOU ALMOST CERTAINLY DID SOMETHING LIKE WHAT IS ILLUSTRATED IN **G**, YOU SHOVED THE ROD OUT AS IF THAT WOULD PUSH THE FLY OUT FURTHER. THINK ABOUT IT, THE LINE ISN'T RIGID SO HOW COULD THAT HELP? GO BACK AND LOOK AT THE ILLUSTRATIONS OF THE OVERHEAD CAST, AS IN **F** THE UPPER ARM HARDLY MOVES.

TROUBLE IS THESE KNOTS CREATE WEAK POINTS IN THE TIPPET WHICH IS ALREADY THE WEAKEST LINK BETWEEN YOU AND YOUR FLY.

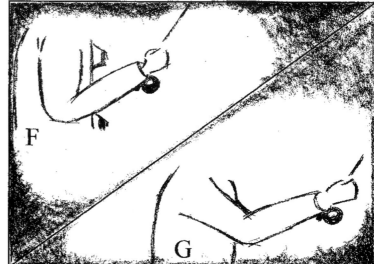

F

G

IT'S GRANDMA'S CURE FOR WIND KNOTS, WORKS GOOD FOR HICCUPS TOO

IF YOU MUST CAST INTO THE WIND AND
IF YOU ARE USING A SINGLE ACTION REEL AND
IF YOU HAVE AN EXTRA SPOOL LOADED WITH "WF" (WEIGHT FORWARD) LINE, USE IT. THIS WILL HELP GET THE WEIGHTED FLY LINE OUT BUT THE WIND WILL STILL TURN THE LEADER—TIPPET—FLY BACK ON YOU. CHANGE TO A SHORTER LEADER AND TIPPET.
IF YOU ARE USING A "LEADER BUTT" AS DESCRIBED IN THE CHAPTER ON KNOTS THIS WILL BE SIMPLE,
IF NOT YOU'LL HAVE TO TIE A "NAIL KNOT"
    (DID YOU BRING ALONG THAT LITTLE STRAW?)

NOTE: IN THE FLY FISHING MAGAZINES AND EVEN THE MANUALS YOU WILL OFTEN SEE BEAUTIFULLY EXECUTED CASTS WITH THE ROD TIP DOWN AROUND 10 O'CLOCK. THIS IS BECAUSE THE PHOTOGRAPHER WAITED FOR THE MOST PICTURESQUE MOMENT. ON THE LAST (AND SO LONGEST) STROKE, WHEN THE LOOP HAD UNFURLED TO WAY AHEAD OF THE CASTER, HE CLICKED THE SHUTTER. THING IS BY THEN THE FISHER HAD LET THE ROD DOWN IN PREPARATION FOR THE LANDING OF THE FLY.
                    BE NOT DECEIVED.

THE FORGOING SHOULD GUIDE YOU THROUGH YOUR PROBLEMS, BUT BE PATIENT WITH YOURSELF, THE OVERHEAD CAST IS NOT THAT EASILY MASTERED.

YOU MAY ACCUSE ME OF PERSEVERATION BUT SOME THINGS ARE TRULY IMPORTANT AND THIS CERTAINLY IS HERE:

KEEP YOUR MIND ON THE LINE
CONCENTRATE ON IT
FLY WITH YOUR LINE
DO THIS AND ALL ELSE WILL FALL INTO PLACE.

I SHOULD REMIND YOU OF THIS TOO
YOU HANDICAP YOURSELF IF YOUR ROD IS NOT DESIGNED FOR THE LINE WEIGHT YOU'RE USING. ON MY ROD, ABOUT A FOOT ABOVE THE CORK HANDLE, IS INSCRIBED "#7 FLY LINE". ON THE BOX IN WHICH MY LINE CAME IS PRINTED "DT—7—F". RECALL FROM THE CHAPTER ON OUTFITTING THAT THIS MEANS THE LINE IS TAPERED AT BOTH ENDS, HAS A WEIGHT RATING OF 7 AND FLOATS. AS A BEGINNER YOU SHOULD MATCH ROD AND LINE.

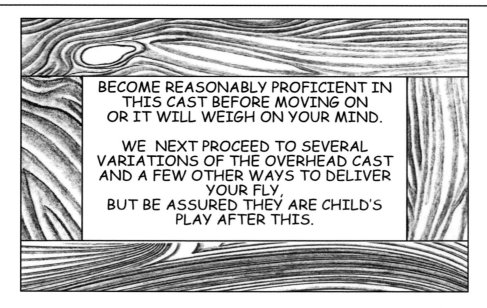

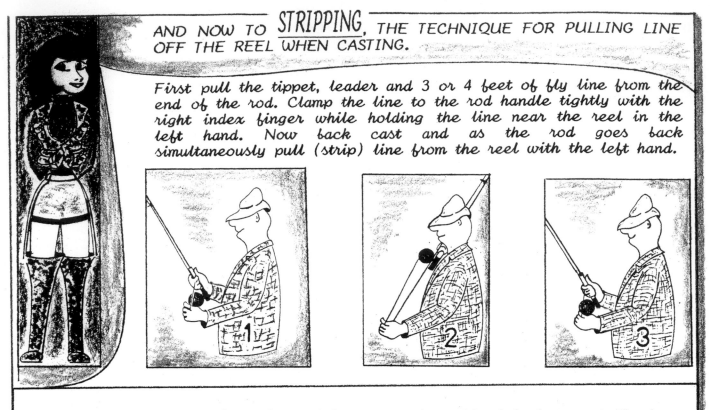

AND NOW TO **STRIPPING**, THE TECHNIQUE FOR PULLING LINE OFF THE REEL WHEN CASTING.

First pull the tippet, leader and 3 or 4 feet of fly line from the end of the rod. Clamp the line to the rod handle tightly with the right index finger while holding the line near the reel in the left hand. Now back cast and as the rod goes back simultaneously pull (strip) line from the reel with the left hand.

On the forward cast, after the rod has stopped at 11 o'clock to <u>set the loop</u>*, relax the right index finger and open the left hand to a loop moving it back up to the reel while the extra line you stripped off on the back cast slips out through the guides (the little loops on the rod).*
Just keep repeating these steps until the fly is out as far as you want.
After the last cast (having stopped to <u>set the loop</u> *at 11 o'clock) let the rod tip down to 10 o'clock and allow the fly to settle gently upon the water (or the lawn).*

TO **INCREASE** YOUR **RANGE** YOU MUST INCREASE THE ARC OF THE CASTING STROKE. USUALLY THE ARC FROM 11 TO 1 O'CLOCK WILL DO, BUT STREAMS TEND TO GATHER AND FORM RIVERS, SO YOU WILL SOMETIMES HAVE TO CAST FURTHER.
FIRST BEGIN CASTING 11-1, WHEN THE LINE GETS OUT SO FAR THAT IT WON'T STAY UP CAST TO 11 (OR 1) AND AFTER THE LOOP IS SET LET THE ROD TIP SETTLE TO 45 DEGREES FROM VERTICAL. WHEN THE LINE STRAIGHTENS OUT POWER THE NEXT CASTING STROKE FROM THERE; STOP ABRUPTLY AT 1 TO SET THE LOOP, LET THE ROD TIP SETTLE TO 45 AND POWER THE NEXT STROKE FROM THERE →(ETC.)

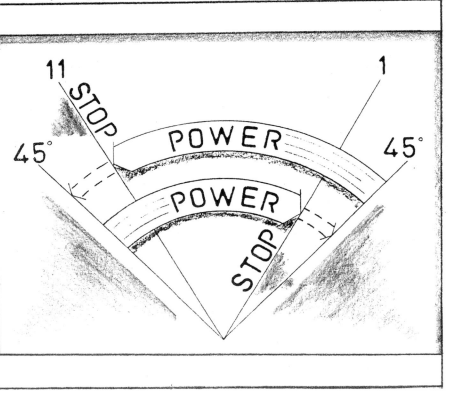

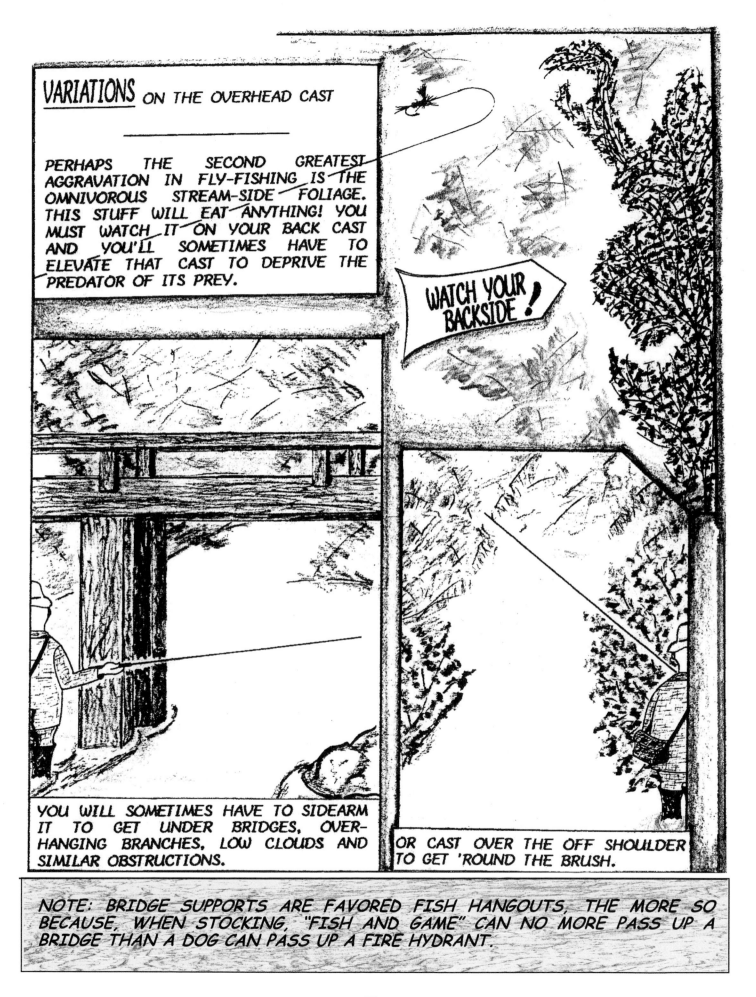

VARIATIONS ON THE OVERHEAD CAST

PERHAPS THE SECOND GREATEST AGGRAVATION IN FLY-FISHING IS THE OMNIVOROUS STREAM-SIDE FOLIAGE. THIS STUFF WILL EAT ANYTHING! YOU MUST WATCH IT ON YOUR BACK CAST AND YOU'LL SOMETIMES HAVE TO ELEVATE THAT CAST TO DEPRIVE THE PREDATOR OF ITS PREY.

WATCH YOUR BACKSIDE !

YOU WILL SOMETIMES HAVE TO SIDEARM IT TO GET UNDER BRIDGES, OVER-HANGING BRANCHES, LOW CLOUDS AND SIMILAR OBSTRUCTIONS.

OR CAST OVER THE OFF SHOULDER TO GET 'ROUND THE BRUSH.

NOTE: BRIDGE SUPPORTS ARE FAVORED FISH HANGOUTS, THE MORE SO BECAUSE, WHEN STOCKING, "FISH AND GAME" CAN NO MORE PASS UP A BRIDGE THAN A DOG CAN PASS UP A FIRE HYDRANT.

THE **SHORT CAST** IS USED TO DELIVER A **DRY** FLY DOWN STREAM.

THE BEST ADVICE TO BE GIVEN ON THIS CAST IS DON'T—UNLESS YOU MUST. FISH HOLD IN PLACE FACING INTO THE CURRENT, WHEN YOU'RE CASTING DOWN STREAM THEY'RE LOOKING RIGHT AT YOU, AND YOU'RE STANDING THERE WAVING YOUR ROD AND FLICKING THAT GAILY COLORED FLY LINE IN THEIR FACE. FRIGHTENED FISH CAN'T BE CAUGHT!

YET THERE ARE TIMES WHEN YOU HAVE TO TAKE THE RISK.

EXAMPLES: WHEN THE WATER IS VERY LOW AND CLEAR AND YOU'RE CASTING UP STREAM THE LEADER AND TIPPET DRIFT BY BEFORE THE FLY, THE SIGHT OF THIS SOMETIMES MAKES THE FISH "LEADER SHY" AND THEY WON'T GO FOR IT. THEN THERE ARE SITUATIONS LIKE THE "DEAD FALL" SHOWN ABOVE. CAST UP STREAM AND THE FLY LANDS BEHIND THE FISH, THEY WON'T SEE IT.

THE SOLUTION IS THE SHORT CAST, YOU SIMPLY MAKE THE REGULAR OVER-HEAD CAST AND, AFTER SETTING THE LOOP AT 11 O'CLOCK, AS THE LINE ROLES OUT PULL THE ROD BACK OVER YOUR SHOULDER. THE FLY LANDS SHORT AND YOU THEN LET THE ROD FORWARD SO THAT THE FLY DOES A PROPER "DEAD DRIFT" DOWN TO THE FALLEN TREE. (YOU CAN GET ABOUT 17 FEET OF DEAD DRIFT WITH AN 8 1/2 FOOT ROD.)

THE ROLL CAST IS USED WHEN YOUR BACK'S TO THE WALL, THAT IS WHEN THE FOLIAGE IS TOO CLOSE TO ALLOW YOU TO PERFORM A BACK CAST.

PROCEED AS FOLLOWS:

1) PULL ALL OF THE LINE TO BE USED IN THE CAST THROUGH THE GUIDES AND OFF THE ROD, JUST THROW IT ON THE WATER AHEAD AND A BIT TO THE RIGHT OF YOU. THEN CLAMP THE LINE TO THE ROD HANDLE WITH YOUR RIGHT INDEX FINGER AS USUAL.
2) BRING THE ROD UP AND BACK AT A NORMAL SPEED (DON'T FLIP ANY LINE OUT BEHIND) UNTIL IT'S IN THE POSITION SHOWN IN ILLUSTRATION **A**, WITH THE LINE CURVED BEHIND AS SHOWN.
3) NOW *THRUST* THE ROD FORWARD AND BRING IT TO AN *ABRUPT* STOP WITH THE ROD TIP STILL HIGH (AS IN ILLUSTRATION **B**). IF THE LINE DOESN'T STRETCH OUT COMPLETELY ON THE FIRST CAST, JUST THROW ANOTHER ROLL, IMMEDIATELY.

IF YOU'VE DONE THIS CORRECTLY THE LOOP WILL ROLL OUT IN FRONT OF YOU PULLING THE LINE OFF THE WATER UNTIL THE FLY IS PULLED UP AND THROWN OUT TO LINE'S END. ALL OF THIS SHOULD HAPPEN *ABOVE* THE WATER, AS IN ILLUSTRATION **C**. IF THE LINE FALLS BACK TO THE SURFACE BEFORE IT FINISHES THE ROLL OUT YOU MAY WELL SCARE THE FISH OFF **(FRIGHTENED FISH CAN'T BE CAUGHT)**. SHOULD THIS HAPPEN TRY ADDING MORE POWER TO YOUR THRUST AND/OR STOPPING THE THRUST HIGHER AND MORE ABRUPTLY.

NOTE: THE WATER'S SURFACE FILM TENDS TO HOLD ON TO THE LINE, SO YOU CAN'T PRACTICE THIS CAST ON THE BACK LAWN.

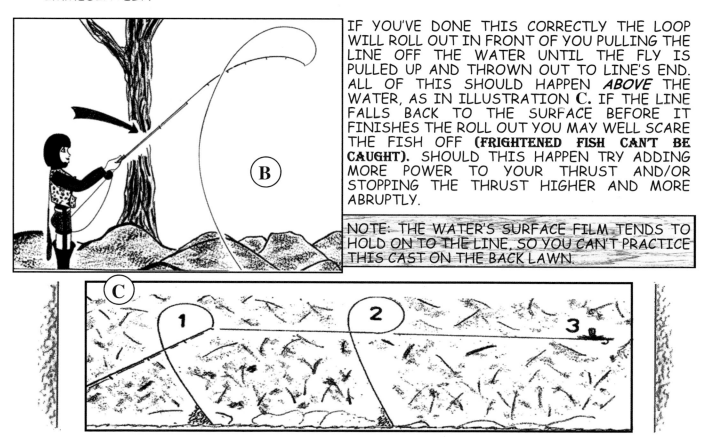

ONCE THE FLY'S OUT THERE YOU CAN LET IT DRIFT PART WAY BACK AND THEN THROW ANOTHER ROLL. TRY THROWING TO A SLIGHTLY DIFFERENT PLACE EACH TIME, THAT WAY YOU CAN COVER ALL THE POSSIBLE FISH HOLDING SPOTS. IN FACT YOU CAN KEEP IT OUT THERE ALL DAY IF THE FISH DON'T FUSS WITH IT.

NOTE: IF THERE'S A CURRENT, SO THAT AS YOU PULL OUT THE LINE AND CHUCK IT UPON THE WATER IT'S DRIFTING DOWN STREAM, AND IF THE OBSTRUCTIONS BELOW ALLOW, LET IT (THOUGH NO FURTHER DOWN THAN YOU PLAN TO CAST UP). WHEN IT GETS DOWN THERE, QUICKLY GO TO THE NEXT PAGE AND READ UP ON THE "WATER LOADED CAST".

THE **_WATER LOADED CAST:_** THE FLY LINE IS SAID TO BE "LOADED" WHEN IT IS STRETCHED OUT EITHER BEHIND OR IN FRONT OF YOU AND READY FOR YOU TO MAKE THE NEXT CASTING STROKE. WITH THE OVERHEAD CAST IT IS HOPEFULLY AT ROD TIP HEIGHT AND KINDA PARALLEL TO THE SURFACE. YOU CAN, HOWEVER, ALLOW THE WATER TO LOAD THE LINE BEHIND YOU PREPARATORY TO THE FORWARD STROKE.

JUST LET THE FLY DRIFT BY ALL THE WAY DOWN UNTIL THE LINE STRAIGHTENS OUT. THIS WILL ALLOW THE FLY TO DRIFT TWICE AS FAR PER CAST, BUT ONCE IT'S PAST YOU THE FISH YOU MIGHT CATCH ARE LOOKING IN YOUR DIRECTION, SO TRY NOT TO BE NOTICED.
(THIS ONE IS MOST OFTEN USED WITH SUBSURFACE FLIES.)

SEE _"THE WATER LOADED CAST"_, IN THE CHAPTER ON **ANGLING TECHNIQUES,** FOR MORE.

TROLLING IS A DEADLY METHOD USED TO FISH SUBSURFACE FLIES DOWN STREAM. (I ADMIT THAT I DON'T KNOW WHAT THIS TECHNIQUE IS CALLED, SO I MADE UP MY OWN NAME.)

TROLLING CAN BE USED IN THOSE SITUATIONS WHERE THE "SHORT CAST" WOULD BE USED WITH DRY FLIES AND IS ABOUT THE ONLY WAY TO FISH WHERE YOU CAN'T CAST AT ALL. THE BEST EXAMPLE WOULD BE A NARROW STRETCH OF STREAM WITH FOLIAGE HANGING OVER BOTH BANKS. THE FLY OF CHOICE WOULD BE A "STREAMER" TO IMITATE A SMALL FISH OR A "WET FLY" TO SUGGEST A SWIMMING BUG. SINCE EITHER IS QUITE SMALL, BUT SIMULATES SOMETHING THAT'S SWIMMING, YOU NEED IMPART TO YOUR LURE SOMETHING OF A SWIMMING ACTION. MOST ESPECIALLY YOU SHOULD REMEMBER THAT SMALL ANIMALS CAN'T EVEN HOLD IN PLACE IN A SWIFT CURRENT.
JUST PLACE YOUR FLY IN THE WATER AND START LETTING IT DOWN A FOOT OR TWO AT A TIME, WITH INTERVENING PAUSES OF FROM ONE TO FIVE SECONDS. IF THERE IS A TONGUE OF FAST CURRENT LET IT DOWN IN THE SLOWER WATER RIGHT NEXT TO THE FAST. TRY TO RETRIEVE IT WITH THE SAME ACTION IN SLOWER, DEEPER WATER.
ALSO REMEMBER **THE FLY MUST STAY DOWN,** IF IT'S SKIMMING THE SURFACE IT'S NOT LIKELY TO FOOL THE FISH.

SEE "ANIMATING SWIMMING FLIES", IN THE CHAPTER ON *ANGELING TECNIQUES,* FOR MORE.

YOU NEEDN'T SPEND PRECIOUS WEEKENDS IN THE BACKYARD PRACTICING YOUR CAST.
WHEN YOU'RE GOOD ENOUGH TO GET THE FLY OUT THERE, MORE OFTEN THAN NOT, AND PLACE IT SOMEWHERE AROUND WHERE YOU INTENDED (AN AFTERNOON'S PRACTICE SHOULD DO), THEN GO FISHING. PERFECT YOUR CAST IN THE WILDERNESS.

BUT MAKE SURE YOU'RE PRACTICING ARIGHT.
YOUR MANTRAS SHOULD BE:
11 O'CLOCK–1 O'CLOCK
POWER (YOUR STROKE)
STOP (LIKE YOU HIT A TREE LIMB)
TIMING (START THE NEXT STROKE WHEN THE LINE IS, OR NEARLY IS, "LOADED").

PRACTICE AWRONG* AND YOU'LL FIND THAT BAD HABITS ARE HARD TO BREAK!

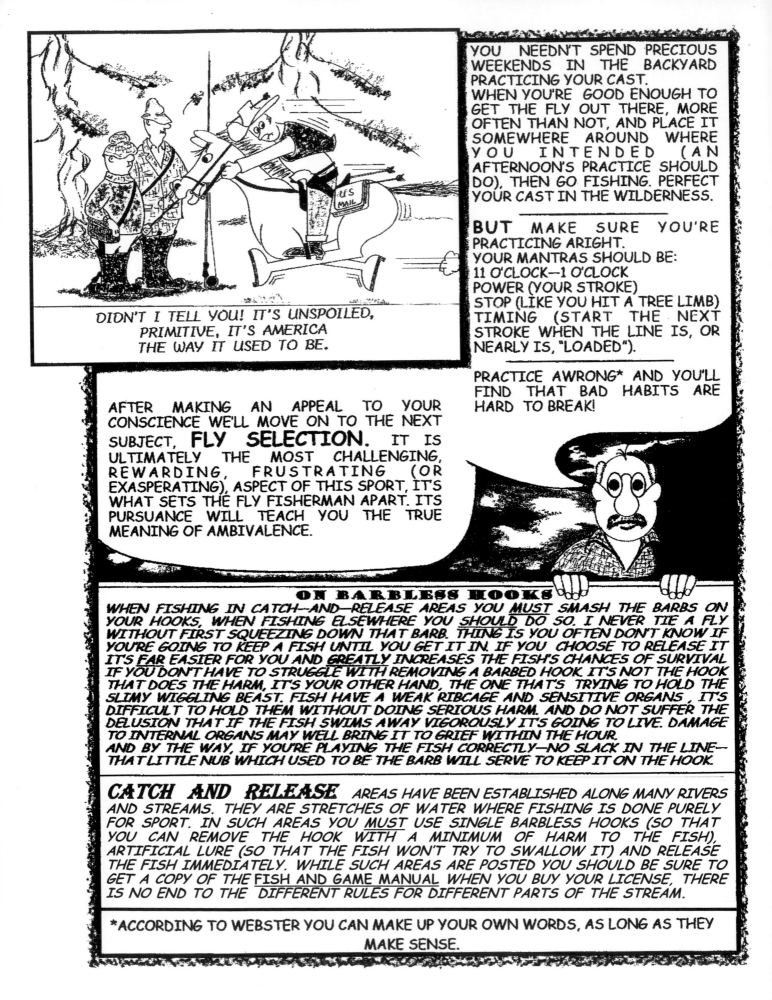

DIDN'T I TELL YOU! IT'S UNSPOILED, PRIMITIVE, IT'S AMERICA THE WAY IT USED TO BE.

AFTER MAKING AN APPEAL TO YOUR CONSCIENCE WE'LL MOVE ON TO THE NEXT SUBJECT, **FLY SELECTION.** IT IS ULTIMATELY THE MOST CHALLENGING, REWARDING, FRUSTRATING (OR EXASPERATING), ASPECT OF THIS SPORT. IT'S WHAT SETS THE FLY FISHERMAN APART. ITS PURSUANCE WILL TEACH YOU THE TRUE MEANING OF AMBIVALENCE.

ON BARBLESS HOOKS

WHEN FISHING IN CATCH--AND--RELEASE AREAS YOU <u>MUST</u> SMASH THE BARBS ON YOUR HOOKS, WHEN FISHING ELSEWHERE YOU <u>SHOULD</u> DO SO. I NEVER TIE A FLY WITHOUT FIRST SQUEEZING DOWN THAT BARB. THING IS YOU OFTEN DON'T KNOW IF YOU'RE GOING TO KEEP A FISH UNTIL YOU GET IT IN. IF YOU CHOOSE TO RELEASE IT IT'S FAR EASIER FOR YOU AND <u>GREATLY</u> INCREASES THE FISH'S CHANCES OF SURVIVAL IF YOU DON'T HAVE TO STRUGGLE WITH REMOVING A BARBED HOOK. IT'S NOT THE HOOK THAT DOES THE HARM, IT'S YOUR OTHER HAND, THE ONE THAT'S TRYING TO HOLD THE SLIMY WIGGLING BEAST. FISH HAVE A WEAK RIBCAGE AND SENSITIVE ORGANS , IT'S DIFFICULT TO HOLD THEM WITHOUT DOING SERIOUS HARM. AND DO NOT SUFFER THE DELUSION THAT IF THE FISH SWIMS AWAY VIGOROUSLY IT'S GOING TO LIVE. DAMAGE TO INTERNAL ORGANS MAY WELL BRING IT TO GRIEF WITHIN THE HOUR.
AND BY THE WAY, IF YOU'RE PLAYING THE FISH CORRECTLY—NO SLACK IN THE LINE— THAT LITTLE NUB WHICH USED TO BE THE BARB WILL SERVE TO KEEP IT ON THE HOOK.

CATCH AND RELEASE AREAS HAVE BEEN ESTABLISHED ALONG MANY RIVERS AND STREAMS. THEY ARE STRETCHES OF WATER WHERE FISHING IS DONE PURELY FOR SPORT. IN SUCH AREAS YOU <u>MUST</u> USE SINGLE BARBLESS HOOKS (SO THAT YOU CAN REMOVE THE HOOK WITH A MINIMUM OF HARM TO THE FISH), ARTIFICIAL LURE (SO THAT THE FISH WON'T TRY TO SWALLOW IT) AND RELEASE THE FISH IMMEDIATELY. WHILE SUCH AREAS ARE POSTED YOU SHOULD BE SURE TO GET A COPY OF THE <u>FISH AND GAME MANUAL</u> WHEN YOU BUY YOUR LICENSE, THERE IS NO END TO THE DIFFERENT RULES FOR DIFFERENT PARTS OF THE STREAM.

*ACCORDING TO WEBSTER YOU CAN MAKE UP YOUR OWN WORDS, AS LONG AS THEY MAKE SENSE.

FLY SELECTION

IN THE BEGINNING I MADE THE RATHER AUDACIOUS ASSERTION THAT A FLY FISHER COULD "OUT FISH HIS OR HER FELLOWS IN THE BAIT-N-BRIC-A-BRAC BUNCH". WHILE I WILL STAND WITH THIS IT IS NECESSARY TO CONCEDE THAT IT IS NOT IN THE LEAST A SIMPLE UNDERTAKING. THE BAIT-N-HARDWARE ENTHUSIASTS USUALLY CARRY FEW DIFFERENT THINGS TO THROW AT THE FISH AND FEW, IF ANY, OF THESE THINGS LOOK LIKE WHAT FISH USUALLY EAT. ON THE OTHER HAND THE VERY ESSENCE OF FLY FISHING IS TO PRESENT FISH WITH REPLICAS OF THEIR NORMAL DIET. THE COMPLICATION IS THAT THE WATERWAYS ARE FOREVER GOING THROUGH NATURAL CYCLES SO THAT WHAT THE FISH ARE TAKING TODAY THEY MAY NOT ON ANOTHER DAY. THE BAIT-N-HARDWARE FISHERS HAVE GOOD AND BAD DAYS AND SO WILL YOU AS LONG AS YOU REMAIN IGNORANT OF WHAT'S GOING ON IN THE STREAM.

IN THIS RATHER PROTRACTED CHAPTER I'LL DO MY BEST TO PUT YOU, IF NOT ON TOP OF IT ALL, THEN AT LEAST ON A FIRM FOOTING IN THE BUSINESS OF FLY SELECTION.

PROVIDED BELOW IS A *SAMPLING* OF *FLY PATTERNS* SO THAT YOU MAY AT LEAST GAIN SOME INSIGHT INTO THIS CORNUCOPIAS WORLD, AND A HEAD START IN LEARNING THE JARGON.

DRY FLIES

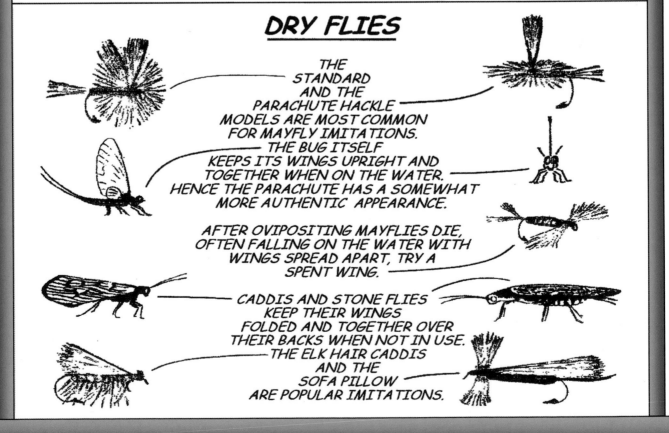

THE STANDARD AND THE PARACHUTE HACKLE MODELS ARE MOST COMMON FOR MAYFLY IMITATIONS.
THE BUG ITSELF KEEPS ITS WINGS UPRIGHT AND TOGETHER WHEN ON THE WATER. HENCE THE PARACHUTE HAS A SOMEWHAT MORE AUTHENTIC APPEARANCE.

AFTER OVIPOSITING MAYFLIES DIE, OFTEN FALLING ON THE WATER WITH WINGS SPREAD APART, TRY A SPENT WING.

CADDIS AND STONE FLIES KEEP THEIR WINGS FOLDED AND TOGETHER OVER THEIR BACKS WHEN NOT IN USE. THE ELK HAIR CADDIS AND THE SOFA PILLOW ARE POPULAR IMITATIONS.

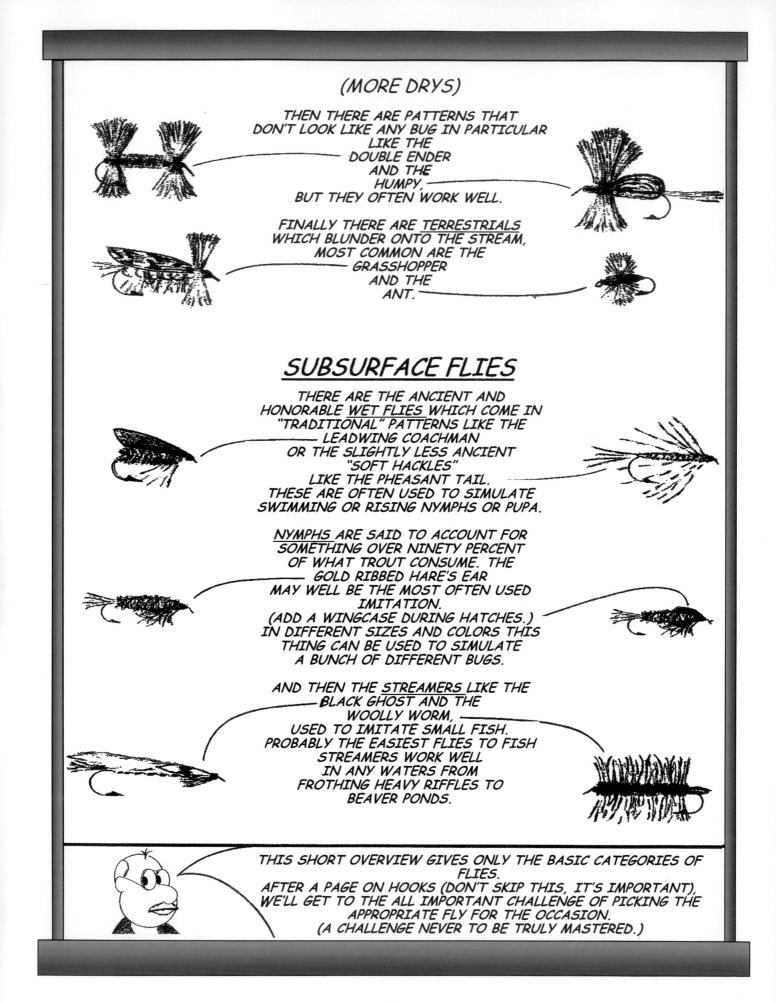

(MORE DRYS)

THEN THERE ARE PATTERNS THAT
DON'T LOOK LIKE ANY BUG IN PARTICULAR
LIKE THE
DOUBLE ENDER
AND THE
HUMPY,
BUT THEY OFTEN WORK WELL.

FINALLY THERE ARE TERRESTRIALS
WHICH BLUNDER ONTO THE STREAM,
MOST COMMON ARE THE
GRASSHOPPER
AND THE
ANT.

SUBSURFACE FLIES

THERE ARE THE ANCIENT AND
HONORABLE WET FLIES WHICH COME IN
"TRADITIONAL" PATTERNS LIKE THE
LEADWING COACHMAN
OR THE SLIGHTLY LESS ANCIENT
"SOFT HACKLES"
LIKE THE PHEASANT TAIL.
THESE ARE OFTEN USED TO SIMULATE
SWIMMING OR RISING NYMPHS OR PUPA.

NYMPHS ARE SAID TO ACCOUNT FOR
SOMETHING OVER NINETY PERCENT
OF WHAT TROUT CONSUME. THE
GOLD RIBBED HARE'S EAR
MAY WELL BE THE MOST OFTEN USED
IMITATION.
(ADD A WINGCASE DURING HATCHES.)
IN DIFFERENT SIZES AND COLORS THIS
THING CAN BE USED TO SIMULATE
A BUNCH OF DIFFERENT BUGS.

AND THEN THE STREAMERS LIKE THE
BLACK GHOST AND THE
WOOLLY WORM,
USED TO IMITATE SMALL FISH.
PROBABLY THE EASIEST FLIES TO FISH
STREAMERS WORK WELL
IN ANY WATERS FROM
FROTHING HEAVY RIFFLES TO
BEAVER PONDS.

THIS SHORT OVERVIEW GIVES ONLY THE BASIC CATEGORIES OF
FLIES.
AFTER A PAGE ON HOOKS (DON'T SKIP THIS, IT'S IMPORTANT),
WE'LL GET TO THE ALL IMPORTANT CHALLENGE OF PICKING THE
APPROPRIATE FLY FOR THE OCCASION.
(A CHALLENGE NEVER TO BE TRULY MASTERED.)

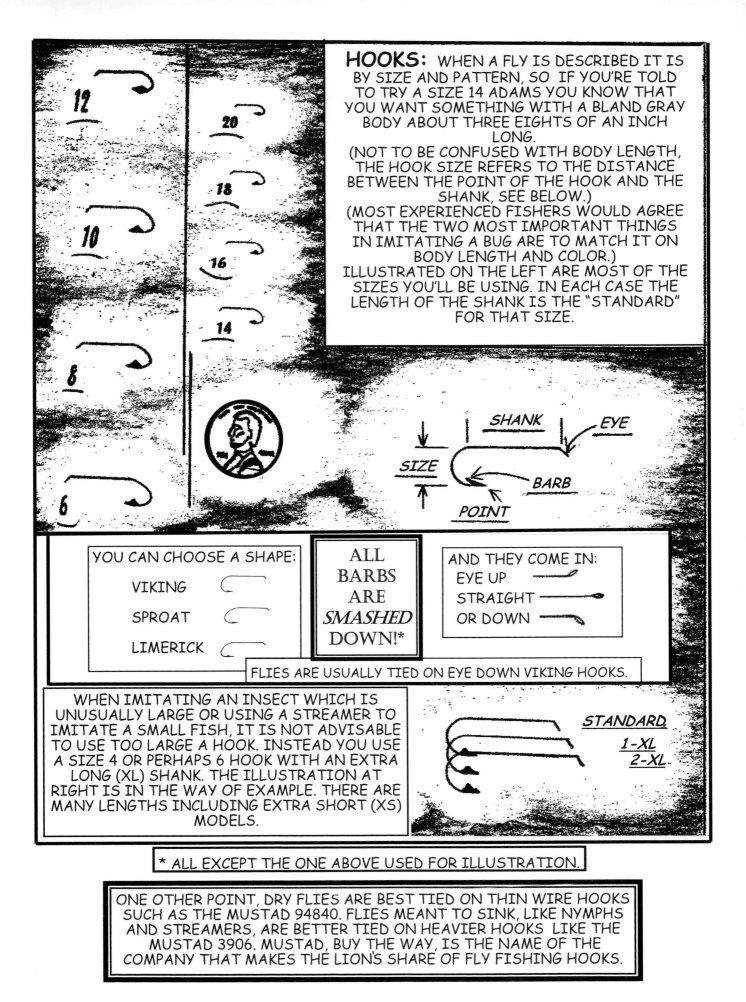

HOOKS: WHEN A FLY IS DESCRIBED IT IS BY SIZE AND PATTERN, SO IF YOU'RE TOLD TO TRY A SIZE 14 ADAMS YOU KNOW THAT YOU WANT SOMETHING WITH A BLAND GRAY BODY ABOUT THREE EIGHTS OF AN INCH LONG.

(NOT TO BE CONFUSED WITH BODY LENGTH, THE HOOK SIZE REFERS TO THE DISTANCE BETWEEN THE POINT OF THE HOOK AND THE SHANK, SEE BELOW.)

(MOST EXPERIENCED FISHERS WOULD AGREE THAT THE TWO MOST IMPORTANT THINGS IN IMITATING A BUG ARE TO MATCH IT ON BODY LENGTH AND COLOR.)

ILLUSTRATED ON THE LEFT ARE MOST OF THE SIZES YOU'LL BE USING. IN EACH CASE THE LENGTH OF THE SHANK IS THE "STANDARD" FOR THAT SIZE.

12 20 18 10 16 14 8 6

SHANK   EYE
SIZE   BARB
POINT

YOU CAN CHOOSE A SHAPE:

VIKING

SPROAT

LIMERICK

ALL BARBS ARE *SMASHED* DOWN!*

AND THEY COME IN:
EYE UP
STRAIGHT
OR DOWN

FLIES ARE USUALLY TIED ON EYE DOWN VIKING HOOKS.

WHEN IMITATING AN INSECT WHICH IS UNUSUALLY LARGE OR USING A STREAMER TO IMITATE A SMALL FISH, IT IS NOT ADVISABLE TO USE TOO LARGE A HOOK. INSTEAD YOU USE A SIZE 4 OR PERHAPS 6 HOOK WITH AN EXTRA LONG (XL) SHANK. THE ILLUSTRATION AT RIGHT IS IN THE WAY OF EXAMPLE. THERE ARE MANY LENGTHS INCLUDING EXTRA SHORT (XS) MODELS.

STANDARD
1-XL
2-XL

* ALL EXCEPT THE ONE ABOVE USED FOR ILLUSTRATION.

ONE OTHER POINT, DRY FLIES ARE BEST TIED ON THIN WIRE HOOKS SUCH AS THE MUSTAD 94840. FLIES MEANT TO SINK, LIKE NYMPHS AND STREAMERS, ARE BETTER TIED ON HEAVIER HOOKS LIKE THE MUSTAD 3906. MUSTAD, BUY THE WAY, IS THE NAME OF THE COMPANY THAT MAKES THE LION'S SHARE OF FLY FISHING HOOKS.

TWITCHES:
THROUGH THE REST OF THIS MANUAL I WILL OFTEN RECOMMEND THE USE OF TWITCHES WHEN YOU ARE "DEAD DRIFTING" A FLY. MANY COMPETENT FLY FISHERS WOULD DISAGREE, BUT THEN THERE ARE OTHERS WHO WOULD SIDE WITH ME. ONE THING IS SURE, IF YOU **OVER TWITCH** YOU'LL **SCARE OFF THE FISH**, SO BE DISCRETE. ALWAYS TRY TO IMAGINE WHAT THE FISH EXPECT TO SEE THE INSECT DOING.

IT IS A COMMON EXPERIENCE TO HAVE A FISH LUNGE FOR YOUR FLY JUST AS YOU TRY TO LIFT IT OFF THE WATER IN PREPARATION FOR ANOTHER CAST. PRESUMABLY THE FISH WAS WATCHING IT BUT WAS UNCERTAIN ABOUT ITS PARENTAGE, WHEN THE THING MOVED THE FISH LIKELY DECIDED IT WAS NOW OR NEVER AND SET ASIDE CAUTION. AN OCCASIONAL TWITCH OF A DRY FLY WHILE IT IS DEAD DRIFTING MAY HAVE THE SAME EFFECT. ON THE OTHER HAND, WHEN YOU TWITCH A DEAD DRIFTING NYMPH YOU ARE SIMPLY SIMULATING ITS EFFORTS TO GET A HOLD ON THE SUBSTRATE AGAIN.

TO TWITCH ARIGHT YOU WILL NEED TO GET MOST (NOT ALL) OF THE SLACK OUT OF YOUR LINE, THEN GIVE THE ROD TIP A SMALL JERK. YOU DO NOT WANT THE FLY TO MOVE MORE THAN HALF ITS LENGTH, MOST OFTEN YOU JUST WANT IT TO APPEAR TO FLINCH. THE SLACK IN THE LINE AND THE RESISTANCE OF THE WATER WILL REDUCE THE MOVEMENT OF THE FLY. BEFORE TRYING THIS ON THE FISH YOU SHOULD CAST A DRY FLY OUT A WAYS AND PRACTICE A BIT.

A FLY FISHER TYPOLOGY:
AS A SORT OF FRAMEWORK FOR THIS EXTENSIVE CHAPTER I'LL TRY TO STUFF FLY FISHERS INTO ONE OF FOUR TYPES, THESE PIGEONHOLES ARE NOT AT ALL ARBITRARY, TROUBLE IS MOST OF US FIT INTO MORE THAN ONE, DEPENDING UPON CIRCUMSTANCES. THE FOUR TYPES ARE: MYOPIC-THE ONE FLY MAN, ECLECTIC-THE GUY WHO STICKS TO A FEW FAVORITES, ACADEMIC-THE ONE WHO ASKS AROUND AND EMPIRICIST- HE WHO MAKES A SCIENCE OF IT ALL.

FELLA UP ON THE SALMON RIVER TOLD ME THAT "IF THEY WON'T TAKE A RENEGADE THEY AIN'T WORTH CATCHIN'." HE IS OF THE TYPE

MYOPIC.

{TO ME A RENEGADE (ILLUSTRATED HERE) WITH IT'S STANDARD HACKLE AT BOTH ENDS AND IT'S EMERALD GREEN PEACOCK HERL BODY LOOKS LIKE A PORCUPINE DRESSED UP FOR ST. PATRICK'S DAY.} BUT THAT IS NOT THE POINT. IF YOU INSIST ON CONFINING YOURSELF TO JUST ONE LURE I'D SUGGEST A SALMON EGG. STILL, THE MANY FLY PATTERNS WHICH HAVE WON SUCH SLAVISH DEVOTION MUST BE PRETTY GOOD, **SOME OF THE TIME.**

SANCTUS
SANCTUS

AN OBVIOUS STEP UP IS THE FISHER I'LL CALL THE **ECLECTIC**, HE KNOWS NOTHING ABOUT WHAT'S GOING ON IN THE STREAM, BUT HE KNOWS ENOUGH TO TRY ANOTHER FLY WHEN THE ONE HE HAS TIED ON ISN'T WORKING.

WE ALL EVOLVE OUR OWN SET OF FAVORED FLIES, MINE WAS SOMEWHAT DIFFERENT A YEAR AGO AND WILL BE A YEAR FROM NOW. MY CURRENT SET IS DESCRIBED BELOW BECAUSE I ASSUME YOU TO BE A NEOPHYTE IN NEED OF A STARTING POINT. IN ADDITION THIS IS A CONVENIENT WAY TO SLIP IN A NUMBER OF OTHER IMPORTANT CONCEPTS.

MANY OF THESE FLIES ARE ILLUSTRATED IN THEIR NATURAL HABITAT, THAT IS, CAUGHT IN A TREE OR BUSH.

WATCH YOUR BACKSIDE!

THERE ARE A FEW UNATTRIBUTED QUOTATIONS HERE, ALL COME FROM SOMEONE CONSIDERED EXPERT IN THE FIELD, EACH HAS PUBLISHED AT LEAST TWO MANUALS ON SOME AREA OF FLY FISHING.

THE **ADAMS** IS MY FAVORITE, IT FALLS INTO THE CATEGORY OF "SEARCHING PATTERNS". SUCH FLIES ARE USUALLY OF A RATHER BLAND COLORING BUT HAVE THE GREAT VIRTUE OF LOOKING SOMEWHAT LIKE A LOT OF BUGS. YOU USE THEM WHEN YOU HAVE NO IDEA WHAT ELSE TO USE (WHICH MEANS QUITE OFTEN).

"THIS FLY HAS LED TO THE DEMISE OF MORE FISH THAN ANY OTHER I KNOW."

"PERHAPS AMERICA'S FAVORITE FLY, THE ADAMS IMITATES A LOT OF THINGS THAT TROUT EAT."

THE **ELK HAIR CADDIS** IS ANOTHER GREAT SEARCHING PATTERN, IT'S SWEPT WING GIVES IT THE PROFILE OF A CADDIS OR STONEFLY.

"THIS IS THE FLY I WOULD TIE ON WHEN IN DOUBT OF WHAT TO USE."

"I RECOMMEND AL TROTH'S ELK HAIR CADDIS AS ONE OF THE MOST VERSATILE FLY PATTERNS TO BE HAD."

THE **ROYAL WULFF** IS WHAT IS CALLED AN "ATTRACTOR PATTERN", THESE ARE GAUDY THINGS THAT DON'T LOOK MUCH LIKE ANY BUG, BUT THERE ARE DAYS WHEN THEY CAN'T BE BEAT. WHEN LEE WULFF, IT'S CREATOR, WAS ASKED WHAT SORT OF INSECT IT WAS SUPPOSED TO IMITATE HE REPORTEDLY RESPONDED "WELL, I DON'T THINK THEY REPRESENT ANY ONE NATURAL INSECT, BUT MORE A DESSERT . . . LIKE STRAWBERRY SHORTCAKE." THERE YOU HAVE A SUCCINCT AND VIVID DEFINITION OF AN ATTRACTOR PATTERN: STRAWBERRY SHORTCAKE.

"THERE ARE FEW PATTERNS THAT OFFER A HIGHER FLOAT, BETTER VISIBILITY TO THE FISHERMAN, AND MORE ATTRACTION TO THE TROUT THAN THIS ONE."

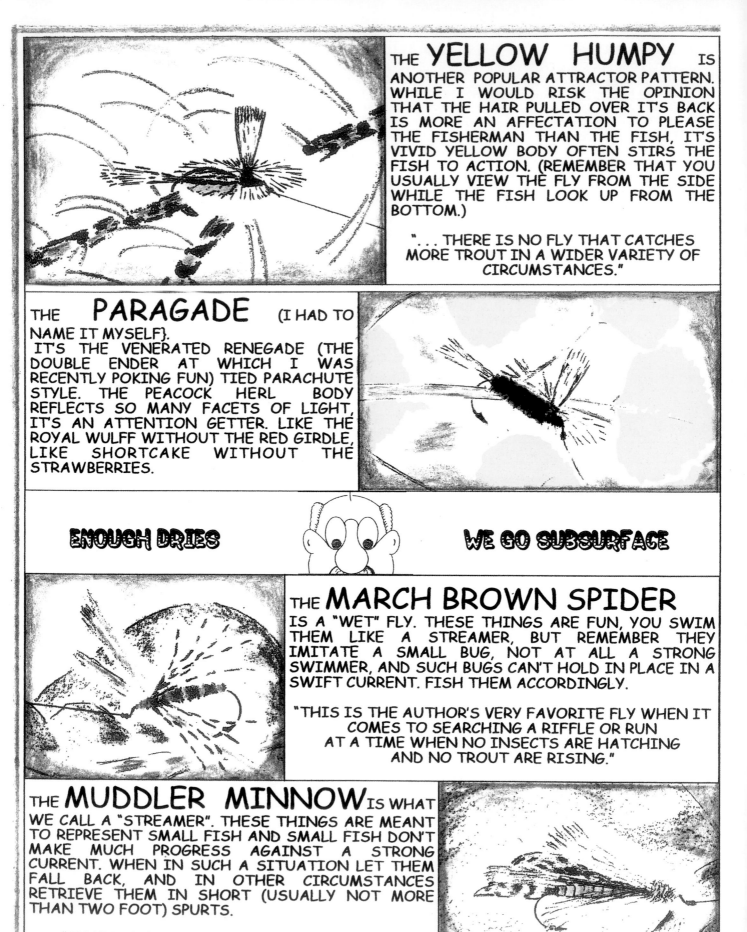

THE YELLOW HUMPY IS

ANOTHER POPULAR ATTRACTOR PATTERN. WHILE I WOULD RISK THE OPINION THAT THE HAIR PULLED OVER IT'S BACK IS MORE AN AFFECTATION TO PLEASE THE FISHERMAN THAN THE FISH, IT'S VIVID YELLOW BODY OFTEN STIRS THE FISH TO ACTION. (REMEMBER THAT YOU USUALLY VIEW THE FLY FROM THE SIDE WHILE THE FISH LOOK UP FROM THE BOTTOM.)

"... THERE IS NO FLY THAT CATCHES MORE TROUT IN A WIDER VARIETY OF CIRCUMSTANCES."

THE PARAGADE (I HAD TO NAME IT MYSELF).

IT'S THE VENERATED RENEGADE (THE DOUBLE ENDER AT WHICH I WAS RECENTLY POKING FUN) TIED PARACHUTE STYLE. THE PEACOCK HERL BODY REFLECTS SO MANY FACETS OF LIGHT, IT'S AN ATTENTION GETTER. LIKE THE ROYAL WULFF WITHOUT THE RED GIRDLE, LIKE SHORTCAKE WITHOUT THE STRAWBERRIES.

ENOUGH DRIES   WE GO SUBSURFACE

THE MARCH BROWN SPIDER

IS A "WET" FLY. THESE THINGS ARE FUN, YOU SWIM THEM LIKE A STREAMER, BUT REMEMBER THEY IMITATE A SMALL BUG, NOT AT ALL A STRONG SWIMMER, AND SUCH BUGS CAN'T HOLD IN PLACE IN A SWIFT CURRENT. FISH THEM ACCORDINGLY.

"THIS IS THE AUTHOR'S VERY FAVORITE FLY WHEN IT COMES TO SEARCHING A RIFFLE OR RUN AT A TIME WHEN NO INSECTS ARE HATCHING AND NO TROUT ARE RISING."

THE MUDDLER MINNOW IS WHAT

WE CALL A "STREAMER". THESE THINGS ARE MEANT TO REPRESENT SMALL FISH AND SMALL FISH DON'T MAKE MUCH PROGRESS AGAINST A STRONG CURRENT. WHEN IN SUCH A SITUATION LET THEM FALL BACK, AND IN OTHER CIRCUMSTANCES RETRIEVE THEM IN SHORT (USUALLY NOT MORE THAN TWO FOOT) SPURTS.

"IN MY OPINION THE MUDDLER MINNOW IS BEYOND ALL DOUBT THE GREATEST FLY EVER TIED."

THE **WOOLLY BUGGER** IS PROBABLY THE MOST POPULAR STREAMER IN THE WEST. IT IS THE TRADITIONAL WOOLLY WORM WITH A VERY SUBSTANTIAL "MARABOU" TAIL TACKED ON. IN THIS ILLUSTRATION I'VE ADDED A MARABOU CAPE. THE TAIL IS OBLIGATORY, THE CAPE OPTIONAL. AND IT MAY BE TIED IN MANY COLORS.

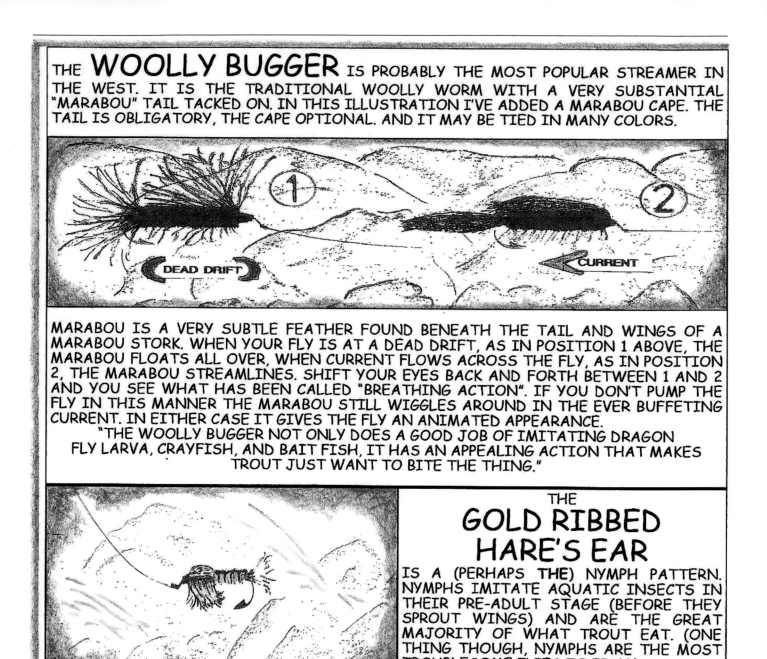

MARABOU IS A VERY SUBTLE FEATHER FOUND BENEATH THE TAIL AND WINGS OF A MARABOU STORK. WHEN YOUR FLY IS AT A DEAD DRIFT, AS IN POSITION 1 ABOVE, THE MARABOU FLOATS ALL OVER, WHEN CURRENT FLOWS ACROSS THE FLY, AS IN POSITION 2, THE MARABOU STREAMLINES. SHIFT YOUR EYES BACK AND FORTH BETWEEN 1 AND 2 AND YOU SEE WHAT HAS BEEN CALLED "BREATHING ACTION". IF YOU DON'T PUMP THE FLY IN THIS MANNER THE MARABOU STILL WIGGLES AROUND IN THE EVER BUFFETING CURRENT. IN EITHER CASE IT GIVES THE FLY AN ANIMATED APPEARANCE.
"THE WOOLLY BUGGER NOT ONLY DOES A GOOD JOB OF IMITATING DRAGON FLY LARVA, CRAYFISH, AND BAIT FISH, IT HAS AN APPEALING ACTION THAT MAKES TROUT JUST WANT TO BITE THE THING."

THE GOLD RIBBED HARE'S EAR

IS A (PERHAPS **THE**) NYMPH PATTERN. NYMPHS IMITATE AQUATIC INSECTS IN THEIR PRE-ADULT STAGE (BEFORE THEY SPROUT WINGS) AND ARE THE GREAT MAJORITY OF WHAT TROUT EAT. (ONE THING THOUGH, NYMPHS ARE THE MOST TROUBLESOME FLIES TO FISH.)

"THE GOLD RIBBED HARE'S EAR IMITATES A GREAT VARIETY OF NYMPHS AND CAN WORK WONDERS ON OTHERWISE SNOBBISH TROUT."
"THIS PATTERN SUGGESTS THE FORM AND COLOR OF SO MANY AQUATIC INSECTS THAT WE ALWAYS CARRY IT IN A FULL RANGE OF SIZES."
"THE OFTEN MENTIONED GOLD RIBBED HARE'S EAR . . . IS ONE OF THE BEST."
"I NOW HEARTILY RECOMMEND THIS ONE TO ANYONE FISHING THE WEST."
". . . GOLD RIBBED HARE'S EAR AND ZUG BUG, TWO OF OUR FAVORITE SEARCHING PATTERNS."

WHILE THE HARE'S EAR DOES WELL AT IMITATING LIGHTER COLORED NYMPHS THE **ZUG BUG** IS **VERY** OFTEN RECOMMENDED FOR THE DARKER ONES.
"IT (THE ZUG BUG) IS AN EXCELLENT SEARCHING PATTERN; LIKE THE GOLD RIBBED HARE'S EAR, IT WILL IMITATE MANY DIFFERENT INSECTS."
"IT HAS TO BE ONE OF THE BEST SLOW WATER NYMPHS EVER INVENTED."

DO YOU GET THE FEELING FROM THE ACCOLADES QUOTED HERE THAT MY SELECTION OF FAVORITES WAS NOT HIT UPON ALTOGETHER INDEPENDENTLY?
FORTUNATELY, THAT IS TRUE.

NOW THE OTHER IMPORTANT THING IS **FLY SIZE.**

WE'RE TALKING ABOUT THE ALL TOO COMMON CASE WHERE YOU DON'T KNOW WHAT'S GOING ON SO BOTH PATTERN AND FLY SIZE ARE SOMETHING OF A GUESS. MY GUESSES ON SIZE (THEY'RE STARTING POINTS) WOULD BE:

> # 14 STANDARD LENGTH HOOK FOR THE ADAMS, ROYAL WULFF, YELLOW HUMPY, PARAGADE, MARCH BROWN SPIDER, GOLD RIBBED HARE'S EAR AND ZUG BUG.
> # 12 STANDARD FOR THE ELK HAIR CADDIS. (IT REPRESENTS A CADDIS OR STONE FLY AND THEY AVERAGE A BIT LARGER THAN MAYFLIES.)
> # 4 3-XL (RECALL THAT MEANS THE HOOK SHANK IS THREE SIZES OVER LENGTH) FOR THE MUDDLER MINNOW AND WOOLLY BUGGER. (THESE PASS FOR LITTLE FISH.)

REMEMBER THE WHOLE IDEA HERE IS TO BE FLEXIBLE, CHANGE PATTERNS WHEN BETTER ONES COME ALONG, AND DON'T GET HOOKED ON JUST ONE SIZE.

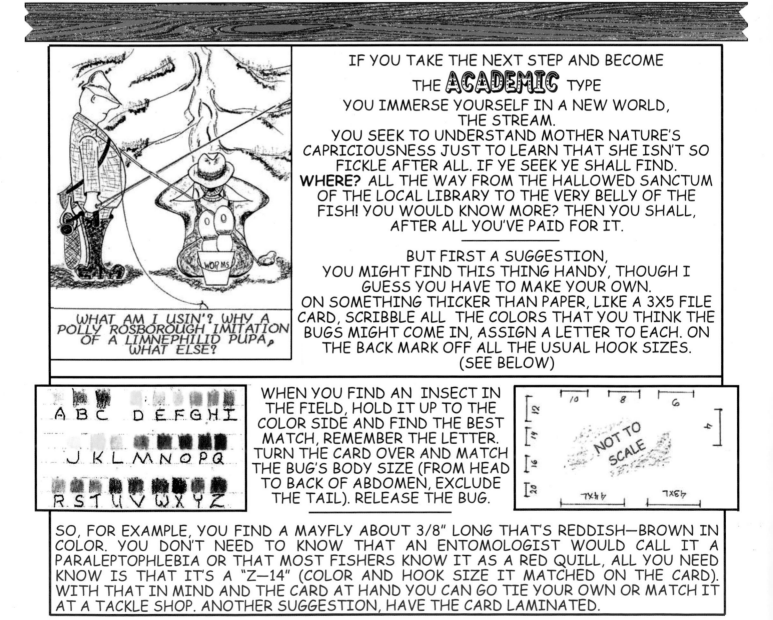

WHAT AM I USIN'? WHY A POLLY ROSBOROUGH IMITATION OF A LIMNEPHILID PUPA, WHAT ELSE?

IF YOU TAKE THE NEXT STEP AND BECOME THE **ACADEMIC** TYPE
YOU IMMERSE YOURSELF IN A NEW WORLD, THE STREAM.
YOU SEEK TO UNDERSTAND MOTHER NATURE'S CAPRICIOUSNESS JUST TO LEARN THAT SHE ISN'T SO FICKLE AFTER ALL. IF YE SEEK YE SHALL FIND. **WHERE?** ALL THE WAY FROM THE HALLOWED SANCTUM OF THE LOCAL LIBRARY TO THE VERY BELLY OF THE FISH! YOU WOULD KNOW MORE? THEN YOU SHALL, AFTER ALL YOU'VE PAID FOR IT.

BUT FIRST A SUGGESTION,
YOU MIGHT FIND THIS THING HANDY, THOUGH I GUESS YOU HAVE TO MAKE YOUR OWN.
ON SOMETHING THICKER THAN PAPER, LIKE A 3X5 FILE CARD, SCRIBBLE ALL THE COLORS THAT YOU THINK THE BUGS MIGHT COME IN, ASSIGN A LETTER TO EACH. ON THE BACK MARK OFF ALL THE USUAL HOOK SIZES.
(SEE BELOW)

WHEN YOU FIND AN INSECT IN THE FIELD, HOLD IT UP TO THE COLOR SIDE AND FIND THE BEST MATCH, REMEMBER THE LETTER. TURN THE CARD OVER AND MATCH THE BUG'S BODY SIZE (FROM HEAD TO BACK OF ABDOMEN, EXCLUDE THE TAIL). RELEASE THE BUG.

SO, FOR EXAMPLE, YOU FIND A MAYFLY ABOUT 3/8" LONG THAT'S REDDISH—BROWN IN COLOR. YOU DON'T NEED TO KNOW THAT AN ENTOMOLOGIST WOULD CALL IT A PARALEPTOPHLEBIA OR THAT MOST FISHERS KNOW IT AS A RED QUILL, ALL YOU NEED KNOW IS THAT IT'S A "Z—14" (COLOR AND HOOK SIZE IT MATCHED ON THE CARD). WITH THAT IN MIND AND THE CARD AT HAND YOU CAN GO TIE YOUR OWN OR MATCH IT AT A TACKLE SHOP. ANOTHER SUGGESTION, HAVE THE CARD LAMINATED.

ANOTHER SUGGESTION, TAKE NOTES. A POCKET SIZE LOOSE LEAF NOTE BOOK IS BEST. IT SHOULD BE LOOSE LEAF BECAUSE EACH NEW ENTRY YOU MAKE SHOULD BE PUT IN PLACE AMONG PREEXISTING PAGES. ORGANIZE IT IN THE WAY THAT SUITS YOU BEST, MINE IS BY MONTH AND WITHIN MONTH BY LOCATION.
AN EXAMPLE (SEE ILLUSTRATION):

IN THE MIDDLE OF SEPTEMBER, IN THE MIDDLE OF THE AFTERNOON UPSTREAM OF THE MARTYR'S BRIDGE ON ST. ANTHONY'S CREEK, AT AN ALTITUDE ESTIMATED AS 6,000 FT. AND WITH A WATER TEMPERATURE MEASURED AS 57 DEGREES, I WAS HAVING NO SUCCESS WITH MY USUAL FAVORITES. THEN I FOUND A MAYFLY IN THE BUSHES AND MATCHED IT TO MY CARD. THE COLOR WAS Z (REDDISH-BROWN) AND THE BODY LENGTH THAT OF A SIZE 14 STANDARD HOOK.

APPARENTLY (I MUST SURMISE, THIS ENTRY WAS MADE 15 YEARS AGO) I HAD NO IMITATION TO MATCH THAT BUT I HAD MY STREAM SIDE FLY TYING STUFF, SO I DID MY BEST TO CREATE ONE, TOOK IT OUT AND TRIED IT AND THE STREAM THAT SEEMED STERILE BEFORE WAS SUDDENLY ALIVE WITH FISH !
THIS IS CLEAR EVIDENCE THAT THERE WAS A Z—14 (RED QUILL) HATCH GOING ON AND THE FISH HAD BECOME SELECTIVE TO THAT BUG.

I WOULD LIKE TO BLAME MY FAILURE TO SPOT THE BUG BEFORE I WASTED TIME TRYING MY USUALS ON TIMING, THE RED QUILLS HAD EMERGED, FLOWN AWAY AND NOT YET RETURNED TO MATE AND OVIPOSIT. (MUCH MORE ON THIS SHORTLY.) IN ANY CASE FISH MAY BECOME SELECTIVE TO VERY SPARSE HATCHES AND THEY WILL CONTINUE SEARCHING FOR THAT PARTICULAR SPECIES LONG AFTER IT HAS LEFT THE STREAM.
(JUST EXCUSES? YOU'RE RIGHT. ALWAYS BE WATCHFUL !)

STOMACH

ESOPHAGUS

THERE IS MORE TO BE GLEANED FROM THIS ENTRY. THE LETTERS "SC" ABBREVIATE **STOMACH CONTENTS.** IF YOU KEEP A FISH YOU'LL BE CLEANING IT AND WHEN YOU DO SO THERE IS MUCH TO BE LEARNED IF YOU TAKE A FEW MORE SECONDS AND OPEN THE STOMACH AND ESOPHAGUS. OBVIOUSLY THERE'S NO MORE CERTAIN WAY TO KNOW WHAT THE FISH HAS BEEN EATING. RECORD WHAT YOU FIND IN YOUR NOTE BOOK. A COMPARISON OF AN ACCUMULATION OF SUCH NOTES WILL SURELY RESULT IN SOME IMPORTANT INSIGHTS.

AN ENTRY WHICH SIMPLY GIVES THE NAME OF THE WATERWAY IS NOT SUFFICIENT, ESPECIALLY IN THE WEST WHERE STREAMS OFTEN FLOW DOWN RATHER STEEP INCLINES. THE SPECIES OF BUG WHICH IS HATCHING AT SOME PARTICULAR POINT TODAY PROBABLY HATCHED LOWER DOWN STREAM A WEEK AGO AND WILL EMERGE FURTHER UP STREAM A WEEK OR SO FROM NOW. BE MORE PRECISE ABOUT LOCATION LIKE "ABOVE MARTYR'S BRIDGE", LACKING SUCH A LANDMARK AT LEAST DO YOUR BEST TO ESTIMATE ALTITUDE.
WATER TEMPERATURE IS IMPORTANT TOO, UNSEASONABLY COLD WATER WILL PROBABLY DELAY A HATCH.

ON YOUR WAY UP THE CREEK STOP BY THE LOCAL # TACKLE SHOP AND ASK

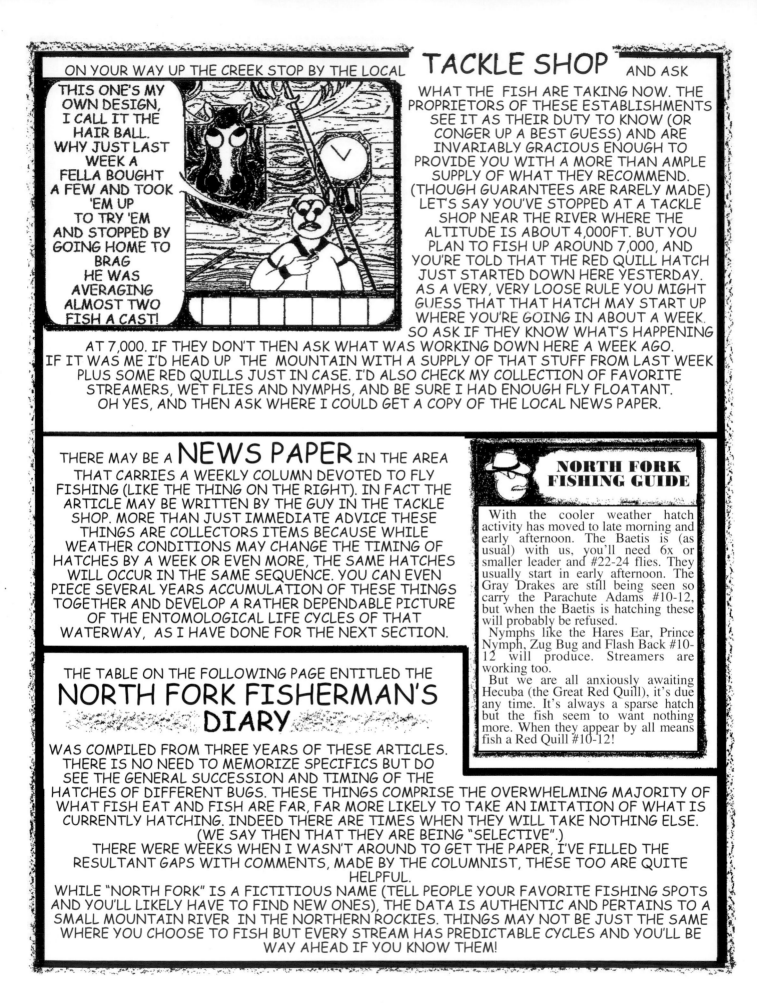

THIS ONE'S MY OWN DESIGN, I CALL IT THE HAIR BALL. WHY JUST LAST WEEK A FELLA BOUGHT A FEW AND TOOK 'EM UP TO TRY 'EM AND STOPPED BY GOING HOME TO BRAG HE WAS AVERAGING ALMOST TWO FISH A CAST!

WHAT THE FISH ARE TAKING NOW. THE PROPRIETORS OF THESE ESTABLISHMENTS SEE IT AS THEIR DUTY TO KNOW (OR CONGER UP A BEST GUESS) AND ARE INVARIABLY GRACIOUS ENOUGH TO PROVIDE YOU WITH A MORE THAN AMPLE SUPPLY OF WHAT THEY RECOMMEND. (THOUGH GUARANTEES ARE RARELY MADE) LET'S SAY YOU'VE STOPPED AT A TACKLE SHOP NEAR THE RIVER WHERE THE ALTITUDE IS ABOUT 4,000FT. BUT YOU PLAN TO FISH UP AROUND 7,000, AND YOU'RE TOLD THAT THE RED QUILL HATCH JUST STARTED DOWN HERE YESTERDAY. AS A VERY, VERY LOOSE RULE YOU MIGHT GUESS THAT THAT HATCH MAY START UP WHERE YOU'RE GOING IN ABOUT A WEEK. SO ASK IF THEY KNOW WHAT'S HAPPENING AT 7,000. IF THEY DON'T THEN ASK WHAT WAS WORKING DOWN HERE A WEEK AGO. IF IT WAS ME I'D HEAD UP THE MOUNTAIN WITH A SUPPLY OF THAT STUFF FROM LAST WEEK PLUS SOME RED QUILLS JUST IN CASE. I'D ALSO CHECK MY COLLECTION OF FAVORITE STREAMERS, WET FLIES AND NYMPHS, AND BE SURE I HAD ENOUGH FLY FLOATANT. OH YES, AND THEN ASK WHERE I COULD GET A COPY OF THE LOCAL NEWS PAPER.

THERE MAY BE A # NEWS PAPER IN THE AREA THAT CARRIES A WEEKLY COLUMN DEVOTED TO FLY FISHING (LIKE THE THING ON THE RIGHT). IN FACT THE ARTICLE MAY BE WRITTEN BY THE GUY IN THE TACKLE SHOP. MORE THAN JUST IMMEDIATE ADVICE THESE THINGS ARE COLLECTORS ITEMS BECAUSE WHILE WEATHER CONDITIONS MAY CHANGE THE TIMING OF HATCHES BY A WEEK OR EVEN MORE, THE SAME HATCHES WILL OCCUR IN THE SAME SEQUENCE. YOU CAN EVEN PIECE SEVERAL YEARS ACCUMULATION OF THESE THINGS TOGETHER AND DEVELOP A RATHER DEPENDABLE PICTURE OF THE ENTOMOLOGICAL LIFE CYCLES OF THAT WATERWAY, AS I HAVE DONE FOR THE NEXT SECTION.

NORTH FORK FISHING GUIDE

With the cooler weather hatch activity has moved to late morning and early afternoon. The Baetis is (as usual) with us, you'll need 6x or smaller leader and #22-24 flies. They usually start in early afternoon. The Gray Drakes are still being seen so carry the Parachute Adams #10-12, but when the Baetis is hatching these will probably be refused.

Nymphs like the Hares Ear, Prince Nymph, Zug Bug and Flash Back #10-12 will produce. Streamers are working too.

But we are all anxiously awaiting Hecuba (the Great Red Quill), it's due any time. It's always a sparse hatch but the fish seem to want nothing more. When they appear by all means fish a Red Quill #10-12!

THE TABLE ON THE FOLLOWING PAGE ENTITLED THE

NORTH FORK FISHERMAN'S DIARY

WAS COMPILED FROM THREE YEARS OF THESE ARTICLES. THERE IS NO NEED TO MEMORIZE SPECIFICS BUT DO SEE THE GENERAL SUCCESSION AND TIMING OF THE HATCHES OF DIFFERENT BUGS. THESE THINGS COMPRISE THE OVERWHELMING MAJORITY OF WHAT FISH EAT AND FISH ARE FAR, FAR MORE LIKELY TO TAKE AN IMITATION OF WHAT IS CURRENTLY HATCHING. INDEED THERE ARE TIMES WHEN THEY WILL TAKE NOTHING ELSE. (WE SAY THEN THAT THEY ARE BEING "SELECTIVE".) THERE WERE WEEKS WHEN I WASN'T AROUND TO GET THE PAPER, I'VE FILLED THE RESULTANT GAPS WITH COMMENTS, MADE BY THE COLUMNIST, THESE TOO ARE QUITE HELPFUL. WHILE "NORTH FORK" IS A FICTITIOUS NAME (TELL PEOPLE YOUR FAVORITE FISHING SPOTS AND YOU'LL LIKELY HAVE TO FIND NEW ONES), THE DATA IS AUTHENTIC AND PERTAINS TO A SMALL MOUNTAIN RIVER IN THE NORTHERN ROCKIES. THINGS MAY NOT BE JUST THE SAME WHERE YOU CHOOSE TO FISH BUT EVERY STREAM HAS PREDICTABLE CYCLES AND YOU'LL BE WAY AHEAD IF YOU KNOW THEM!

NORTH FORK FISHERMAN'S DIARY

Month—Week

YEAR	6-1	6-2	6-3	7-1	7-2	7-3	7-4	8-1	8-4	9-2	9-3	9-4
90	large nymphs #8-12, woolly bugger (fish deep)	same as 6-1	unfishable	GN D, gn d, WQ	p adams #10-14	p adams, royal wulff #12-14; BAETIS #20; elk hair caddis #12 (late evening)	p adams #14-16; CADDIS (late evening)	p adams, royal wulff #14; p adams #10-12; BAETIS #16-18; GY D	RD Q #12-14; BAETIS #22; TRICO #20-22; HOPPERS	RD Q; rd q #12; TRICO	RD Q; rd q, grey wulff #12; TRICO #22; p adams #18-20	RD Q; GY D #12; BAETIS #22; TRICO; MIDGES
92	large nymphs #10 (zug bug, hare's ear, flashback, prince nymph) (fish deep)	unfishable		GN D, gn d; p adams #10	GN D, gn d, WQ; p adams #10-14	BAETIS #20-22; p adams #14-16; CADDIS #14-18 (late evening); HOPPERS	royal wulff, humpies, elk hair caddis #10-12; HOPPERS	GN D, gn d #10; p adams, stimulator #10-14; CADDIS; rusty spinner #14-16 (evening)	RD Q #12-14; BAETIS #22; TRICO #20-22; HOPPERS	RD Q; rd q #12; TRICO	RD Q; rd q, grey wulff #12; TRICO #22; p adams #18-20	RD Q; rd q #12; BAETIS #22; GY D; HOPPERS
93				large nymphs #8 (fish deep)	GN D, GY D, WQ, gn d; p adams #10-12; STONES; stimulator #10; CADDIS; HOPPERS			GN D, gn d #10; p adams, stimulator, tor #12-14; CADDIS; hopper #10-12		p adams #12-18; HOPPERS; dave's hopper #10-12	p adams #18-20	RD Q; rd q #12; BAETIS #22; GY D; p adams #12

Pertinent notes (in script), by year:

- **90:** *Daring spring run off fish back waters, side channels, beaver ponds, anything slower.*
- **90:** *The RD Q hatch usually peaks mid September and ends early October.*
- **92:** *It is noted in the 7-3 column that recent hard rains have probably prematurely ended the GN D and WQ hatches.*
- **93:** *The columnist warns that last winter's unusually deep snow pack should result in the delay of this season's hatches.*
- **93:** *Unseasonably cold water delays the maturation of nymphs and thus postpones their hatches.*
- **93:** *Very low, clear water calls for longer, finer leaders (eg. 12' of 7x).*

NOTES: THE NAMES OF INSECTS ARE PRINTED IN ALL CAPS. Suggested fly patterns are given in lower case. Pertinent notes, taken from the columns, are in script.

Abbreviations were necessary, decode them as follows: GN D = Green Drake, GY D = Gray Drake, WQ = Western Quill, RD Q = Red Quill, TRICO = Tricorythodes (a very small mayfly). HOPPERS = grasshoppers, and the fly pattern "p adams" = parachute adams.

NORTH FORK IS JUST A FEW HUNDRED MILES SOUTH OF CANADA AND AVERAGES ABOUT 6,000 FT. IN ALTITUDE. UP HERE SPRING SLEEPS IN AND THE RUN OFF FROM SNOW MELT DOESN'T USUALLY BECOME SERIOUS UNTIL THE BEGINNING OF JUNE. GENERALLY, UNTIL THE END OF JUNE, THE WATER RUNS HIGH, FAST, DIRTY AND COLD. IF THE STREAMS ARE FISHABLE AT ALL YOU SHOULD USE STREAMERS OR LARGE NYMPHS AND THESE SHOULD BE HEAVILY WEIGHTED TO GET THEM DOWN AND KEEP THEM THERE IN THE SWIFT CURRENT.

BUT I KNOW A LITTLE MEADOW, AT LEAST IT'S A MEADOW AGAIN COME AUGUST, WHICH BECOMES A BACK WATER POND DURING RUN OFF. THE WATER IS STILL, THE SEDIMENT SETTLES OUT, IT WARMS IN THE SUN AND I FISH DRY FLIES WHILE THE FOLKS BACK ON THE RIVER ARE USING NYMPHS TIED BY WRAPPING MOORING ROPE AROUND MEAT HOOKS. SEEK OUT THESE BACK WATERS, SIDE CHANNELS AND BEAVER PONDS WHEN THE MAINSTREAM IS RUNNING HIGH.

WHEN THE FLOOD SUBSIDES, USUALLY BY THE BEGINNING OF JULY, THE HATCHES (AND SO THE DRY FLY ACTION) BEGIN. FIRST COMES THE GREEN DRAKE, IT WILL PROBABLY BE AROUND FOR FROM TWO TO FOUR WEEKS. DURING THIS TIME THERE WILL BE PERIODS OF SPARSE AND SPORADIC EMERGENCE WITH ONE OR MORE PEAKS IN INTENSITY. THE PROPER IMITATION IS A GOOD BET THROUGHOUT, BUT ESPECIALLY DURING THE PEAKS. OVERLAPPING THE GREEN DRAKE PERIOD WILL COME THE GRAY DRAKE HATCH*. THIS INSECT MAY CONTINUE TO SHOW UP FOR MONTHS (SO HAVE A #12 PARACHUTE ADAMS AT HAND). TO COMPLICATE MATTERS BOTH THE GOLDEN AND THE LITTLE YELLOW STONE FLIES WILL PROBABLY APPEAR.

ABOUT THE MIDDLE OF JULY ALL THIS INTENSE HATCH ACTIVITY BACKS OFF AND YOU CAN TRY OUT SOME OTHER FLIES, LIKE THOSE GAUDY ATTRACTOR PATTERNS (EG. THE ROYAL WULFF OR THE YELLOW HUMPY), BUT THERE IS A FLY IN THE OINTMENT (SORRY). NOTE IN THE "DIARY" THAT THE DREADED NAME <u>BAETIS</u> APPEARS AND THEN LINGERS ON LIKE THE TASTE OF A DENVER OMELET. THE BAETIS IS A MAYFLY WITH A VERY SHORT LIFE SPAN, THEY GO THROUGH THREE OR FOUR GENERATIONS IN A SEASON, SO THEY SEEM TO BE FOREVER HATCHING. IN ADDITION THE FISH ARE VERY FOND OF THEM AND ARE KNOWN TO SOMETIMES IGNORE OTHER CONCURRENT HATCHES AND TARGET THE BAETIS. SO WHAT'S WRONG? GO BACK TO THE "DIARY" AND NOTE THE SUGGESTED FLY SIZES, USUALLY #20-22! A FLY THAT SMALL IS ALMOST IMPOSSIBLE TO KEEP TRACK OF ON THE WATER AND MUST BE TIED ON WITH A VERY FINE TIPPET. GET THAT HOOK INTO A GOOD SIZED TROUT AND YOU'RE CONNECTED TO IT BY MONOFILAMENT THAT'S PROBABLY RATED AT 3 1/2 LBS. OR LESS. IF YOU LAND THAT FISH YOU HAVE SOMETHING TO BRAG ABOUT— BUT WHO'LL BELIEVE YOU? THE GRASSHOPPER ALSO BECOMES IMPORTANT ABOUT NOW, CATCH ONE AND MATCH IT ON SIZE AND COLOR, AT LEAST YOU CAN SEE THE FOOL THING!

*TOO OFTEN THE LOCALS WILL HAVE THEIR OWN NAME FOR AN INSECT AND TOO OFTEN THAT NAME IS USED INTERCHANGEABLY WITH THE MORE COMMON ONE. BUT IF YOU MATCHED THE BUG ON SIZE AND COLOR USING THE CARD SUGGESTED A FEW PAGES BACK, YOU CAN'T GO MUCH WRONG.

continued ➤

AND NOW IT'S SEPTEMBER AGAIN AND THE "GREAT RED QUILL" IS ON THE WATER.

THEY'LL USUALLY START EMERGING IN LATE AUGUST AND CONTINUE FOR A MONTH OR A LITTLE MORE, SO COME PREPARED WITH SOME #10-14 IMITATIONS. THE GRAY DRAKE IS OFTEN STILL AROUND SO HAVE THE P ADAMS IN #12-14. THE HOPPERS CONTINUE TO BE A GOOD BET— AND THEN THERE IS THAT BLASTED BAETIS (SO BRING SOME MAGNIFYING GLASSES AND A BOTTLE OF ASPIRIN).

THERE WERE SOME OTHER POINTS IN THESE ARTICLES THAT I COULDN'T FIT IN SO THEY ARE TACKED ON BELOW.

THE FISH AREN'T USUALLY BEING SELECTIVE EVEN WHEN THERE IS AN ONGOING HATCH SO YOU CAN TRY OTHER PATTERNS, BUT YOU SHOULD CARRY APPROPRIATE IMITATIONS OF THAT HATCH—THEY COULD SAVE THE DAY.

IN THE WAY OF "I TOLD YOU SO" PLEASE NOTE THAT THE PARACHUTE ADAMS IS THE MOST OFTEN RECOMMENDED FLY BUT ALSO NOTE THAT IT IS SOMETIMES RECOMMENDED IN DIFFERENT SIZES. RECALL THAT IT'S A "SEARCHING PATTERN", USED TO IMITATE MANY DIFFERENT SPECIES AND THESE COME IN MANY DIFFERENT SIZES.
TO BE FAIR I SHOULD ADD THAT THERE ARE OTHER GRAY-BODIED PATTERNS THAT WOULD SERVE, LIKE THE HENDRICKSON OR THE GRAY WULFF.

THE CADDISFLY IS OFTEN RECOMMENDED BUT USUALLY WITH A NOTE LIKE "LATE EVENING". THIS IS A RATHER INCONVENIENT HABIT OF CADDISFLIES, EMERGING LATE IN THE DAY. IF YOU WISH TO "FISH OVER" THE HATCH, THAT IS TO DO IT WHILE THE BUG IS EMERGING, REMEMBER TO BRING YOUR PEN LIGHT. HOWEVER YOU MAY FIND AN APPROPRIATE IMITATION EFFECTIVE AT OTHER TIMES OF THE DAY.

THERE ARE MANY OTHER PATTERNS THAT MAY BE EFFECTIVE, VERY IMPORTANT AMONG THESE IS THE ANT. WHEN YOU FIND THEM CRAWLING OUT ON BRANCHES THAT OVERHANG THE WATER, ESPECIALLY ON WINDY DAYS WHEN A GUST MAY SHAKE THEM OFF, TRY FLOATING A FACSIMILE DOWN BENEATH THOSE BRANCHES.

WHEN THE WEATHER IS COOL OR MODERATE HATCHES USUALLY BEGIN IN LATE MORNING AND CONTINUE TILL MID AFTERNOON. BUT WHEN THE HEAT IS ON EMERGENCE TIMES USUALLY MOVE TO EARLY MORNING OR LATE AFTERNOON.

AT ANY TIME DURING THE SEASON STREAMERS AND NYMPHS WILL PROBABLY BE EFFECTIVE.

FROM THE NOTES IN THE "DIARY" YOU CAN SEE THAT WEATHER CAN BE AN IMPORTANT FACTOR IN THE TIMING OF HATCHES, BUT ALSO OBSERVE THAT THE SAME HATCHES OCCUR IN THE SAME ORDER.

IF THERE IS A NEWS PAPER WITH FISHING ARTICLES THEN THERE IS PROBABLY A LIBRARY WHICH ARCHIVES THEM. GO THERE AND SEEK THEM OUT. YOU MAY LEARN MORE IN AN HOUR THAN YOU WOULD FISHING THE RIVER BY TRIAL AND ERROR IN YEARS.

ONLY SOME IDGIT THAT'D SPEND YEARS DRAWIN' UP AN OVERSTUFFED FLY FISHIN' MANUEL WOULD ALSO THINK TO COME UP WITH SOMETHIN' LIKE THE "DIARY". (DO YOU REALIZE THAT THING WAS NEAR 20 YEARS IN THE MAKIN'?) BUT IT WAS WORTH IT IF IT'S GIVEN YOU SOME FEEL FOR THE COMING AND GOING OF THE FISH FOOD. STILL, YOU AREN'T LIKELY TO FIND ONE FOR YOUR STREAM. FORTUNATELY, WHERE SANITY (MORE OFTEN) PREVAILS YOU MAY FIND THESE THINGS CALLED **EMERGENCE TABLES.** THESE TABLES SHOW AVERAGE START AND END TIMES FOR THE ANNUAL HATCHES. EVEN KNOWING THIS YOU MAY FIND THAT THE EXPECTED HATCH ISN'T OCCURRING WHEN YOU GET THERE, BUT YOU WERE FOREWARNED SO YOU HAVE NO EXCUSE FOR SHOWING UP WITHOUT THE CORRECT FLY PATTERN IF THE USUAL HATCH IS IN PROGRESS. WHAT FOLLOWS IS AN EXAMPLE OF SUCH A TABLE BASED ON SEVEN YEARS OF ACCUMULATED NEWS PAPER ARTICLES FOR "NORTH FORK".

EMERGENCE TABLE: NORTH FORK

	JULY	AUGUST	SEPTEMBER
GREEN DRAKE	▬▬▬▬▬▬▬▬		
GRAY DRAKE	▬▬▬▬▬		▬▬▬▬
GOLDEN STONE	▬▬		
LITTLE YELLOW STONE	▬▬▬▬		
RED QUILL			▬▬▬▬▬▬▬
BAETIS	▬	▬	▬
TRICO	▬	▬	▬ ▬
CREAM DUNS	▬▬▬		

THE NUMEROUS CADDISFLY HATCHES HAVE BEEN OMITTED BECAUSE THE COLUMNIST, APPARENTLY ASSUMING THAT NO ONE WANTED TO FISH IN THE LATE EVENING, DIDN'T MENTION THE GENUS OR SPECIES OF THE EMERGING INSECT. BUT I'LL BET IF YOU FISH AN IMITATION OF THAT BUG THE NEXT DAY THE FISH WILL NOT HAVE FORGOTTEN.

WHILE ALL THIS PERTAINS TO JUST ONE RIVER THERE SHOULD BE MANY WITHIN THAT REGION FOR WHICH IT WOULD BE ACCURATE, BUT IN FAR-FLUNG ENVIRONS YOU WOULD NEED TO SEEK OUT INFORMATION ABOUT THAT LOCALE. ASK AT THE TACKLE SHOP. AS AN EXAMPLE IN *THE COMPLETE BOOK OF WESTERN HATCHES* (AN EXCELLENT TEXT FOR THOSE WHO WISH TO KNOW MORE ABOUT AQUATIC ENTOMOLOGY) THE AUTHORS INDICATE THAT THE GRAY DRAKE EMERGES IN THE (WESTERN) COASTAL MOUNTAINS EARLY IN THE SEASON AND IN THE ROCKIES DURING LATE SEASON. ON "NORTH FORK" IT DOES BOTH. THE LESSON?

KNOW YOUR WATERS

FINALLY, THE **EMPIRICIST.** THIS ONE SHAKES THE BUSHES, TURNS OVER THE ROCKS, DIPS A FINE NET IN THE FAST CURRENTS AND IF HE CAN'T FIND ANY APPROPRIATE BUGS HE REVERTS TO AN "ECLECTIC" AND TRIES ALL HIS "SEARCHING" PATTERNS. THEN, WHEN HE FINALLY GETS A FISH, HE CHECKS STOMACH CONTENTS AND FINDS SOMETHING TO IMITATE. (WANT TO BET IT'S A BAETIS?) HE TIES HIS OWN FLIES, HE EVEN HAS AN AQUARIUM IN THE LIVING ROOM, NOTHING IN IT BUT BUGS. HE IS OBSESSED! AND HE CATCHES MORE FISH, AND HIS WIFE HAS PROBABLY LEFT HIM.

IF YOU ARE TO IMITATE THESE BUGS THEN THERE IS NOTHING FOR IT BUT TO DEVELOP A RUDIMENTARY KNOWLEDGE OF

THE LIFE CYCLES OF SELECTED AQUATIC INSECTS
WHILE THERE ARE OTHERS, THREE ARE OF SERIOUS CONCERN TO THE FLY FISHER, THESE ARE:

THE STONEFLY,
THE MAYFLY AND
THE CADDISFLY.

YOU MAY HAVE THOUGHT, JUST FLEETINGLY, THAT THREE SEEMS A MANAGEABLE NUMBER BUT SURELY BY NOW YOU HAVE BEEN DISABUSED OF SUCH HOPES. THE STONE, MAY AND CADDISFLIES ARE NOT SPECIES BUT WHAT TAXONOMISTS CALL ORDERS. THERE ARE OVER 150 SPECIES OF STONES, 200 OF MAYS AND 300 OF CADDIS IN THE WESTERN U.S. ALONE. THEY RANGE IN SIZE FROM UNDER 1/16" TO OVER 2"; IN COLOR FROM NEAR WHITE TO ALMOST BLACK WITH MANY A LOVELY HUE BETWEEN. AND WHILE MATCHING THE INSECT IS WELL ENOUGH DONE BY SIMULATING ITS SIZE AND COLOR, WHEN FISHING YOUR IMITATION YOU MUST ALSO BE CONCERNED ABOUT THE SORT OF BEHAVIORS THE FISH EXPECT FROM THE THING.
LET US EXAMINE THIS—YOU'LL SEE.
WE'LL BEGIN WITH STONEFLIES, THEIR STORY IS THE SIMPLEST TO TELL.

STONEFLY LIFE CYCLE: AFTER STONES HATCH (THIS IS NOT WHAT FISHERS CALL A "HATCH" SO LET'S SAY BREAK OUT OF THE EGG) THEY WILL BE "NYMPHS" UNTIL THEY METAMORPHOSE TO WINGED ADULTS. THIS STAGE MAY BE LESS THAN A YEAR FOR SOME SPECIES AND UP TO FOUR YEARS FOR OTHERS. DURING THIS MAJOR PART OF THEIR LIFE THEY'RE CRAWLING AROUND ON THE BOTTOM EATING ALGA, VEGETATIVE MATTER OR OTHER INSECTS. THEY NEED A LOT OF OXYGEN SO THEY FREQUENT FASTER STRETCHES OF THE STREAM, OFTEN WHITE WATER AREAS LIKE HEAVY RIFFLES. AS NYMPHS THEY AREN'T USUALLY AVAILABLE TO THE FISH BUT THEY SOMETIMES LOSE THEIR GRIP AND, BECAUSE THEY'RE POOR SWIMMERS, DRIFT SOME DISTANCE BEFORE GRABBING THE BOTTOM AGAIN. WHILE IN THE DRIFT THEY'RE VULNERABLE TO THE FISH SO PRESENTING AN IMITATION, ESSENTIALLY "DEAD DRIFTED" WITH PERHAPS AN OCCASIONAL LITTLE JERK, MAY CATCH FISH AT ANYTIME OF YEAR. THIS IS BEST DONE IN OR BELOW THOSE FASTER WATERS.

NOW COMES WHAT FISHERS CALL THE **HATCH.** DURING THIS PERIOD THE EMERGING INSECT BECOMES AVAILABLE IN SUCH GREAT NUMBERS THAT THE FISH MAY BECOME **SELECTIVE** TO JUST THAT SPECIES. SELECTIVE MEANS THEY WANT NO OTHER LURE AND THEY OFTEN CONSUME THE HATCHING SPECIES WITH RECKLESS ABANDON.

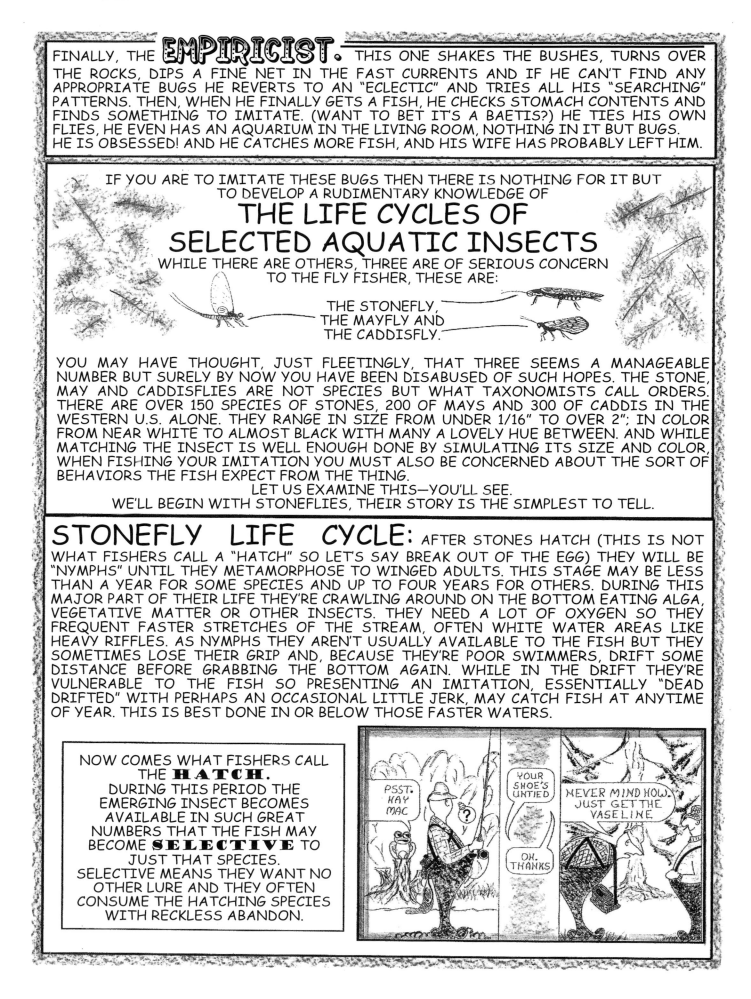

Stonefly Hatch:

SOMEHOW NATURE STIMULATES THEM AND THEY BEGIN A PILGRIMAGE TOWARD SHORE.

ALONG THE WAY MANY LOSE THEIR GRIP AND ARE SWEPT INTO THE CURRENT. THE FISH SOON BECOME AWARE OF THIS AND THE "HATCH" IS ON?

TERRAFIRMA

SURE WE'RE GOING THE RIGHT WAY?

OOORPHH!!

USE A NYMPH,

DEAD DRIFT WITH TWITCHES.

YUP, THE GUIDE BOOK SAID FOLLOW THE ARROWS

THE SURVIVORS CRAWL ASHORE (A) AND UP INTO THE BUSH OR ONTO STREAM SIDE ROCKS WHERE THEY BREAK OUT OF THEIR EXOSKELETONS (B) AND TAKE WING (C). YOU'LL SOMETIMES FIND THE ROCKS LITTERED WITH THESE "SHUCKS" (D).

FOR FROM AS FEW AS TWO DAYS TO MORE THAN TWO WEEKS, DEPENDING UPON SPECIES, THE ADULTS WILL LINGER AROUND THE STREAM.
THEY'RE CLUMSY FLIERS SO THERE WILL BE THOSE WHO CRASH INTO THE WATER, THE FISH ARE WAITING.
THEY OFTEN CONGREGATE ON BRANCHES THAT OVERHANG THE WATER, A GUST OF WIND AND SOME FALL IN, THE FISH ARE WAITING.

CAST A DRY IMITATION TOWARD SHORE, ESPECIALLY WHERE BRANCHES OVERHANG DEEPER WATER. FISH DEAD DRIFT WITH TWITCHES.

AND THEN THEY MATE, DISCREETLY, IN THE BRUSH

THE FEMALE THEN FILES BACK TO THE STREAM TO OVIPOSIT. THE FEMALES OF MOST SPECIES WILL DIP THEIR ABDOMEN TO THE SURFACE AND RELEASE A SAC OF EGGS. THIS IS REPEATED SEVERAL TIMES. BUT THEIR AWKWARD FLYING OFTEN RESULTS IN THEIR SPLASHING IN. THE FISH ARE WAITING.

USE A DRY FLY, DEAD DRIFT WITH TWITCHES

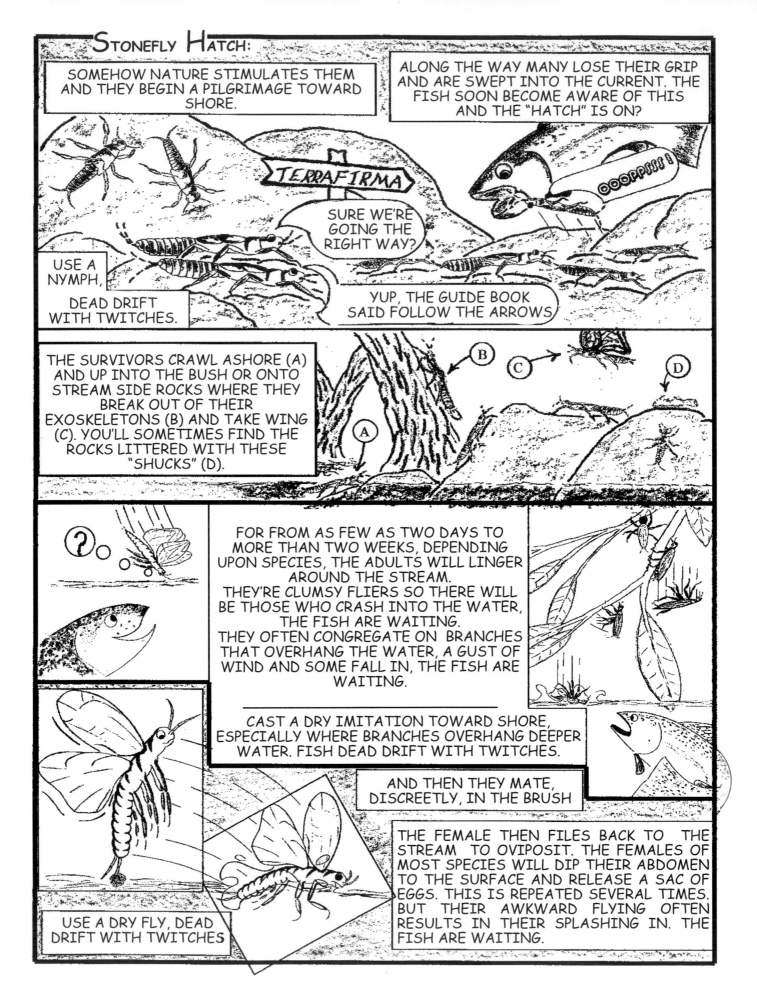

MAYFLY LIFE CYCLE: HERE THINGS ARE MORE COMPLICATED.

FROM THE BEGINNING, THAT IS THE NYMPHAL PERIOD WHICH EXTENDS THROUGH MOST OF THEIR LIFE, THE 200 SPECIES OF MAYFLIES ARE DIVIDED INTO FOUR GROUPS BASED UPON THEIR BEHAVIOR. THESE GROUPS ARE:

1. THE **BURROWERS** ARE OF LITTLE INTEREST TO FISHERS, THE NYMPHS DIG A "U" SHAPED TUNNEL IN THE STREAM FLOOR AND SPEND THEIR DAYS THERE, COMING OUT TO FEED AT NIGHT WHEN WE'RE NOT AROUND. IT'S ONLY DURING THE HATCH THAT WE NEED TO DEAL WITH THEIR KIND.

2. THE **CRAWLERS** AND 3. THE **CLINGERS** CAN BE TREATED TOGETHER FOR OUR PURPOSES.

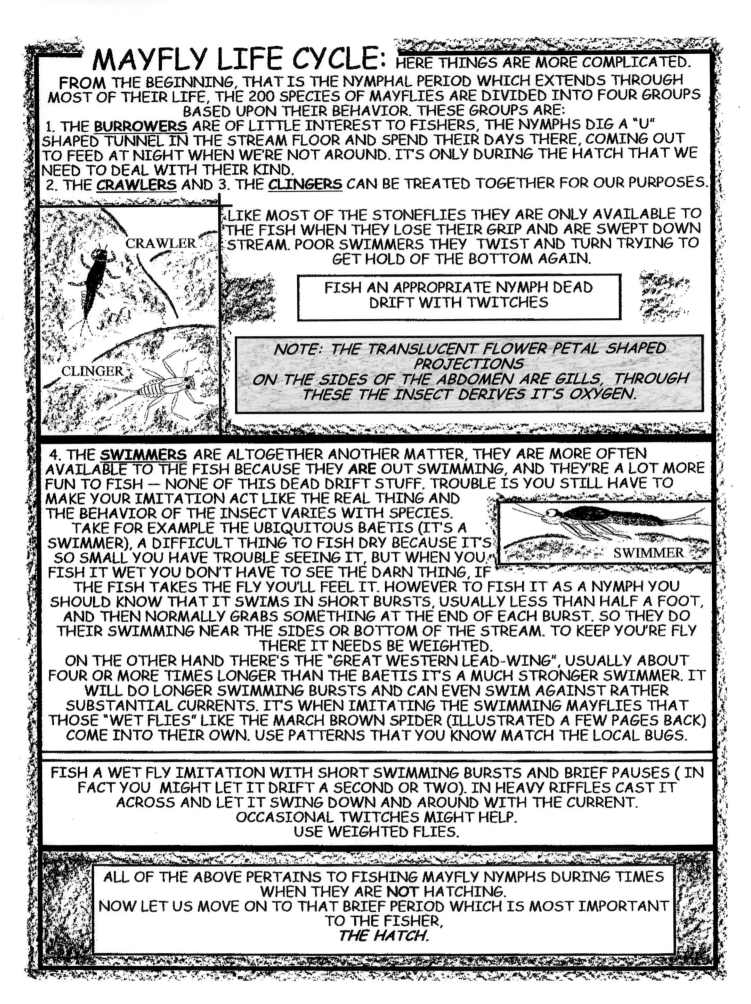

CRAWLER

CLINGER

LIKE MOST OF THE STONEFLIES THEY ARE ONLY AVAILABLE TO THE FISH WHEN THEY LOSE THEIR GRIP AND ARE SWEPT DOWN STREAM. POOR SWIMMERS THEY TWIST AND TURN TRYING TO GET HOLD OF THE BOTTOM AGAIN.

FISH AN APPROPRIATE NYMPH DEAD DRIFT WITH TWITCHES

NOTE: THE TRANSLUCENT FLOWER PETAL SHAPED PROJECTIONS ON THE SIDES OF THE ABDOMEN ARE GILLS, THROUGH THESE THE INSECT DERIVES IT'S OXYGEN.

4. THE **SWIMMERS** ARE ALTOGETHER ANOTHER MATTER, THEY ARE MORE OFTEN AVAILABLE TO THE FISH BECAUSE THEY **ARE** OUT SWIMMING, AND THEY'RE A LOT MORE FUN TO FISH — NONE OF THIS DEAD DRIFT STUFF. TROUBLE IS YOU STILL HAVE TO MAKE YOUR IMITATION ACT LIKE THE REAL THING AND THE BEHAVIOR OF THE INSECT VARIES WITH SPECIES.

TAKE FOR EXAMPLE THE UBIQUITOUS BAETIS (IT'S A SWIMMER), A DIFFICULT THING TO FISH DRY BECAUSE IT'S SO SMALL YOU HAVE TROUBLE SEEING IT, BUT WHEN YOU FISH IT WET YOU DON'T HAVE TO SEE THE DARN THING, IF

SWIMMER

THE FISH TAKES THE FLY YOU'LL FEEL IT. HOWEVER TO FISH IT AS A NYMPH YOU SHOULD KNOW THAT IT SWIMS IN SHORT BURSTS, USUALLY LESS THAN HALF A FOOT, AND THEN NORMALLY GRABS SOMETHING AT THE END OF EACH BURST. SO THEY DO THEIR SWIMMING NEAR THE SIDES OR BOTTOM OF THE STREAM. TO KEEP YOU'RE FLY THERE IT NEEDS BE WEIGHTED.

ON THE OTHER HAND THERE'S THE "GREAT WESTERN LEAD-WING", USUALLY ABOUT FOUR OR MORE TIMES LONGER THAN THE BAETIS IT'S A MUCH STRONGER SWIMMER. IT WILL DO LONGER SWIMMING BURSTS AND CAN EVEN SWIM AGAINST RATHER SUBSTANTIAL CURRENTS. IT'S WHEN IMITATING THE SWIMMING MAYFLIES THAT THOSE "WET FLIES" LIKE THE MARCH BROWN SPIDER (ILLUSTRATED A FEW PAGES BACK) COME INTO THEIR OWN. USE PATTERNS THAT YOU KNOW MATCH THE LOCAL BUGS.

FISH A WET FLY IMITATION WITH SHORT SWIMMING BURSTS AND BRIEF PAUSES (IN FACT YOU MIGHT LET IT DRIFT A SECOND OR TWO). IN HEAVY RIFFLES CAST IT ACROSS AND LET IT SWING DOWN AND AROUND WITH THE CURRENT. OCCASIONAL TWITCHES MIGHT HELP. USE WEIGHTED FLIES.

ALL OF THE ABOVE PERTAINS TO FISHING MAYFLY NYMPHS DURING TIMES WHEN THEY ARE **NOT** HATCHING. NOW LET US MOVE ON TO THAT BRIEF PERIOD WHICH IS MOST IMPORTANT TO THE FISHER, *THE HATCH.*

Mayfly Hatch:

SOME SPECIES WILL RISE TO THE SURFACE FROM THEIR NATURAL HABITAT EVEN IF IT'S IN SWIFT CURRENT.

MORE WILL CRAWL OR SWIM TO CALMER WATERS BEFORE RISING.

WINGCASE

THEN THERE ARE SOME THAT WILL CRAWL ASHORE OR UP SOMETHING THAT PROJECTS ABOVE THE WATER, ANYTHING TO GET OUT OF THE FISH'S REACH.

THESE MATURE NYMPHS, READY TO BREAK OUT AND BECOME WINGED ADULTS, ARE CALLED "**EMERGERS**". THEY ARE DISTINGUISHED BY A VERY THICK WINGCASE ABOVE THE THORACIC AREA.

WHEN THOSE SPECIES THAT DON'T CRAWL OUT OF THE WATER RISE THERE ARE SOME THAT MOLT (IE. BREAK OUT OF THE EXOSKELETON) AS THEY RISE, THEY ARE THEN ADULTS BUT THEIR WINGS AREN'T FULLY EXTENDED, SO AN IMITATION WITH CLIPPED WINGS IS APPROPRIATE. THIS WE CALL AN "EMERGER" PATTERN.

OTHERS RISE TO THE SURFACE AND REMAIN IN OR BELOW THE SURFACE FILM WHILE THEY MOLT. THEY THEN CLIMB OUT ON TOP.

WHATEVER THEIR WAY, THAT WHICH BREAKS FREE OF THE SHUCK IS A FIRST-STAGE ADULT CALLED A "**DUN**" THE DUN MUST REMAIN BRIEFLY ON THE SURFACE, PRESUMABLY TO DRY IT'S WINGS, BEFORE TAKING FLIGHT. THIS IS WHEN MOST FISH ARE TAKEN DURING THE EMERGENCE STAGE OF THE HATCH. (UNFORTUNATELY THERE ARE TIMES WHEN THE FISH ARE SO CAUTIOUS THAT YOU MIGHT HAVE TO USE AN EMERGER PATTERN FISHED JUST BELOW THE SURFACE, FORTUNATELY THIS IS UNCOMMON.)

USE A DRY (DUN) IMITATION DEAD DRIFT WITH OCCASIONAL TWITCHES. CAST IT ABOVE WHERE FISH ARE RISING OR WHERE YOU THINK THEY MAY BE HOLDING. LET IT DRIFT DOWN THROUGH.

IT IS AN AXIOM THAT THE BODY COLOR OF A DUN IMITATION SHOULD MATCH THE BELLY COLOR OF THE NATURAL. I STRONGLY SUGGEST THAT IT BE RIBBED IN THE BACK COLOR.

AND NOW THAT BRIEF TERRESTRIAL PERIOD OF THEIR LIVES. YOU WILL SURELY ANTICIPATE MY SAYING THAT HOW LONG THIS LASTS DEPENDS UPON THE SPECIES: FOR SOME A FEW HOURS, FOR SOME A FEW DAYS. DURING THIS TIME THEY WILL MOLT, MATE, OVIPOSIT AND DIE. DETAILS ON NEXT PAGE.

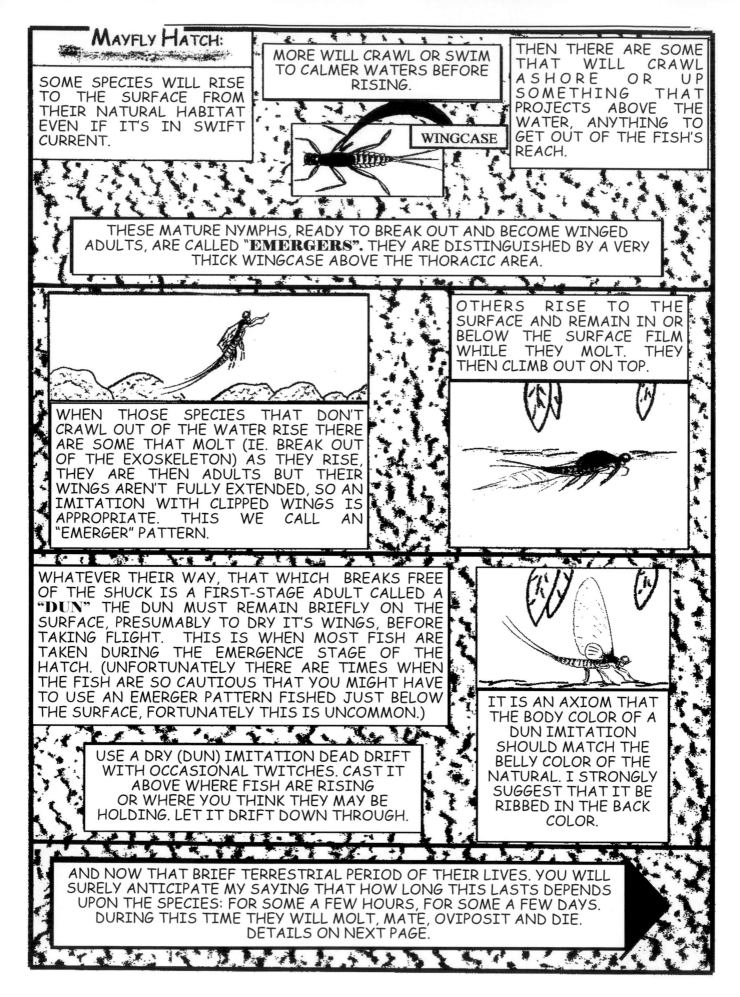

ANOTHER PECULIAR THING ABOUT MAYFLIES, THEIR BRIEF ADULT LIFE IS IN TWO STAGES. AFTER THE DUN FLIES OFF IT WILL MOLT AGAIN TO BECOME A **SPINNER.** THIS TAKES PLACE AWAY FROM THE STREAM AND SO IS OF NO IMMEDIATE SIGNIFICANCE TO US, BUT THE SPINNER DOESN'T LOOK JUST LIKE THE DUN SO WHEN THEY RETURN TO OVIPOSIT A SOMEWHAT DIFFERENT FLY PATTERN IS ADVISABLE. WHILE DUN AND SPINNER ARE THE SAME SIZE, THE SPINNER USUALLY HAS CLEARER WINGS AND A MORE DISTINCT BODY COLOR.

AFTER THIS LAST MOLT THE MALES WILL RETURN TO THE STREAM AND SWARM OVER THE TYPE OF WATER (RIFFLES, POOLS, ETC.) APPROPRIATE TO THEIR SPECIES. THE FEMALES WILL FLY INTO THE SWARM AND MATING TAKES PLACE IN A FEW SECONDS OF FREE FALL (THEY CAN'T USE THEIR WINGS WHILE COPULATING).

WHEN INSEMINATION IS COMPLETE THE MALES WILL FLY BACK TO THE BUSH AND DIE, THE FEMALES WILL TURN TO THEIR FINAL ACT— OVIPOSITING. SOME SPECIES FIND OBJECTS PROTRUDING FROM THE WATER AND CLIMB DOWN WHILE OTHERS DIP TO THE WATER'S SURFACE AND DROP BUNDLES OR EGGS LIKE MOST STONEFLIES.

SHORTLY AFTER ALL THE EGGS ARE LAID THE FEMALE DIES AND FALLS TO THE WATER WITH WINGS SPREAD WIDE. THIS IS WHEN THAT FLY PATTERN CALLED THE "SPENT WING" IS USED. WE CALL THIS FINAL STAGE OF THE HATCH A **SPINNER FALL.**

FLOAT A MATCHING SPENT WING PATTERN DOWN THROUGH THE AREA WHERE OVIPOSITING IS OCCURRING AND A WAYS BELOW. FISH DEAD DRIFT.

SUBJECT: MAYFLIES, COPULATION, AERIAL, EXTRINSIC HAZARDS IN:

SURE HOPE HE'S HAD HIS TETANUS SHOT

CADDISFLY LIFE CYCLE:

MAY AND STONEFLIES GO THROUGH WHAT IS CALLED "INCOMPLETE METAMORPHOSIS", THAT IS FROM EGG TO NYMPH TO ADULT. THE CADDISFLY UNDERGOES "COMPLETE METAMORPHOSIS" WHICH MEANS EGG TO LARVA TO PUPA TO ADULT.

THE **LARVAL** STAGE TAKES UP THE MAJORITY OF THEIR LIFE SPAN AND HERE THERE IS ANOTHER INTERESTING PHENOMENON; WHILE SOME SPECIES ARE NOT, MOST ARE "CASE BUILDERS". THE KEY TO THIS MARVEL IS A FINE, SILK LIKE AND VERY STICKY THREAD THEY PRODUCE AND USE TO BIND TOGETHER THE STUFF OF WHICH THE CASE IS MADE.

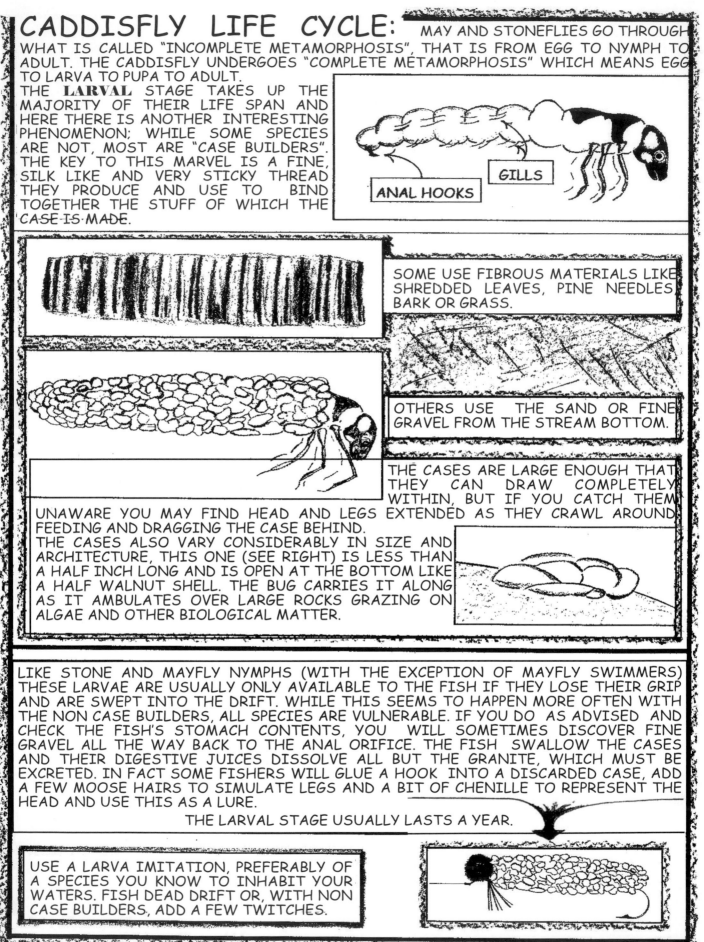

ANAL HOOKS

GILLS

SOME USE FIBROUS MATERIALS LIKE SHREDDED LEAVES, PINE NEEDLES BARK OR GRASS.

OTHERS USE THE SAND OR FINE GRAVEL FROM THE STREAM BOTTOM.

THE CASES ARE LARGE ENOUGH THAT THEY CAN DRAW COMPLETELY WITHIN, BUT IF YOU CATCH THEM UNAWARE YOU MAY FIND HEAD AND LEGS EXTENDED AS THEY CRAWL AROUND FEEDING AND DRAGGING THE CASE BEHIND.

THE CASES ALSO VARY CONSIDERABLY IN SIZE AND ARCHITECTURE, THIS ONE (SEE RIGHT) IS LESS THAN A HALF INCH LONG AND IS OPEN AT THE BOTTOM LIKE A HALF WALNUT SHELL. THE BUG CARRIES IT ALONG AS IT AMBULATES OVER LARGE ROCKS GRAZING ON ALGAE AND OTHER BIOLOGICAL MATTER.

LIKE STONE AND MAYFLY NYMPHS (WITH THE EXCEPTION OF MAYFLY SWIMMERS) THESE LARVAE ARE USUALLY ONLY AVAILABLE TO THE FISH IF THEY LOSE THEIR GRIP AND ARE SWEPT INTO THE DRIFT. WHILE THIS SEEMS TO HAPPEN MORE OFTEN WITH THE NON CASE BUILDERS, ALL SPECIES ARE VULNERABLE. IF YOU DO AS ADVISED AND CHECK THE FISH'S STOMACH CONTENTS, YOU WILL SOMETIMES DISCOVER FINE GRAVEL ALL THE WAY BACK TO THE ANAL ORIFICE. THE FISH SWALLOW THE CASES AND THEIR DIGESTIVE JUICES DISSOLVE ALL BUT THE GRANITE, WHICH MUST BE EXCRETED. IN FACT SOME FISHERS WILL GLUE A HOOK INTO A DISCARDED CASE, ADD A FEW MOOSE HAIRS TO SIMULATE LEGS AND A BIT OF CHENILLE TO REPRESENT THE HEAD AND USE THIS AS A LURE.

THE LARVAL STAGE USUALLY LASTS A YEAR.

USE A LARVA IMITATION, PREFERABLY OF A SPECIES YOU KNOW TO INHABIT YOUR WATERS. FISH DEAD DRIFT OR, WITH NON CASE BUILDERS, ADD A FEW TWITCHES.

THEN COMES **PUPATION**. THE CASE BUILDERS WILL SEAL THEMSELVES WITHIN. THE OTHERS WILL BREAK DOWN AND MAKE A CASE. DURING THIS STAGE, WHICH MAY LAST ONLY TWO WEEKS OR STRETCH TO FOUR MONTHS, DEPENDING ON SPECIES, A MOST THOROUGHGOING METAMORPHOSIS OCCURS. FOR EXAMPLE REPRODUCTIVE ORGANS DEVELOP, AND A WAY TO DERIVE OXYGEN FROM THE AIR. EXTERNALLY THEY GROW VERY LONG ANTENNAS, THE SHORT STOCKY LEGS BECOME LONG AND SLENDER, THE ANAL HOOKS DISAPPEAR TO BE REPLACED BY GENITAL CLASPS (IMAGINE WHAT SIGMUND FREUD WOULD HAVE MADE OF THAT) AND, OF COURSE, FOUR WINGS BLOSSOM.

THEN — THE HATCH.

Caddisfly Hatch:

AFTER THE PUPAE BREAK OUT OF THE CASE SOME SPECIES WILL CRAWL ASHORE AND MOLT ABOVE THE WATER LINE. MOST WILL EITHER SWIM TO THE SURFACE OR BE ELEVATED THERE BY GAS BUBBLES THAT FORM BENEATH THE EXOSKELETON. THESE RISERS WILL STOP AT THE SURFACE FILM AND MOLT IN OR JUST BENEATH IT. THE ADULT THEN CLIMBS ATOP THE FILM AND IS USUALLY OFF AND FLYING VERY QUICKLY (A SECOND OR TWO). BECAUSE THE WHOLE THING HAPPENS RATHER EXPEDITIOUSLY THE FISH SOMETIMES GO INTO A FEEDING FRENZY AND SINCE MOST ADULTS REMAIN ON THE SURFACE SO BRIEFLY THE FISH OFTEN BECOME SELECTIVE TO THE RISING OR MOLTING PUPA.

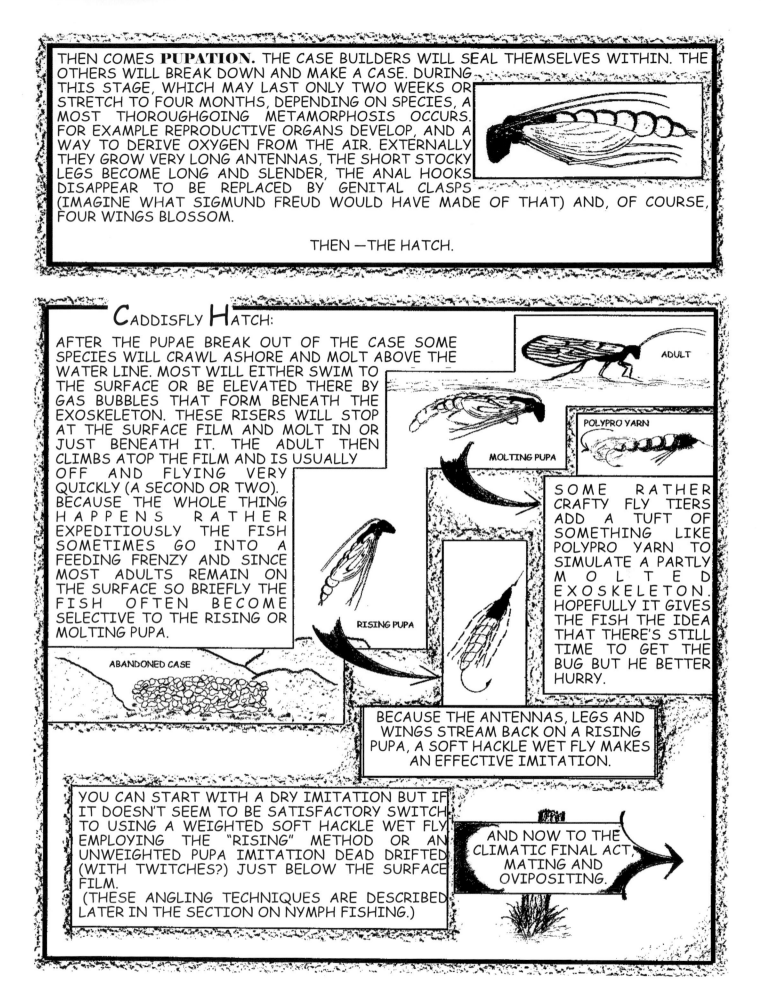

ADULT

MOLTING PUPA

POLYPRO YARN

RISING PUPA

ABANDONED CASE

SOME RATHER CRAFTY FLY TIERS ADD A TUFT OF SOMETHING LIKE POLYPRO YARN TO SIMULATE A PARTLY MOLTED EXOSKELETON. HOPEFULLY IT GIVES THE FISH THE IDEA THAT THERE'S STILL TIME TO GET THE BUG BUT HE BETTER HURRY.

BECAUSE THE ANTENNAS, LEGS AND WINGS STREAM BACK ON A RISING PUPA, A SOFT HACKLE WET FLY MAKES AN EFFECTIVE IMITATION.

YOU CAN START WITH A DRY IMITATION BUT IF IT DOESN'T SEEM TO BE SATISFACTORY SWITCH TO USING A WEIGHTED SOFT HACKLE WET FLY EMPLOYING THE "RISING" METHOD OR AN UNWEIGHTED PUPA IMITATION DEAD DRIFTED (WITH TWITCHES?) JUST BELOW THE SURFACE FILM.
(THESE ANGLING TECHNIQUES ARE DESCRIBED LATER IN THE SECTION ON NYMPH FISHING.)

AND NOW TO THE CLIMATIC FINAL ACT, MATING AND OVIPOSITING.

WHEN THE URGE PREVAILS THEY WILL **MATE.** THIS OCCURS AWAY FROM THE STREAM, OUT IN THE BUSHES, AND IT SEEMS RATHER MODESTLY DONE WHEN YOU CONSIDER THE SHOW THAT THE MAYFLIES MAKE OF IT. THE MALES WILL THEN EXPIRE AND THE FEMALES WILL RETURN TO THE WATER TO DEPOSIT THEIR EGGS IN ONE OF SEVERAL WAYS AS ALWAYS, DEPENDING UPON SPECIES.

OVIPOSITING

A FEW WILL LAY THEIR EGGS JUST ABOVE THE WATER LINE, WHEN THE LARVAE BREAK OUT THEY WILL CLIMB DOWN INTO THE STEAM.

AND, AS ALWAYS, THERE ARE THOSE THAT FAVOR AERIAL DELIVERY. THEY WILL DROP DOWN SEVERAL TIMES TO RELEASE ANOTHER BUNDLE.

FAR MORE WILL CRAWL DOWN AND AFFIX THE EGG BUNDLES TO AN APPROPRIATE OBJECT, THEN SWIM BACK TO THE SURFACE.

IF YOU'RE FISHING OVER THE HATCH OF A SPECIES THAT CRAWLS DOWN INTO THE STREAM TO DEPOSIT THE EGGS AND THEN SWIMS BACK TO THE SURFACE, YOU'LL PROBABLY DO BEST IF YOU STICK WITH A WEIGHTED WET FLY FISHED BY THE RISING METHOD. IF THE FLY GETS BACK UP AND THERE IS STILL FISHABLE WATER DOWN STREAM, GIVE IT JUST ENOUGH SLACK TO SINK BACK DOWN AND THEN RAISE IT AGAIN. YOU CAN CONTINUE THIS YO-YOING TILL DAY AFTER TOMORROW IF YOU STILL THINK THE WATER FISHABLE.

IF THE FEMALES ARE DIPPING TO THE SURFACE TO OVIPOSIT A DRY FLY IS CALLED FOR. CAST IT UPSTREAM OF THE ACTION AND LET IT DRIFT DOWN THROUGH. BUT WATCH THE NATURALS, IF THEY ARE SKIPPING AROUND ON THE SURFACE THEN RAISE YOUR ROD TIP AS HIGH AS POSSIBLE (THESE ARE THE TIMES YOU WISH YOU BOUGHT A LONGER ROD) AND WITH LITTLE FLICKS TRY TO IMITATE THE REAL BUG. WE CALL THIS "SKITTERING". IF YOUR FLY SINKS TRY LETTING IT DEAD DRIFT WITH A MINIMUM OF LINE SLACK, THIS SIMULATES A DROWNED ADULT.

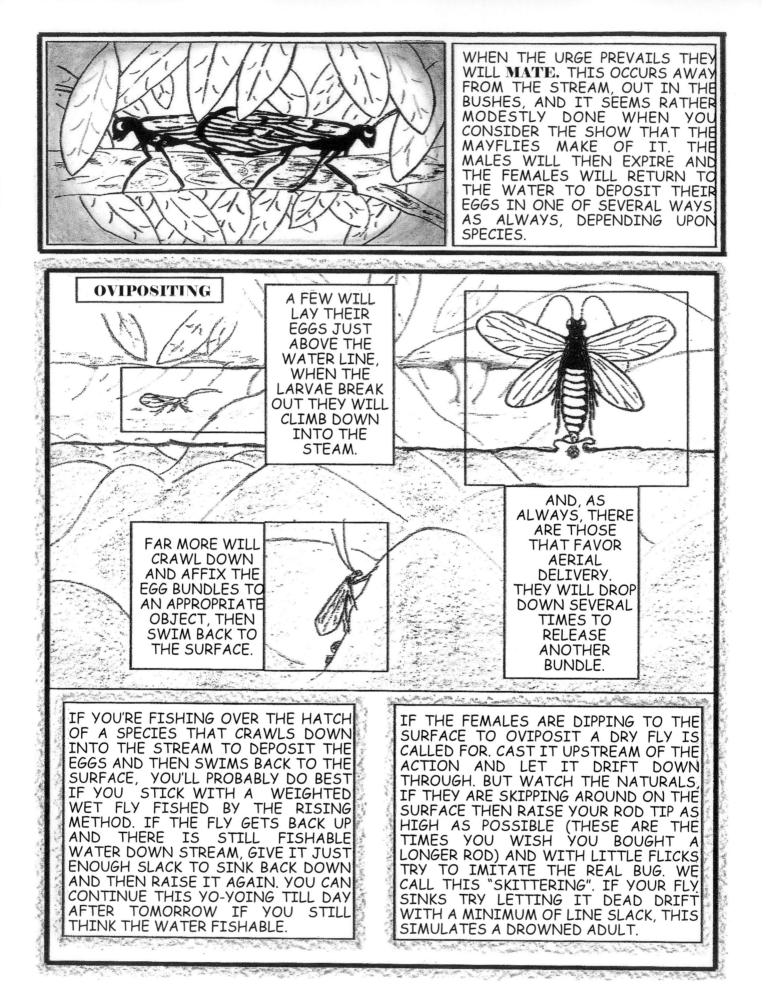

THE **MIDGE** MUST BE ADDED HERE. YOU WILL RARELY FIND THEM IN THOSE ARTICLES IN THE PAPER BECAUSE THEY DON'T HATCH IN THE <u>SORT OF</u> PREDICTABLE AND <u>SOMETIMES</u> SPECTACULAR WAY THAT THE STONES, MAYS AND CADDIS DO. THEIR "HATCHES" ARE SEEMINGLY MINOR EVENTS. HOWEVER THEY GO ON YEAR AROUND.. AT ANY TIME, EVEN IN THE DEAD OF WINTER, MIDGES MAY BE EMERGING AND THE FISH WILL LIKELY BE TAKING THEM.

LIKE THAT OF THE CADDIS FLY, THEIR LIFE INVOLVES "COMPLETE METAMORPHOSIS". THEIR LARVA MAY BE "BURROWERS", "CASE BUILDERS" OR "FREE SWIMMING'" AND THE DIFFERENT SPECIES DEPOSIT THEIR EGGS IN THEIR OWN WAY (ALL PREVIOUSLY DESCRIBED).

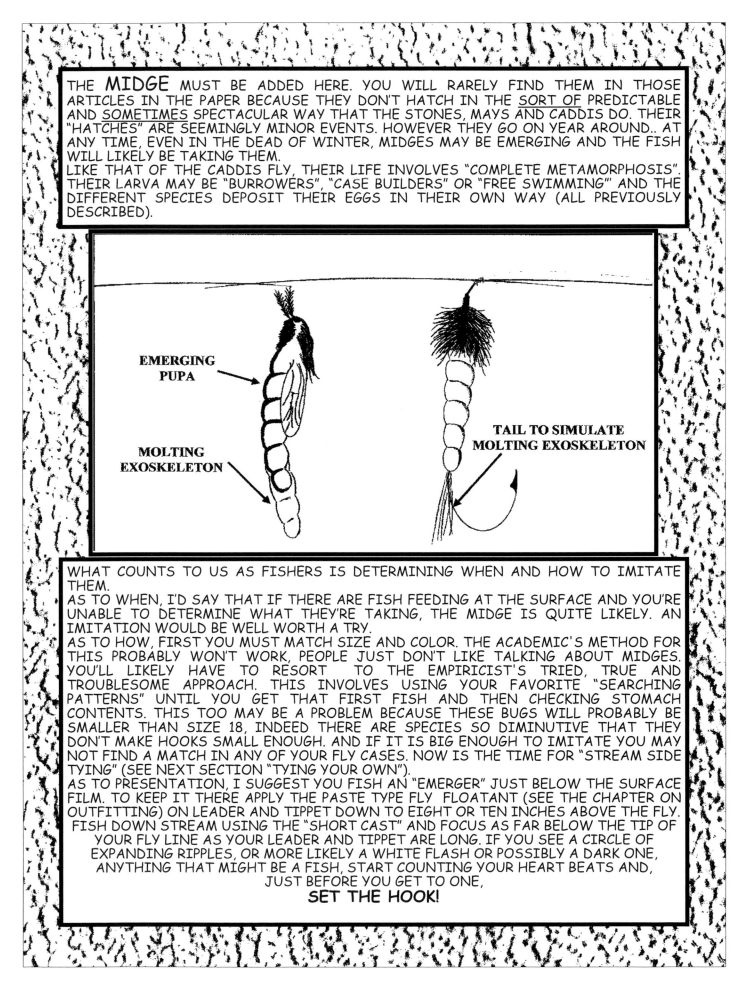

EMERGING PUPA

MOLTING EXOSKELETON

TAIL TO SIMULATE MOLTING EXOSKELETON

WHAT COUNTS TO US AS FISHERS IS DETERMINING WHEN AND HOW TO IMITATE THEM.

AS TO WHEN, I'D SAY THAT IF THERE ARE FISH FEEDING AT THE SURFACE AND YOU'RE UNABLE TO DETERMINE WHAT THEY'RE TAKING, THE MIDGE IS QUITE LIKELY. AN IMITATION WOULD BE WELL WORTH A TRY.

AS TO HOW, FIRST YOU MUST MATCH SIZE AND COLOR. THE ACADEMIC'S METHOD FOR THIS PROBABLY WON'T WORK, PEOPLE JUST DON'T LIKE TALKING ABOUT MIDGES. YOU'LL LIKELY HAVE TO RESORT TO THE EMPIRICIST'S TRIED, TRUE AND TROUBLESOME APPROACH. THIS INVOLVES USING YOUR FAVORITE "SEARCHING PATTERNS" UNTIL YOU GET THAT FIRST FISH AND THEN CHECKING STOMACH CONTENTS. THIS TOO MAY BE A PROBLEM BECAUSE THESE BUGS WILL PROBABLY BE SMALLER THAN SIZE 18, INDEED THERE ARE SPECIES SO DIMINUTIVE THAT THEY DON'T MAKE HOOKS SMALL ENOUGH. AND IF IT IS BIG ENOUGH TO IMITATE YOU MAY NOT FIND A MATCH IN ANY OF YOUR FLY CASES. NOW IS THE TIME FOR "STREAM SIDE TYING" (SEE NEXT SECTION "TYING YOUR OWN").

AS TO PRESENTATION, I SUGGEST YOU FISH AN "EMERGER" JUST BELOW THE SURFACE FILM. TO KEEP IT THERE APPLY THE PASTE TYPE FLY FLOATANT (SEE THE CHAPTER ON OUTFITTING) ON LEADER AND TIPPET DOWN TO EIGHT OR TEN INCHES ABOVE THE FLY.

FISH DOWN STREAM USING THE "SHORT CAST" AND FOCUS AS FAR BELOW THE TIP OF YOUR FLY LINE AS YOUR LEADER AND TIPPET ARE LONG. IF YOU SEE A CIRCLE OF EXPANDING RIPPLES, OR MORE LIKELY A WHITE FLASH OR POSSIBLY A DARK ONE, ANYTHING THAT MIGHT BE A FISH, START COUNTING YOUR HEART BEATS AND, JUST BEFORE YOU GET TO ONE,

SET THE HOOK!

TYING YOUR OWN

IT IS TRADITION THAT WE BEGIN WITH THE QUESTION __WHY__? SO FIRST, IT'S A WHOLE LOT CHEAPER, AND THEN TOO, MANY JUST CONSIDER IT A PART OF THE SPORT, CATCHING FISH ON FLIES THEY TIED THEMSELVES SEEMS A GREATER ACCOMPLISHMENT. AND YOU CAN CREATE YOUR OWN PATTERNS, THEN GO OUT AND TEST YOUR JUDGMENT. YOU ALSO HAVE COMPLETE CONTROL OVER SUCH THINGS AS HOW MUCH HACKLE IS USED AND, MORE IMPORTANT, HOW MUCH WEIGHT IS IN YOUR SUBSURFACE FLIES. THEN THERE WILL BE TIMES WHEN NOTHING YOU HAVE IS WORKING AND YOU DISCOVER, PERHAPS BY FINDING A BUG IN THE BUSH, OR FROM ANOTHER, SUCCESSFUL, FLY FISHER, WHAT THE FISH ARE TAKING, BUT YOU DON'T HAVE ONE. FOR SUCH OCCASIONS THERE IS __"STREAM SIDE TYING"__. YOU CAN CARRY TOOLS AND BASIC TYING MATERIALS ENOUGH IN A LUNCH BOX TO MAKE AN IMITATION OF JUST ABOUT ANYTHING YOU COVET.
AND HEED THIS, YOU NEED NOT BE AN ARTIST TO TIE YOUR OWN. ALMOST EVERY FLY I'VE EVER FISHED I TIED MYSELF, THEY'VE SERVED ME WELL, BUT I DOUBT THERE WAS ONE PRETTY ENOUGH TO BE SOLD IN A TACKLE SHOP. GUESS IT'S 'CAUSE BUGS ARE UGLY THAT FLIES CAN BE TOO.

THE TYING OF BUT ONE FLY IS ILLUSTRATED HERE, THIS SECTION IS SIMPLY INTENDED TO SHOW THAT IT'S NOT AS DIFFICULT AS YOU MAY THINK. HOWEVER, IF VARIED IN SIZE AND COLOR THIS PATTERN CAN BE USED TO IMITATE __ANY__ MAYFLY AND MANY "SEARCHING" AND "ATTRACTER" PATTERNS TOO.

THE __GALLOWS__ IS AN UNCOMPLICATED CONTRAPTION WHICH SERVES TO GREATLY SIMPLIFY THE TYING OF PARACHUTE HACKLE FLIES.
(some assembly required)

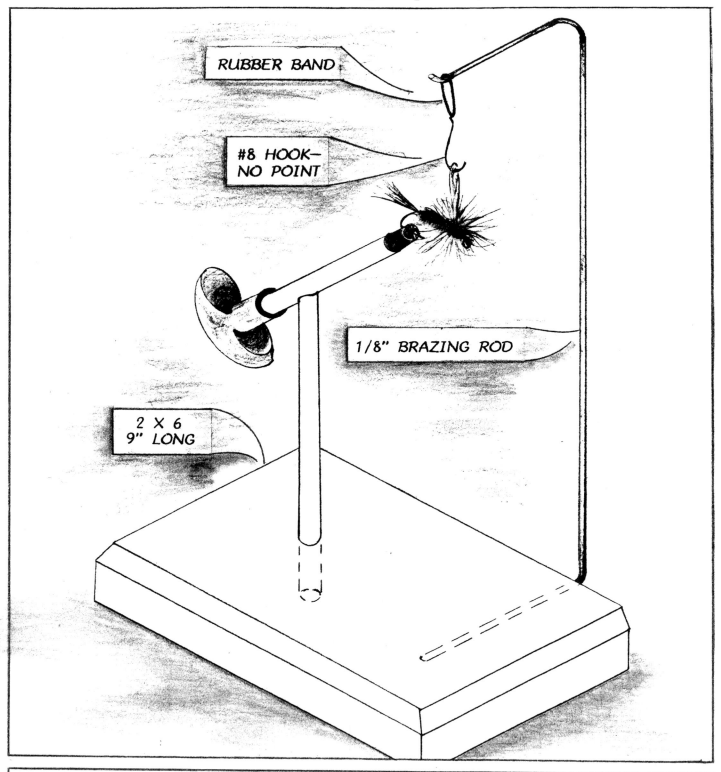

RUBBER BAND

#8 HOOK— NO POINT

1/8" BRAZING ROD

2 X 6 9" LONG

REMOVE THE MAST AND ARM FROM ONE OF THOSE VICES THAT CLAMP TO THE EDGE OF YOUR BENCH. DRILL A HOLE JUST LARGE ENOUGH TO ACCEPT THE MAST (TIGHTLY) IN THE 2 X 6. NEXT DRILL A 3/16" HOLE IN THE SIDE OF THE 2 X 6, HERE YOU WANT A HOLE INTO WHICH THE BRAZING ROD WILL FIT LOOSELY.
(THESE HOLES ARE ILLUSTRATED BY THE DASHED LINES) (ANY QUESTIONS?)

TO THE **TYING:** THERE WILL BE A "RECIPE", THIS SPECIFIES THE MATERIALS TO BE USED FOR THE FLY YOU'RE TYING, IN THE CASE OF THE FLY TO BE CONSTRUCTED HERE IT IS AS FOLLOWS:

RIBBED PARACHUTE ADAMS
HOOK: *Mustad 94840, # 6-2O.*
THREAD: *Dark gray.*
WING: *White polypro yarn or calf tail.*
TAIL: *Deer hair.*
BODY: *Muskrat fur or light gray yarn.*
RIB: *Dark gray tying thread.*
HACKLE: *Grizzly, tied parachute.*

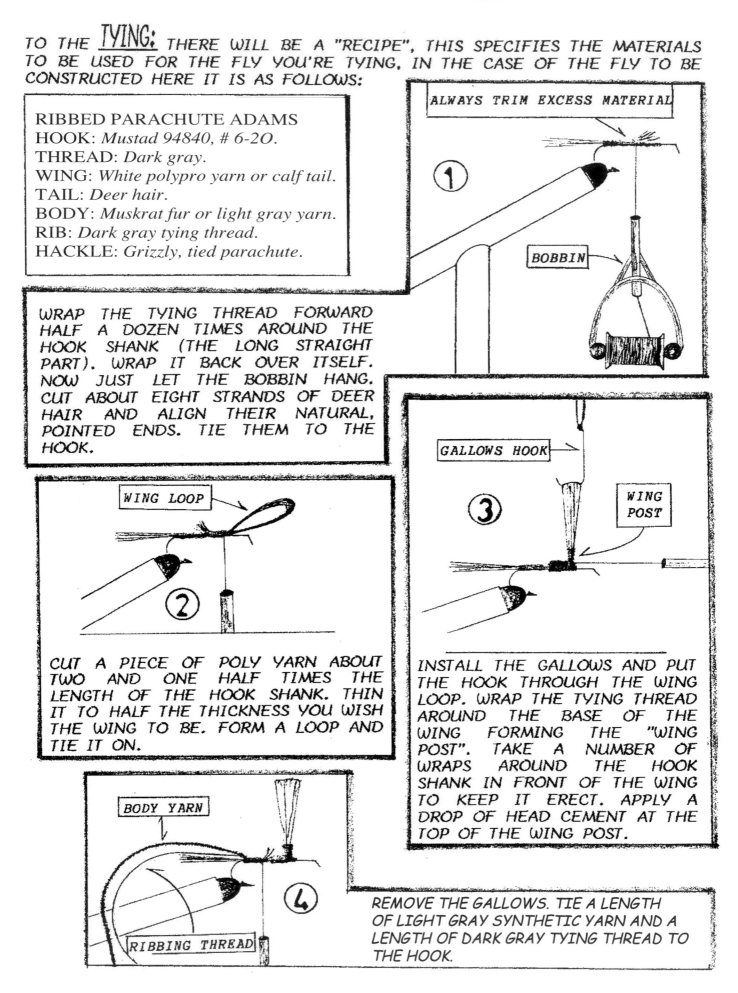

ALWAYS TRIM EXCESS MATERIAL

① **BOBBIN**

WRAP THE TYING THREAD FORWARD HALF A DOZEN TIMES AROUND THE HOOK SHANK (THE LONG STRAIGHT PART). WRAP IT BACK OVER ITSELF. NOW JUST LET THE BOBBIN HANG. CUT ABOUT EIGHT STRANDS OF DEER HAIR AND ALIGN THEIR NATURAL, POINTED ENDS. TIE THEM TO THE HOOK.

GALLOWS HOOK

③ **WING POST**

WING LOOP

②

CUT A PIECE OF POLY YARN ABOUT TWO AND ONE HALF TIMES THE LENGTH OF THE HOOK SHANK. THIN IT TO HALF THE THICKNESS YOU WISH THE WING TO BE. FORM A LOOP AND TIE IT ON.

INSTALL THE GALLOWS AND PUT THE HOOK THROUGH THE WING LOOP. WRAP THE TYING THREAD AROUND THE BASE OF THE WING FORMING THE "WING POST". TAKE A NUMBER OF WRAPS AROUND THE HOOK SHANK IN FRONT OF THE WING TO KEEP IT ERECT. APPLY A DROP OF HEAD CEMENT AT THE TOP OF THE WING POST.

BODY YARN

④

RIBBING THREAD

REMOVE THE GALLOWS. TIE A LENGTH OF LIGHT GRAY SYNTHETIC YARN AND A LENGTH OF DARK GRAY TYING THREAD TO THE HOOK.

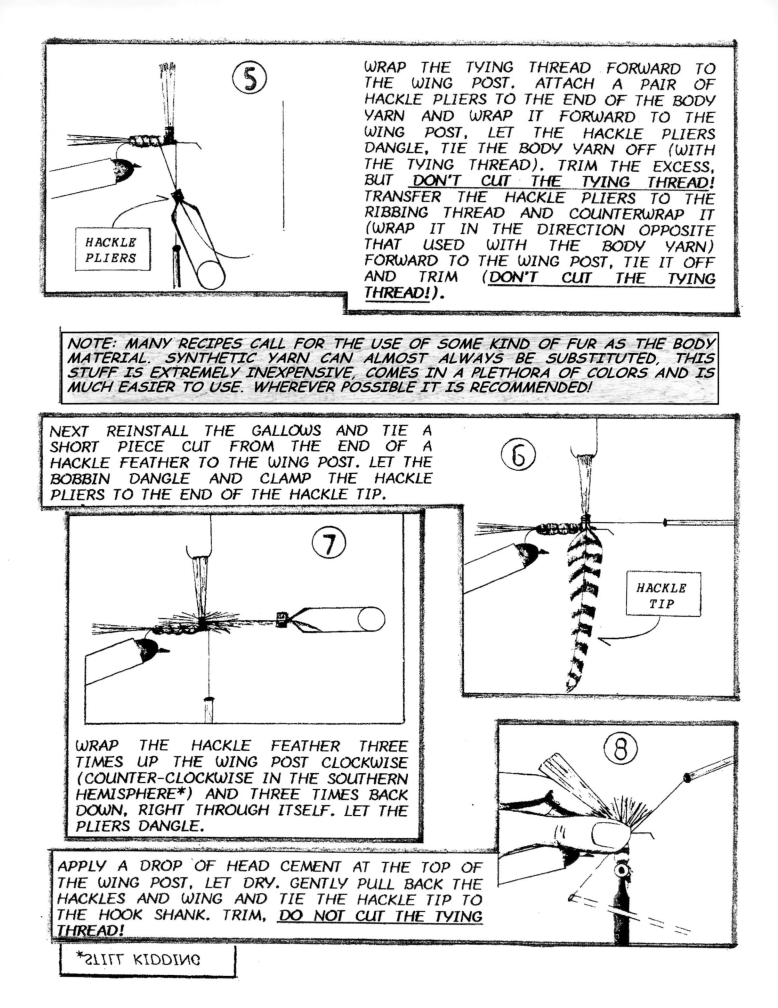

⑤

WRAP THE TYING THREAD FORWARD TO THE WING POST. ATTACH A PAIR OF HACKLE PLIERS TO THE END OF THE BODY YARN AND WRAP IT FORWARD TO THE WING POST, LET THE HACKLE PLIERS DANGLE, TIE THE BODY YARN OFF (WITH THE TYING THREAD). TRIM THE EXCESS, BUT <u>DON'T CUT THE TYING THREAD!</u> TRANSFER THE HACKLE PLIERS TO THE RIBBING THREAD AND COUNTERWRAP IT (WRAP IT IN THE DIRECTION OPPOSITE THAT USED WITH THE BODY YARN) FORWARD TO THE WING POST, TIE IT OFF AND TRIM (<u>DON'T CUT THE TYING THREAD!</u>).

HACKLE PLIERS

NOTE: MANY RECIPES CALL FOR THE USE OF SOME KIND OF FUR AS THE BODY MATERIAL. SYNTHETIC YARN CAN ALMOST ALWAYS BE SUBSTITUTED, THIS STUFF IS EXTREMELY INEXPENSIVE, COMES IN A PLETHORA OF COLORS AND IS MUCH EASIER TO USE. WHEREVER POSSIBLE IT IS RECOMMENDED!

NEXT REINSTALL THE GALLOWS AND TIE A SHORT PIECE CUT FROM THE END OF A HACKLE FEATHER TO THE WING POST. LET THE BOBBIN DANGLE AND CLAMP THE HACKLE PLIERS TO THE END OF THE HACKLE TIP.

⑥

HACKLE TIP

⑦

WRAP THE HACKLE FEATHER THREE TIMES UP THE WING POST CLOCKWISE (COUNTER-CLOCKWISE IN THE SOUTHERN HEMISPHERE*) AND THREE TIMES BACK DOWN, RIGHT THROUGH ITSELF. LET THE PLIERS DANGLE.

⑧

APPLY A DROP OF HEAD CEMENT AT THE TOP OF THE WING POST, LET DRY. GENTLY PULL BACK THE HACKLES AND WING AND TIE THE HACKLE TIP TO THE HOOK SHANK. TRIM, <u>DO NOT CUT THE TYING THREAD!</u>

*JUST KIDDING

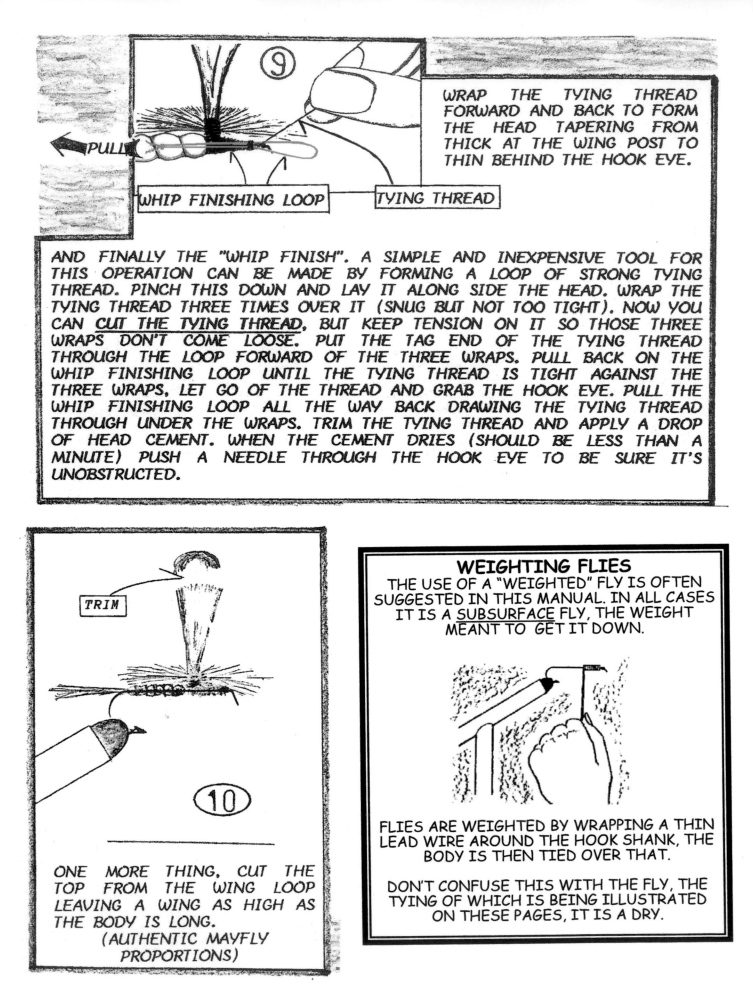

⑨

PULL

WHIP FINISHING LOOP

TYING THREAD

WRAP THE TYING THREAD FORWARD AND BACK TO FORM THE HEAD TAPERING FROM THICK AT THE WING POST TO THIN BEHIND THE HOOK EYE.

AND FINALLY THE "WHIP FINISH". A SIMPLE AND INEXPENSIVE TOOL FOR THIS OPERATION CAN BE MADE BY FORMING A LOOP OF STRONG TYING THREAD. PINCH THIS DOWN AND LAY IT ALONG SIDE THE HEAD. WRAP THE TYING THREAD THREE TIMES OVER IT (SNUG BUT NOT TOO TIGHT). NOW YOU CAN CUT THE TYING THREAD, BUT KEEP TENSION ON IT SO THOSE THREE WRAPS DON'T COME LOOSE. PUT THE TAG END OF THE TYING THREAD THROUGH THE LOOP FORWARD OF THE THREE WRAPS. PULL BACK ON THE WHIP FINISHING LOOP UNTIL THE TYING THREAD IS TIGHT AGAINST THE THREE WRAPS, LET GO OF THE THREAD AND GRAB THE HOOK EYE. PULL THE WHIP FINISHING LOOP ALL THE WAY BACK DRAWING THE TYING THREAD THROUGH UNDER THE WRAPS. TRIM THE TYING THREAD AND APPLY A DROP OF HEAD CEMENT. WHEN THE CEMENT DRIES (SHOULD BE LESS THAN A MINUTE) PUSH A NEEDLE THROUGH THE HOOK EYE TO BE SURE IT'S UNOBSTRUCTED.

TRIM

⑩

ONE MORE THING, CUT THE TOP FROM THE WING LOOP LEAVING A WING AS HIGH AS THE BODY IS LONG.
(AUTHENTIC MAYFLY PROPORTIONS)

WEIGHTING FLIES
THE USE OF A "WEIGHTED" FLY IS OFTEN SUGGESTED IN THIS MANUAL. IN ALL CASES IT IS A SUBSURFACE FLY, THE WEIGHT MEANT TO GET IT DOWN.

FLIES ARE WEIGHTED BY WRAPPING A THIN LEAD WIRE AROUND THE HOOK SHANK, THE BODY IS THEN TIED OVER THAT.

DON'T CONFUSE THIS WITH THE FLY, THE TYING OF WHICH IS BEING ILLUSTRATED ON THESE PAGES, IT IS A DRY.

A SIMPLE VARIATION ON THIS PATTERN CALLED THE "HAIR BALL" PRODUCES A SOMEWHAT MORE AUTHENTIC LOOKING FLY. IT IS TIED AS FOLLOWS:

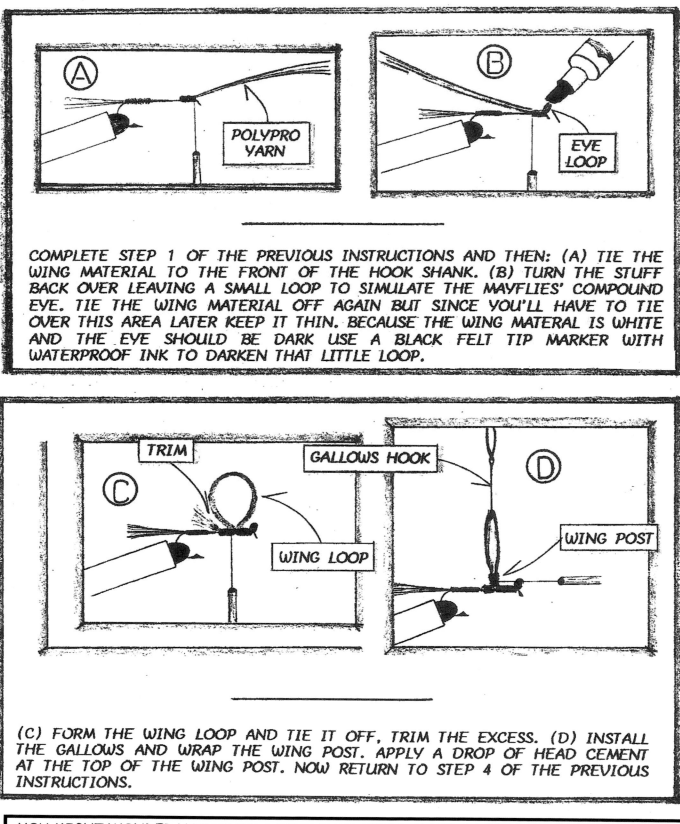

COMPLETE STEP 1 OF THE PREVIOUS INSTRUCTIONS AND THEN: (A) TIE THE WING MATERIAL TO THE FRONT OF THE HOOK SHANK. (B) TURN THE STUFF BACK OVER LEAVING A SMALL LOOP TO SIMULATE THE MAYFLIES' COMPOUND EYE. TIE THE WING MATERIAL OFF AGAIN BUT SINCE YOU'LL HAVE TO TIE OVER THIS AREA LATER KEEP IT THIN. BECAUSE THE WING MATERAL IS WHITE AND THE EYE SHOULD BE DARK USE A BLACK FELT TIP MARKER WITH WATERPROOF INK TO DARKEN THAT LITTLE LOOP.

(C) FORM THE WING LOOP AND TIE IT OFF, TRIM THE EXCESS. (D) INSTALL THE GALLOWS AND WRAP THE WING POST. APPLY A DROP OF HEAD CEMENT AT THE TOP OF THE WING POST. NOW RETURN TO STEP 4 OF THE PREVIOUS INSTRUCTIONS.

YOU MIGHT WONDER HOW SUCH A TINY BUMP COULD MAKE A DIFFERENCE AND I WOULD RESPOND: IF YOU'RE GOING TOO SUCK SOMETHING INTO YOUR MOUTH YOU HAVE TO GET VERY CLOSE.

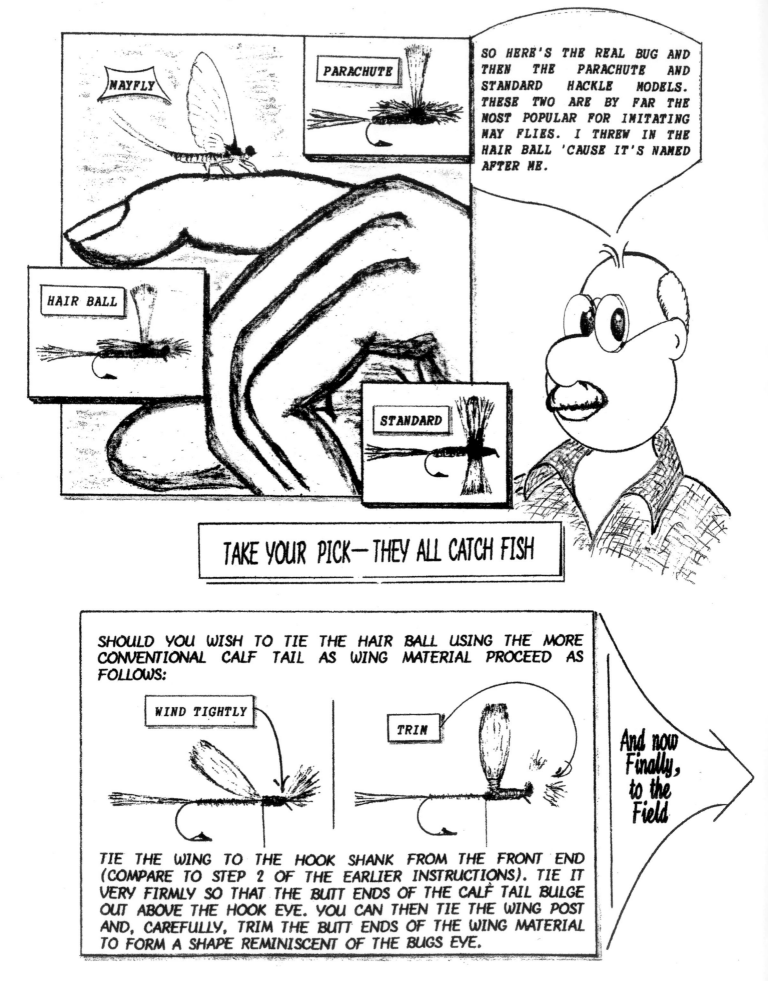

MAYFLY

PARACHUTE

HAIR BALL

STANDARD

SO HERE'S THE REAL BUG AND THEN THE PARACHUTE AND STANDARD HACKLE MODELS. THESE TWO ARE BY FAR THE MOST POPULAR FOR IMITATING MAY FLIES. I THREW IN THE HAIR BALL 'CAUSE IT'S NAMED AFTER ME.

TAKE YOUR PICK—THEY ALL CATCH FISH

SHOULD YOU WISH TO TIE THE HAIR BALL USING THE MORE CONVENTIONAL CALF TAIL AS WING MATERIAL PROCEED AS FOLLOWS:

WIND TIGHTLY

TRIM

And now Finally, to the Field

TIE THE WING TO THE HOOK SHANK FROM THE FRONT END (COMPARE TO STEP 2 OF THE EARLIER INSTRUCTIONS). TIE IT VERY FIRMLY SO THAT THE BUTT ENDS OF THE CALF TAIL BULGE OUT ABOVE THE HOOK EYE. YOU CAN THEN TIE THE WING POST AND, CAREFULLY, TRIM THE BUTT ENDS OF THE WING MATERIAL TO FORM A SHAPE REMINISCENT OF THE BUGS EYE.

Stalking Fish

THERE IS NOTHING IN THE WORLD OF ANGLING SO MUCH LIKE HUNTING AS FISHING DRY FLIES ON A MOUNTAIN STREAM.
1. YOU MUST FIND YOUR QUARRY,
2. YOU MUST MAKE SURE IT DOESN'T KNOW YOU'RE TRYING,
3. YOU MUST PLACE YOUR FLY WITH GREAT ACCURACY.
IN OTHER WAYS THE FISHER'S JOB IS THE GREATER CHALLENGE BECAUSE:
4. IT IS MUCH EASIER TO CHOOSE THE RIGHT BULLET THAN THE RIGHT FLY AND
5. ONCE THE FLY IS ON THE WATER YOU MUST ATTEND TO IT CONSTANTLY, IF IT BEHAVES IN A WAY INCONSISTENT WITH WHAT THE FISH EXPECT YOU MUST CORRECT ITS MOVEMENT IMMEDIATELY (WE CALL THIS "MINDING AND MENDING").
6. IF IT DISAPPEARS IN A CIRCLE OF RIPPLES YOU MUST "SET THE HOOK", DO THIS IN LESS THAN A SECOND AND
7. YOU HAVE A FISH TO "PLAY AND LAND".
8. ONE MORE NICE THING, YOU DON'T HAVE TO KILL TO ENJOY THIS SPORT.

STEALTH,
THE BUSINESS OF NOT ALERTING THE FISH. TRY SNEAKING UP TO A STREAM AND REMAINING BEHIND THE BUSHES. PEAK THROUGH THE BRANCHES AND FOCUS ON THE WATER, YOU WILL PROBABLY SEE NO FISH, BUT WHEN YOU THEN STEP BOLDLY OUT AND TO STEAM SIDE THERE MAY BE DARK STREAKS ALL OVER, MOST DASHING UP STREAM WHILE AN OCCASIONAL ONE TURNS AND DISAPPEARS DOWN. THOSE WERE FISH, AND IN PERHAPS A QUARTER OF AN HOUR THEY'LL BE BACK AND CATCHABLE AGAIN *IF LEFT UNDISTURBED.* **FRIGHTENED FISH CAN'T BE CAUGHT!!**

WHAT FRIGHTENS THEM ?

YOU: STAY OUT OF SIGHT AS MUCH AS POSSIBLE
MOVE SLOWLY, LIQUIDLY
FISH UPSTREAM WHEN YOU CAN
(FISH HOLD IN PLACE FACING INTO THE CURRENT)
DON'T WEAR BRIGHT OR CONTRASTING CLOTHING

ANY UNUSUAL MOVING OBJECTS
INCLUDING SHADOWS
SOMETIMES EVEN THAT OF YOUR ROD TIP

SOUNDS: LIKE THE ROCKS GRINDING UNDER YOUR FEET WHETHER YOU'RE WADING OR AT STREAM SIDE, AND CRASHING THROUGH THE BRUSH (SOUND TRAVELS WELL FROM GROUND TO WATER)

SUDDEN CHANGES IN WATER LEVEL OR CLARITY LIKE AFTER ONE OF THOSE SHORT BUT ENERGETIC MOUNTAIN THUNDERSTORMS

IF YOU SCARE ONE FISH AND HE GOES STREAKING PAST OTHERS THEY TOO WILL TAKE FLIGHT
(FISH DON'T WAIT TO ASK QUESTIONS)

IF YOU MUST CAST DOWN STREAM DON'T STIR UP SAND OR SILT THAT MAY FLOW DOWN STREAM INTO THEIR FACES

THE EFFORTS YOU MAKE TO SECRET YOURSELF FROM THE FISH WILL DEFINITELY PAY OFF!!

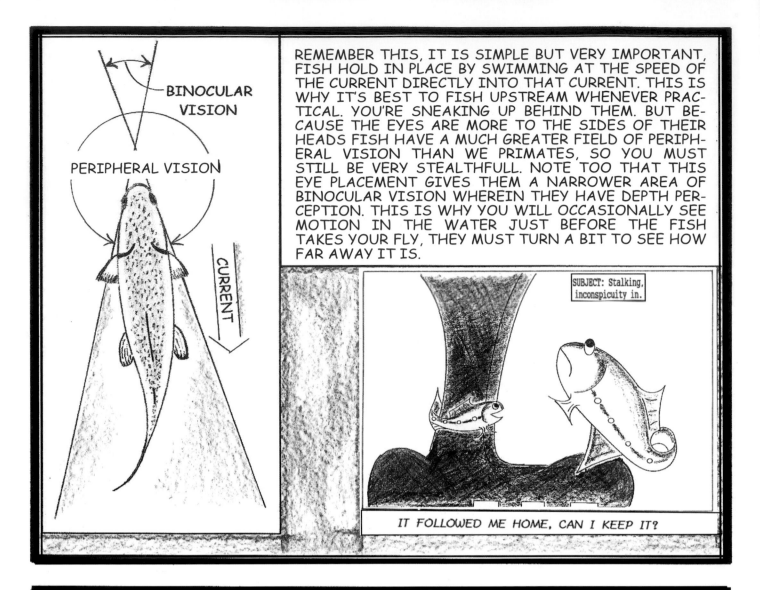

BINOCULAR VISION

PERIPHERAL VISION

CURRENT

REMEMBER THIS, IT IS SIMPLE BUT VERY IMPORTANT, FISH HOLD IN PLACE BY SWIMMING AT THE SPEED OF THE CURRENT DIRECTLY INTO THAT CURRENT. THIS IS WHY IT'S BEST TO FISH UPSTREAM WHENEVER PRACTICAL. YOU'RE SNEAKING UP BEHIND THEM. BUT BECAUSE THE EYES ARE MORE TO THE SIDES OF THEIR HEADS FISH HAVE A MUCH GREATER FIELD OF PERIPHERAL VISION THAN WE PRIMATES, SO YOU MUST STILL BE VERY STEALTHFULL. NOTE TOO THAT THIS EYE PLACEMENT GIVES THEM A NARROWER AREA OF BINOCULAR VISION WHEREIN THEY HAVE DEPTH PERCEPTION. THIS IS WHY YOU WILL OCCASIONALLY SEE MOTION IN THE WATER JUST BEFORE THE FISH TAKES YOUR FLY, THEY MUST TURN A BIT TO SEE HOW FAR AWAY IT IS.

SUBJECT: Stalking, inconspicuity in.

IT FOLLOWED ME HOME, CAN I KEEP IT?

AND NOW TO THE _ART_ OF **READING WATER.** FISH ARE NOT IN THE HABIT OF FOREVER SWIMMING ABOUT THE STREAM. THEY WILL FIND A PLACE THAT SUITS THEM AND THEN JUST HANG AROUND. SUCH NOOKS ARE CALLED *"HOLDING WATER"* AND TO FIND THE FISH YOU MUST LEARN TO SPOT THESE PLACES FROM A DISTANCE. YOU DO _NOT_ WANT TO MAKE VISUAL CONTACT. BRINGS TO MIND ANOTHER OF THOSE OLD SAYINGS *"IF YOU CAN SEE THEM THEY CAN SEE YOU"* AND THIS YOU DO NOT WANT. AS AN AID IN FINDING THESE PLACES CONSIDER THE FISH'S NEEDS:

A FISH'S WISH LIST

1. FOOD
2. SHELTER FROM STRONG CURRENTS
3. SHELTER FROM PREDATORS
(EVEN THOUGH MAN HAS ELIMINATED
OR TAKEN THE PLACE OF MOST
OF THESE, THE INSTINCTS REMAIN)
4. WATER TEMPERATURE
(IN THE MID FIFTIES TO MID SIXTIES)
5. OXYGEN
(MOST ABUNDANT IN OR BELOW AREAS
OF WHITE WATER)

THESE ARE SIMPLY BASIC NEEDS, OBVIOUSLY CIRCUMSTANCES DETERMINE WHICH IS MOST IMPORTANT AT A GIVEN TIME. POINT IS YOU NEED CONSIDER THEM ALL IN YOUR SEARCH FOR GOOD HOLDING WATER. NORMALLY WATER TEMPERATURE AND OXYGEN WON'T BE THAT IMPORTANT, BUT THEN NEITHER WILL SHELTER FROM PREDATORS UNTIL THE FISH CATCH SIGHT OF YOU. THEN YOU'LL SEE HOW QUICKLY THEIR PRIORITIES CAN CHANGE!

"FISH THE MARGINS" MY UNCLE ALBERT WAS MOST FOND OF SAYING, AND WHILE THERE IS A BIT MORE TO IT, STILL IT WAS A SAGE OBSERVATION. THE MAJORITY OF FISH TAKEN FROM MOVING WATERS WERE FOUND IN "THE MARGINS". IT'S SIMPLE TO DEFINE MARGINS BUT SOMETIMES NOT THAT SIMPLE TO FIND THEM, THE DEFINITION GOES LIKE THIS:

WHERE AN AREA OF SLOWER WATER IS CONTIGUOUS TO
AN AREA OF FASTER WATER THE INTERFACE BETWEEN THESE
AREAS IS CALLED A *MARGIN*. (ANY QUESTIONS?)

MOST OF THE REMAINDER OF THIS CHAPTER WILL DEAL WITH THE BUSINESS OF FINDING THEM AND, IN SO DOING, FINDING THE FISH.
ANYTHING WHICH PARTIALLY OBSTRUCTS THE WATERS FLOW CREATES A CURRENT SHELTERED AREA, COULD BE A BRIDGE SUPPORT OR A GRAVEL BAR OR A DEAD FALL OR . . . BUT A LOT MORE OFTEN THAN NOT IT'LL BE A ROCK, SO WE'LL START THERE.

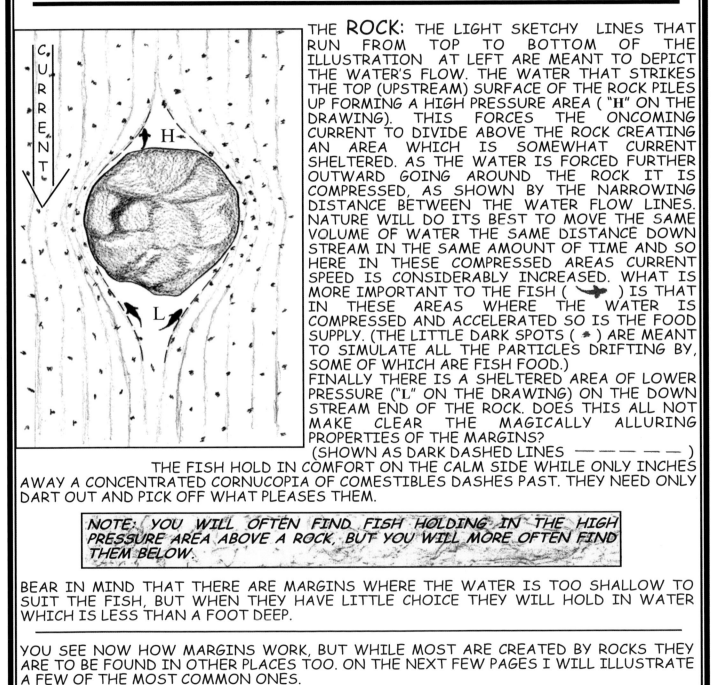

THE **ROCK**: THE LIGHT SKETCHY LINES THAT RUN FROM TOP TO BOTTOM OF THE ILLUSTRATION AT LEFT ARE MEANT TO DEPICT THE WATER'S FLOW. THE WATER THAT STRIKES THE TOP (UPSTREAM) SURFACE OF THE ROCK PILES UP FORMING A HIGH PRESSURE AREA ("**H**" ON THE DRAWING). THIS FORCES THE ONCOMING CURRENT TO DIVIDE ABOVE THE ROCK CREATING AN AREA WHICH IS SOMEWHAT CURRENT SHELTERED. AS THE WATER IS FORCED FURTHER OUTWARD GOING AROUND THE ROCK IT IS COMPRESSED, AS SHOWN BY THE NARROWING DISTANCE BETWEEN THE WATER FLOW LINES. NATURE WILL DO ITS BEST TO MOVE THE SAME VOLUME OF WATER THE SAME DISTANCE DOWN STREAM IN THE SAME AMOUNT OF TIME AND SO HERE IN THESE COMPRESSED AREAS CURRENT SPEED IS CONSIDERABLY INCREASED. WHAT IS MORE IMPORTANT TO THE FISH ( ) IS THAT IN THESE AREAS WHERE THE WATER IS COMPRESSED AND ACCELERATED SO IS THE FOOD SUPPLY. (THE LITTLE DARK SPOTS ( ) ARE MEANT TO SIMULATE ALL THE PARTICLES DRIFTING BY, SOME OF WHICH ARE FISH FOOD.)
FINALLY THERE IS A SHELTERED AREA OF LOWER PRESSURE ("**L**" ON THE DRAWING) ON THE DOWN STREAM END OF THE ROCK. DOES THIS ALL NOT MAKE CLEAR THE MAGICALLY ALLURING PROPERTIES OF THE MARGINS?
(SHOWN AS DARK DASHED LINES — — — — —)
THE FISH HOLD IN COMFORT ON THE CALM SIDE WHILE ONLY INCHES AWAY A CONCENTRATED CORNUCOPIA OF COMESTIBLES DASHES PAST. THEY NEED ONLY DART OUT AND PICK OFF WHAT PLEASES THEM.

> *NOTE: YOU WILL OFTEN FIND FISH HOLDING IN THE HIGH PRESSURE AREA ABOVE A ROCK, BUT YOU WILL MORE OFTEN FIND THEM BELOW.*

BEAR IN MIND THAT THERE ARE MARGINS WHERE THE WATER IS TOO SHALLOW TO SUIT THE FISH, BUT WHEN THEY HAVE LITTLE CHOICE THEY WILL HOLD IN WATER WHICH IS LESS THAN A FOOT DEEP.

YOU SEE NOW HOW MARGINS WORK, BUT WHILE MOST ARE CREATED BY ROCKS THEY ARE TO BE FOUND IN OTHER PLACES TOO. ON THE NEXT FEW PAGES I WILL ILLUSTRATE A FEW OF THE MOST COMMON ONES.

GRAVEL BARS: ON THE LEFT OF THIS ILLUSTRATION A BAR OF STONES AND GRAVEL PROTRUDES INTO THE CURRENT. JUST AS WITH THE ROCK ON THE PRIOR PAGE, THE WATER IS COMPRESSED AND ACCELERATED ALONG WITH THE FISH FOOD AND A MARGIN IS CREATED.

THE ROOTS OF THE TREE ON THE RIGHT HAVE BEEN RETARDING EROSION FOR YEARS (THOUGH IT APPEARS THE BATTLE WILL SOON BE LOST). THIS HAS CAUSED ANOTHER REROUTING OF THE WATER'S FLOW, AND SO ANOTHER MARGIN.

THE **BRIDGE SUPPORTS** AND THE **DEAD FALL** (DOWNED TREE) ALSO CREATE MARGINS. IN THE CASE OF THE TREE THE MARGINS WOULD CONTINUE BELOW THE SURFACE AT AN ANGLE AND BE MORE ABOVE AND BELOW THE FISH THAN TO THE SIDE, THE FISH DON'T SEEM TO CARE.

OWING TO CHANGES IN PERSPECTIVE THE MARGINS NOW LOOK LIKE (- - - - - - -) AND THE FISH (🐟) ARE VIEWED TAIL ON.

THERE ARE TWO OTHER WAYS IN WHICH THE BRIDGE AND THE DEAD FALL SUIT THE FISH'S NEEDS, THEY PROVIDE PROTECTION FROM OVERHEAD PREDATORS AND SHADE DURING THE DEAD OF SUMMER (I READ SOMEWHERE THAT FISH CAN EVEN GET SUNBURNED)*, THOUGH TO TAKE ADVANTAGE THEY WOULD HAVE TO GET UNDERNEATH.

*PLEASE DON'T QUOTE ME.

70

RUNS

RUNS ARE MODERATELY DEEP STRETCHES OF WATER WHERE THE SURFACE SHOWS LITTLE OR NO INDICATION OF WHETHER THERE IS "HOLDING WATER" BENEATH. YOU CAN PASS THESE BY IN SEARCH OF WATER YOU CAN READ, BUT IF YOU DO YOU MAY PASS BY A LOT OF GOOD FISHING. IF YOU CHOOSE TO FISH A RUN THE RECOMMENDED PROCEDURE IS TO SWEEP THAT SUBMERGED TERRA INCOGNITA SYSTEMATICALLY FROM ITS UP TO ITS DOWN STREAM EXTREMITY. I SUGGEST A WEIGHTED SUBSURFACE FLY ATTACHED TO A FAIRLY LONG LEADER/TIPPET (SAY 8ft OR MORE) WHICH IS TIED TO FLOATING FLY LINE. IF THE WATERWAY IS WIDE ENOUGH CAST ACROSS AND LET THE CURRENT SWING YOUR FLY DOWN AND AROUND. IF THE WATER IS NOT THAT WIDE CAST ACROSS AND DOWN AND LET IT SWING. AFTER MAYBE TWO CASTS MOVE DOWN STREAM A FEW FEET AND START AGAIN. ON A NARROW STREAM CAST UP AND RETRIEVE JUST FASTER THAN THE CURRENT, STRIPPING THE LINE IN WITH IRREGULAR SPEED.

THING IS, IF THERE ARE OBJECTS DOWN THERE BIG ENOUGH TO BLOCK THE CURRENT'S FLOW THERE ARE PROBABLY FISH, IF NOT, YOU'RE LIKELY WASTING YOUR TIME.

WHEN THE TOP OF A ROCK IS NOT TOO DEEP IT CREATES A SURFACE DISTURBANCE WHICH IS MOST VISIBLE SOME DISTANCE DOWN STREAM, LIKE THE ROOSTER TAIL BEHIND A SPEEDING BOAT. BECAUSE YOU WANT TO CAST WELL UPSTREAM OF THE ROCK, SO THAT YOUR FLY DRIFTS PAST NATURALLY, YOU MUST LAND THE FLY QUITE A BIT ABOVE THAT SURFACE DISTURBANCE.

A **TRIBUTARY STREAM** IS ALWAYS A VERY GOOD BET, THEIR WATERS USUALLY CARRY SUBSTANTIALLY MORE FOOD AND HAVE A HIGHER OXYGEN CONTENT THAN THE MAINSTREAM. BUT THERE IS ONE PECULIARITY, WHILE THEIR WATER IS USUALLY COOLER, SO THEY PROVIDE RELIEF TO THE FISH IN THE HEAT OF SUMMER (REMEMBER THAT FISH ARE COLD BLOODED, THEY MUST COUNT ON THEIR ENVIRONMENT TO MAINTAIN PROPER BODY TEMPERATURE), SOME STREAMS ARE FED BY HOT SPRINGS AND SO RUN WARMER THAN THE RIVER DURING THE EARLY SEASON. AT SUCH TIMES FIND THEM AND DON'T JUST FISH AT THE MOUTH, IF THEY'RE LARGE ENOUGH WORK YOUR WAY UP STREAM, FOR MANY REASONS IT CAN MAKE FOR A BETTER DAY.
A TIP, FORESTRY MAPS USUALLY SHOW HOT SPRINGS.

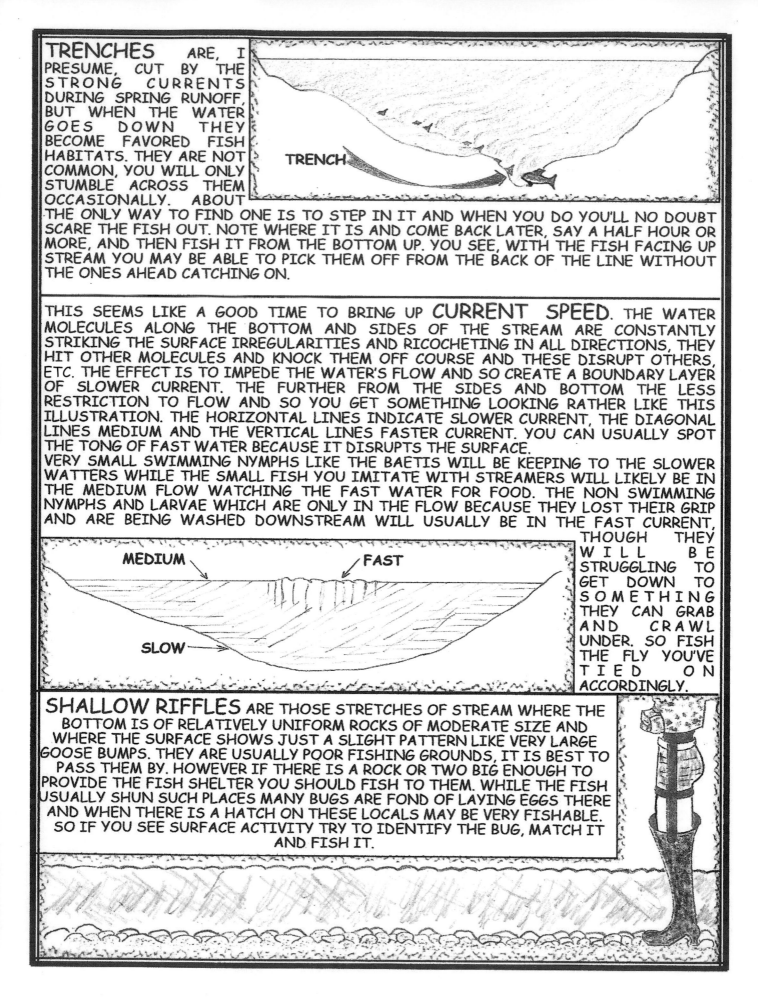

TRENCHES ARE, I PRESUME, CUT BY THE STRONG CURRENTS DURING SPRING RUNOFF, BUT WHEN THE WATER GOES DOWN THEY BECOME FAVORED FISH HABITATS. THEY ARE NOT COMMON, YOU WILL ONLY STUMBLE ACROSS THEM OCCASIONALLY. ABOUT THE ONLY WAY TO FIND ONE IS TO STEP IN IT AND WHEN YOU DO YOU'LL NO DOUBT SCARE THE FISH OUT. NOTE WHERE IT IS AND COME BACK LATER, SAY A HALF HOUR OR MORE, AND THEN FISH IT FROM THE BOTTOM UP. YOU SEE, WITH THE FISH FACING UP STREAM YOU MAY BE ABLE TO PICK THEM OFF FROM THE BACK OF THE LINE WITHOUT THE ONES AHEAD CATCHING ON.

THIS SEEMS LIKE A GOOD TIME TO BRING UP CURRENT SPEED. THE WATER MOLECULES ALONG THE BOTTOM AND SIDES OF THE STREAM ARE CONSTANTLY STRIKING THE SURFACE IRREGULARITIES AND RICOCHETING IN ALL DIRECTIONS, THEY HIT OTHER MOLECULES AND KNOCK THEM OFF COURSE AND THESE DISRUPT OTHERS, ETC. THE EFFECT IS TO IMPEDE THE WATER'S FLOW AND SO CREATE A BOUNDARY LAYER OF SLOWER CURRENT. THE FURTHER FROM THE SIDES AND BOTTOM THE LESS RESTRICTION TO FLOW AND SO YOU GET SOMETHING LOOKING RATHER LIKE THIS ILLUSTRATION. THE HORIZONTAL LINES INDICATE SLOWER CURRENT, THE DIAGONAL LINES MEDIUM AND THE VERTICAL LINES FASTER CURRENT. YOU CAN USUALLY SPOT THE TONG OF FAST WATER BECAUSE IT DISRUPTS THE SURFACE.
VERY SMALL SWIMMING NYMPHS LIKE THE BAETIS WILL BE KEEPING TO THE SLOWER WATTERS WHILE THE SMALL FISH YOU IMITATE WITH STREAMERS WILL LIKELY BE IN THE MEDIUM FLOW WATCHING THE FAST WATER FOR FOOD. THE NON SWIMMING NYMPHS AND LARVAE WHICH ARE ONLY IN THE FLOW BECAUSE THEY LOST THEIR GRIP AND ARE BEING WASHED DOWNSTREAM WILL USUALLY BE IN THE FAST CURRENT, THOUGH THEY WILL BE STRUGGLING TO GET DOWN TO SOMETHING THEY CAN GRAB AND CRAWL UNDER. SO FISH THE FLY YOU'VE TIED ON ACCORDINGLY.

MEDIUM   FAST

SLOW

SHALLOW RIFFLES ARE THOSE STRETCHES OF STREAM WHERE THE BOTTOM IS OF RELATIVELY UNIFORM ROCKS OF MODERATE SIZE AND WHERE THE SURFACE SHOWS JUST A SLIGHT PATTERN LIKE VERY LARGE GOOSE BUMPS. THEY ARE USUALLY POOR FISHING GROUNDS, IT IS BEST TO PASS THEM BY. HOWEVER IF THERE IS A ROCK OR TWO BIG ENOUGH TO PROVIDE THE FISH SHELTER YOU SHOULD FISH TO THEM. WHILE THE FISH USUALLY SHUN SUCH PLACES MANY BUGS ARE FOND OF LAYING EGGS THERE AND WHEN THERE IS A HATCH ON THESE LOCALS MAY BE VERY FISHABLE. SO IF YOU SEE SURFACE ACTIVITY TRY TO IDENTIFY THE BUG, MATCH IT AND FISH IT.

HEAVY RIFFLES, BY CONTRAST, ARE MADE OF BIG ROCKS, SO THERE'S LOTS OF HOLDING WATER. OFTEN A GOOD DEAL OF WHITE WATER TOO, SO THERE'S MORE OXYGEN. FORTY TWO FISH IN FIFTY SIX MINUTES, MY PERSONAL RECORD, I DON'T *JUST* MEAN TO BRAG, THERE ARE A FEW LESSONS HERE. FIRST I WAS FISHING "HEAVY RIFFLES" THE MOST PRODUCTIVE WATER IN THESE MOUNTAINS, AND THEY WERE ONLY ABOUT FIFTY YARDS ABOVE A BRIDGE (RECALL MY SAYING THAT *FISH AND GAME* CAN'T PASS UP A BRIDGE WHEN STOCKING? MY TIMING MUST HAVE BEEN QUITE LUCKY). I WAS USING A BLACK WOOLLY BUGGER, MY FAVORITE STREAMER. STILL, YOU'RE THINKING, THAT'S NEAR A FISH A MINUTE. SO I'LL ADMIT, I COULDN'T HAVE DONE IT WITHOUT THAT BARBLESS HOOK, IT MAKES RELEASING THEM (I LET FORTY GO, KEPT TWO FOR DINNER) QUICK AND EASY. BUT HERE'S THE POINT I MOST WISH TO MAKE, FORTY TWO FISH HOOKED, FORTY TWO FISH LANDED, NOT A ONE SLIPPED THAT BARBLESS HOOK! IF YOU'RE PLAYING THE FISH PROPERLY (NEXT CHAPTER) YOU'LL USUALLY FIND THAT WHEN YOU LOSE A FISH YOU'VE ALSO LOST A FLY.
YOU LET HIM BUST YOUR TIPPET.

"HEAVY RIFFLES" ARE ALSO ABOUT THE SIMPLEST THINGS TO FISH,. START AT THE TOP, WADE OUT FAR ENOUGH TO MAKE ROOM FOR YOUR BACK CAST AND THEN CAST STRAIGHT ACROSS TO THE FAR SIDE (POSITION **A** IN THE ABOVE ILLUSTRATION) *AND*
——————— WATCH YOUR BACKSIDE!———————
NOW LET THE CURRENT PULL YOUR FLY DOWN AND AROUND (FOLLOW THE ARROWS). WHEN THE FLY'S STRAIGHT DOWN STREAM FROM YOU (POSITION **B**), STRIP IN SOME LINE AND CAST ACROSS AGAIN. AFTER TWO OR THREE CASTS FROM THE SAME SPOT MOVE DOWN STREAM ABOUT FIVE FEET AND START AGAIN. A "STREAMER" IS YOUR BEST BET HERE AND <u>DEFINITELY</u> USE <u>FLOATING</u> LINE (SINKING LINE WILL OFTEN GO DOWN AND GET CAUGHT ON THE ROCKS). FOR THE SAME REASON A SHORTER LEADER/TIPPET (SAY SIX ft.) IS BEST, THOUGH USUALLY NOT CRITICAL.
WHY START AT THE TOP? THE WATER SURFACE IS ROUGH SO IF YOU AREN'T FOOL ENOUGH TO WEAR A BRIGHT RED SHIRT THE FISH AREN'T LIKELY TO SEE YOU AND YOUR FLY SWINGS DOWN AND AROUND SO YOU'RE STANDING UPSTREAM OF THEM ANYWAY. HOWEVER, IF YOU WADE UPSTREAM, YOU'LL WALK RIGHT THROUGH SOME OF THE FISH YOU'RE ABOUT TO TRY TO CATCH.

POOLS ARE FAVORED SPOTS ON SMALL STREAMS. SOME FISHERS WILL TREK THE DISTANCE FROM POOL TO POOL AND PASS BY HALF THE FISH IN THE WATER. STILL, THEY ARE GOOD FISHING. FOR OUR PURPOSES THEY HAVE THREE IMPORTANT PARTS, IN THE ORDER YOU ARE ADVISED TO FISH THEM THESE ARE: THE **"TAIL OUT"**, THE **"BELLY"** AND THE **"HEAD"**. YOU WORK YOUR WAY UP STREAM HERE, AS IN MOST PLACES, SO THAT YOU CAN PICK THE FISH OFF FROM BELOW WITH MUCH LESS CHANCE THAT THE FISH UP STREAM WILL GET WISE. REMEMBER, THEY'RE HOLDING INTO THE CURRENT AND WATCHING FOR THE FOOD DRIFTING DOWN TOWARD THEM.

THE **TAIL OUT** IS THE BOTTOM OF THE POOL WHERE THE WATER GETS SHALLOW AND ACCELERATES. I REALLY CAN'T SAY WHY THERE WOULD BE FISH HERE BUT I ASSURE YOU THERE OFTEN ARE, DON'T PASS IT UP.

MOST OF THE FISH ARE IN THE **BELLY**, THIS IS THE PART THE SPRING RUNOFF HAS SPENT YEARS CUTTING DEEP. POOLS ARE OFTEN AT A BEND IN THE STREAM AND THE BELLY IS AT THE OUTSIDE OF THAT BEND. BECAUSE OF ITS DEPTH AND THE USUAL OVERHANGING WILLOWS IT IS OFTEN A BEAUTIFUL EMERALD GREEN.

THE **HEAD** IS WHERE THE WATER RUSHES INTO THE POOL AND WHERE, MOST OF THE TIME, MOST OF THE FOOD ENTERS. HERE YOU SHOULD CAST TO THE WATER ABOVE AND LET YOUR FLY SURGE DOWN THROUGH THE POOL'S ENTRANCE. EVEN A DRY FLY MAY WORK BUT IT WILL BE KNOCKED UNDER SO KEEP THE SLACK OUT OF YOUR LINE SO YOU CAN FEEL A "TAKE" (WHEN THE FISH TAKES THE FLY IN ITS MOUTH). IN FACT IT'S A GOOD IDEA TO KEEP THE ROD TIP VERY HIGH SO THAT THERE IS NO FLOATING FLY LINE ON THE WATER. (FISHING THE HEAD IS CLOSE WORK, MORE ON THIS SHORTLY.)

THE POOL IS WHERE YOU MIGHT SPOT ONE OF THOSE GUYS I CALL THE "EMPIRICIST" TYPE (THE ONE WITH THE AQUARIUM FULL OF BUGS IN HIS LIVING ROOM). HE'LL LOOK AT THE POOL AND, IF THERE'S NO SURFACE FEEDING, HE'LL WALK AROUND AND ENTER THE WATER UPSTREAM. HERE HE'LL TURN OVER A FEW ROCKS FROM THE BOTTOM AND PROBABLY DISCOVER PLENTY OF NYMPHS NO LARGER THAN SIZE 24. NO PROBLEM, HE'S SURELY GOT JUST THE THING IN ONE OF THOSE VEST POCKETS, ALONG WITH 15 FT. OF 10x LEADER AND TIPPET WITH WHICH TO TIE IT ON. (SOMETIMES BEING THE BEST CAN BE AWFULLY TEDIOUS.) BUT BET ON IT, IF YOU CHECKED THE STOMACH CONTENTS OF ONE OF THE FISH FROM THAT POOL THEY'D LOOK VERY MUCH LIKE WHAT HE FOUND UNDER THOSE ROCKS UPSTREAM.

PLUNGE POOLS

FLY LINE

LEADER

CASCADES ARE FOUND IN MANY DIFFERENT TYPES OF WATER, FOR EXAMPLE THE CLASSIC POOL DESCRIBED ON THE PRIOR PAGE MAY HAVE A CASCADE AT ITS HEAD. FURTHER UP THE MOUNTAIN, WHERE THE STREAM FLOWS DOWN A STEEPER GRADIENT, YOU'LL FIND WHAT I'VE HEARD CALLED "PLUNGE POOLS" (SEE ILLUSTRATION), THEY'RE TOO SHORT TO HAVE A BELLY, YOU FISH THE CASCADE AT THEIR HEAD. THE MOUTH OF A TRIBUTARY STREAM, SIDE CHANNELS AND, LATE IN THE SEASON WHEN THE WATER IS QUITE LOW, EVEN THE RIVER BED MAY HAVE CASCADES. BUT WHEREVER FOUND THEY ARE FISHED IN THE SAME WAY.

WHERE THE WATER PLUNGES OVER THE ROCKS IT DIGS A SIZEABLE HOLE IN THE BOTTOM OF THE POOL BELOW. THE FISH HOLD IN THE CALMER WATER AT THE SIDES OF THIS HOLE AND WATCH FOR THE FOOD POURING IN. YOU SIMPLY ADD YOUR FLY TO THAT FOOD. THIS IS VERY CLOSE WORK AND YOU MORE FLIP THAN CAST YOUR FLY UP TO THE POINT LABELED **A** IN THE ILLUSTRATION BELOW. THEN HOLD THE ROD TIP VERY HIGH WITH YOUR ARM EXTENDED (BACK TO THE DRAWING ABOVE) AND LET THE FLY DRIFT OVER THE CASCADE AND INTO THE WATER BELOW. KEEP SLACK TO A MINIMUM AND *KEEP THAT COLORED FLY LINE OFF THE WATER*. THIS IS AS CLOSE AS YOU'LL COME TO FISHING OFF A PIER ON A MOUNTAIN STREAM, SO BE STEALTHFULL, BUT YOU HAVE TWO ADVANTAGES: FIRST THE FISH WILL BE UNDER THE WHITE WATER SO IT'S DIFFICULT FOR THEM TO SEE YOU, THEN THE SOUND OF THE CASCADE WILL HELP COVER THE GRINDING OF ROCKS UNDER YOUR FEET. IF YOUR FLY LINE DOES FLOW OVER THE CASCADE IT WILL TWIST 'ROUND IN THE SWIRLING CURRENT AND THE FISH CAN'T HELP BUT SEE IT, ERGO YOU MAY HAVE TO TIE ON A LONGER LEADER (SEE "LEADER BUTT" IN THE NEXT CHAPTER). YOU SHOULD DO BEST FISHING A WEIGHTED NYMPH OR PERHAPS A WEIGHTED WET FLY.

ANGLING TECHNIQUES

MUCH HAS BEEN SAID ON TECHNIQUE IN PRIOR CHAPTERS, IT JUST SORTA CAME UP WHERE IT SEEMED APPROPRIATE, BUT EVEN WHILE I'LL TRY TO MINIMIZE REPETITION THERE IS A GOOD DEAL MORE TO BE COVERED, LET US BEGIN WITH **"MINDING AND MENDING"**

MINDING: WHEN FISHING "DRIES" YOU <u>MUST</u> KEEP YOUR EYE ON THE FLY! IF YOU LOSE SIGHT OF IT A FISH CAN SUCK IT IN, TASTE IT AND SPIT IT OUT WITHOUT YOU EVER KNOWING. IF YOU DO LOSE TRACK OF THE DARN THING SIGHT DOWN YOUR LINE AND FOCUS GENERALLY ON THE AREA BEYOND ITS END, ABOUT AS FAR OUT AS YOUR LEADER AND TIPPET WOULD PLACE IT. IF YOU SEE ANYTHING UNUSUAL, A SMALL CIRCLE OF RIPPLES OR A FLASH JUST BENEATH THE SURFACE FOR EXAMPLE, _SET THE HOOK_!

WHEN YOU HAVE THE FLY IN SIGHT MAKE SURE IT'S DRIFTING NATURALLY AND, IN YOUR LOWER PERIPHERAL VISION, ATTEND TO THE LINE. IF IT BEGINS TO BOW, EITHER UP STREAM OR DOWN, YOU WILL HAVE TO TOSS IN A **"MEND"**.

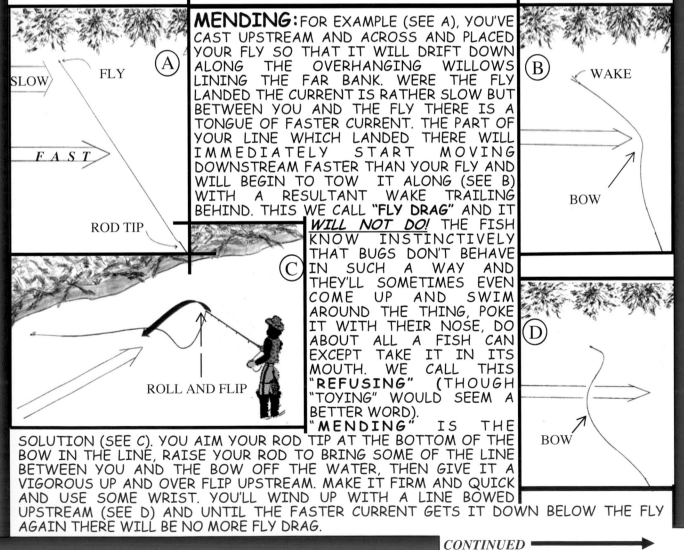

MENDING: FOR EXAMPLE (SEE A), YOU'VE CAST UPSTREAM AND ACROSS AND PLACED YOUR FLY SO THAT IT WILL DRIFT DOWN ALONG THE OVERHANGING WILLOWS LINING THE FAR BANK. WERE THE FLY LANDED THE CURRENT IS RATHER SLOW BUT BETWEEN YOU AND THE FLY THERE IS A TONGUE OF FASTER CURRENT. THE PART OF YOUR LINE WHICH LANDED THERE WILL IMMEDIATELY START MOVING DOWNSTREAM FASTER THAN YOUR FLY AND WILL BEGIN TO TOW IT ALONG (SEE B) WITH A RESULTANT WAKE TRAILING BEHIND. THIS WE CALL **"FLY DRAG"** AND IT _WILL NOT DO!_ THE FISH KNOW INSTINCTIVELY THAT BUGS DON'T BEHAVE IN SUCH A WAY AND THEY'LL SOMETIMES EVEN COME UP AND SWIM AROUND THE THING, POKE IT WITH THEIR NOSE, DO ABOUT ALL A FISH CAN EXCEPT TAKE IT IN ITS MOUTH. WE CALL THIS **"REFUSING"** (THOUGH "TOYING" WOULD SEEM A BETTER WORD).

"MENDING" IS THE SOLUTION (SEE C). YOU AIM YOUR ROD TIP AT THE BOTTOM OF THE BOW IN THE LINE, RAISE YOUR ROD TO BRING SOME OF THE LINE BETWEEN YOU AND THE BOW OFF THE WATER, THEN GIVE IT A VIGOROUS UP AND OVER FLIP UPSTREAM. MAKE IT FIRM AND QUICK AND USE SOME WRIST. YOU'LL WIND UP WITH A LINE BOWED UPSTREAM (SEE D) AND UNTIL THE FASTER CURRENT GETS IT DOWN BELOW THE FLY AGAIN THERE WILL BE NO MORE FLY DRAG.

FLY

SLOW

FAST

ROD TIP

ROLL AND FLIP

WAKE

BOW

BOW

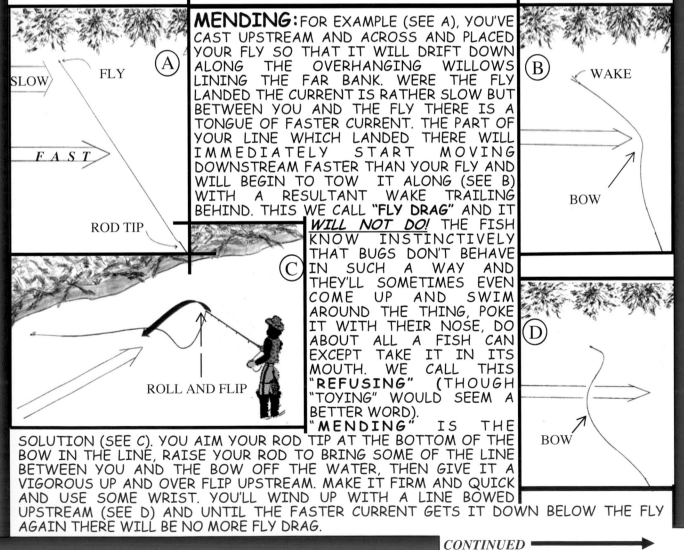

CONTINUED ➡

MENDING, A FEW IMPORTANT POINTS:

SOMETIMES YOUR FLY WILL BE IN THE FASTER WATER SO THAT YOUR LINE BOWS UPSTREAM, IN SUCH A CASE TOSS A DOWNSTREAM MEND.

OFTEN, AS IN THE EXAMPLE ON THE PRIOR PAGE, THE LINE WILL START TO BOW AND THE FLY TO DRAG AS SOON AS THEY LAND ON THE WATER, SO THROW YOUR MEND IMMEDIATELY! DON'T WAIT UNTIL THE FISH HAVE SEEN THE FLY MISBEHAVING.

TO SIMPLIFY THIS, IF THE LINE BOWS DOWNSTREAM MEND UP, IF IT BOWS UPSTREAM MEND DOWN, AND DON'T WASTE TIME THINKING ABOUT IT!

THE SURFACE FILM COHERES WITH ANYTHING WHICH GETS INTO IT, THIS IS WHY YOU RAISE YOUR ROD TO GET SOME OF YOUR LINE OFF THE WATER JUST BEFORE MENDING. IN THE BALANCE THIS HOLDING ACTION IS IN YOUR FAVOR BECAUSE IT HELPS KEEP THE LINE BETWEEN THE BOW AND THE FLY IN PLACE SO THAT THE FLY ISN'T YANKED OFF THE WATER AND SLAPPED DOWN A FOOT OR TWO UPSTREAM.
THIS COHESIVE FORCE IS ALSO THE REASON THAT THERE IS LITTLE SENSE IN PRACTICING MENDING AND ROLL CASTS ON THE BACK LAWN.

IF THE BOW IS FURTHER OUT YOU MUST BRING THE ROD TIP HIGHER AND MEND WITH A MORE VIGOROUS FLIP OVER A WIDER ARK.

MENDING ISN'T ONLY NEEDED WITH DRY FLIES, IF YOU HAD BEEN USING A DRIFTING NYMPH, IN THE EXAMPLE GIVEN, THE BOWING OF THE LINE WOULD HAVE DRAGGED IT UNNATURALLY THROUGH THE SLOWER CURRENT AND RAISED IT FROM NEAR THE BOTTOM WHERE IT SHOULD BE. WHEN THE FISH SAW THIS THEY'D REFUSE THE FLY. THE SOLUTION IS EXACTLY THE SAME AS WITH THE DRY, AN UPSTREAM MEND.

THIS BOWING AND MENDING RESULTS IN MORE SLACK ON THE WATER SO YOU MUST BE SURE THAT THERE ISN'T SO MUCH SLACK THAT IT WILL KEEP YOU FROM BEING ABLE TO SET THE HOOK SHOULD A FISH TAKE THE FLY.

STRIPPING LINE IN:

THINK OF THE REEL AS A PLACE TO STORE YOUR LINE, YOU DON'T USE REELS MUCH WHILE FLY FISHING. AFTER CASTING, WHILE YOUR FLY IS DRIFTING BACK DOWN TOWARD YOU, YOU "STRIP" IN THE SLACK. WHEN YOU'VE HOOKED A FISH AND ARE TRYING TO LAND IT, YOU HAVE MUCH BETTER CONTROL IF YOU "STRIP" IN THE LINE RATHER THAN TRYING TO CRANK IT IN WITH THE REEL.
TO STRIP SIMPLY REACH YOUR LEFT HAND UP AND GRASP THE LINE JUST WHERE IT'S EMERGING BEHIND THE RIGHT INDEX FINGER, WHICH IS HOLDING IT AGAINST THE ROD HANDLE. RELAX THE RIGHT INDEX FINGER AND PULL THROUGH AS MUCH LINE AS YOU WISH. LET THE LINE YOU'VE PULLED IN DANGLE DOWN ON THE WATER AND DRIFT DOWN STREAM, IT WON'T BE A HINDRANCE AS LONG AS YOU REMEMBER NOT TO STEP IN IT.

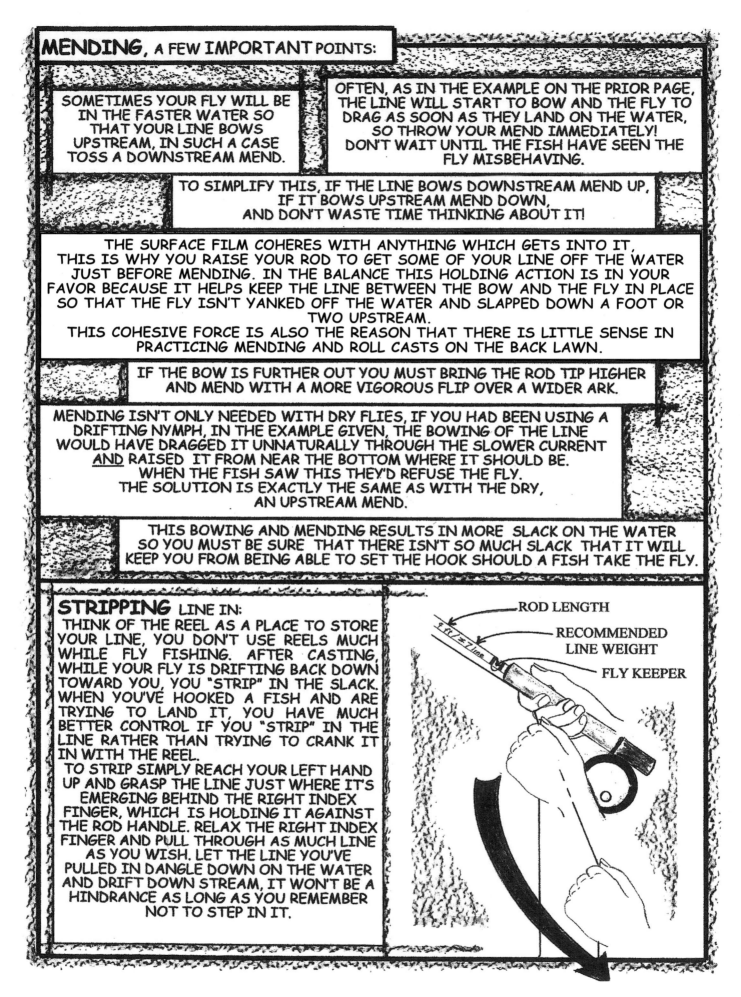

ROD LENGTH

RECOMMENDED LINE WEIGHT

FLY KEEPER

77

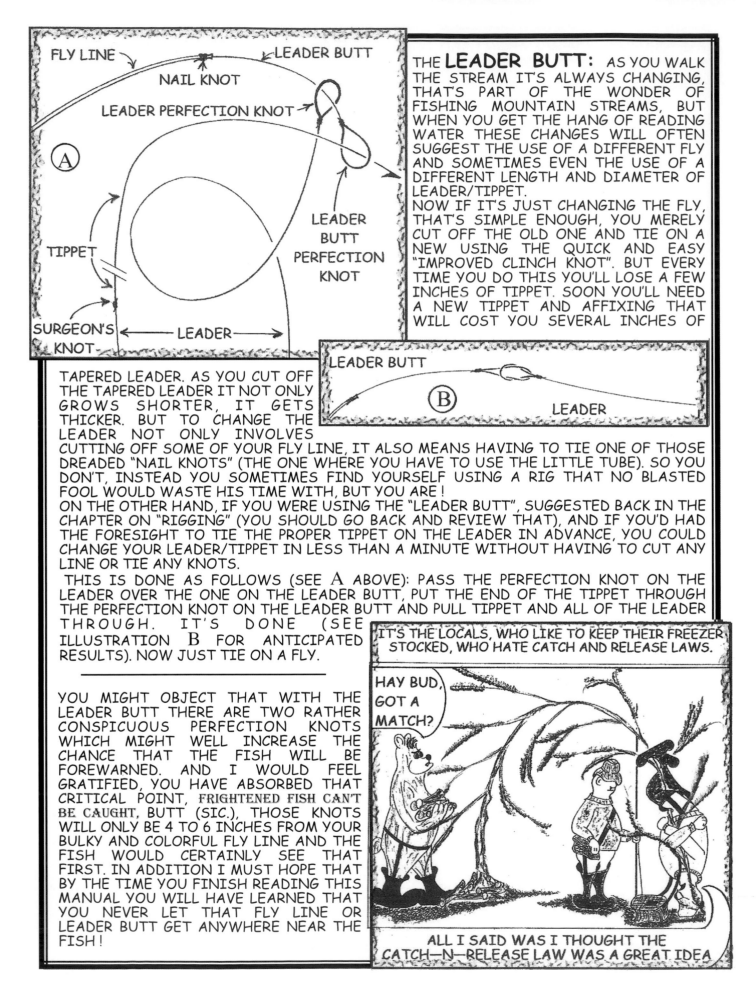

FLY LINE — LEADER BUTT

NAIL KNOT

LEADER PERFECTION KNOT →

Ⓐ

LEADER BUTT PERFECTION KNOT

TIPPET

SURGEON'S KNOT

←— LEADER —→

THE **LEADER BUTT:** AS YOU WALK THE STREAM IT'S ALWAYS CHANGING, THAT'S PART OF THE WONDER OF FISHING MOUNTAIN STREAMS, BUT WHEN YOU GET THE HANG OF READING WATER THESE CHANGES WILL OFTEN SUGGEST THE USE OF A DIFFERENT FLY AND SOMETIMES EVEN THE USE OF A DIFFERENT LENGTH AND DIAMETER OF LEADER/TIPPET.

NOW IF IT'S JUST CHANGING THE FLY, THAT'S SIMPLE ENOUGH, YOU MERELY CUT OFF THE OLD ONE AND TIE ON A NEW USING THE QUICK AND EASY "IMPROVED CLINCH KNOT". BUT EVERY TIME YOU DO THIS YOU'LL LOSE A FEW INCHES OF TIPPET. SOON YOU'LL NEED A NEW TIPPET AND AFFIXING THAT WILL COST YOU SEVERAL INCHES OF

LEADER BUTT

Ⓑ

LEADER

TAPERED LEADER. AS YOU CUT OFF THE TAPERED LEADER IT NOT ONLY GROWS SHORTER, IT GETS THICKER. BUT TO CHANGE THE LEADER NOT ONLY INVOLVES CUTTING OFF SOME OF YOUR FLY LINE, IT ALSO MEANS HAVING TO TIE ONE OF THOSE DREADED "NAIL KNOTS" (THE ONE WHERE YOU HAVE TO USE THE LITTLE TUBE). SO YOU DON'T, INSTEAD YOU SOMETIMES FIND YOURSELF USING A RIG THAT NO BLASTED FOOL WOULD WASTE HIS TIME WITH, BUT YOU ARE !

ON THE OTHER HAND, IF YOU WERE USING THE "LEADER BUTT", SUGGESTED BACK IN THE CHAPTER ON "RIGGING" (YOU SHOULD GO BACK AND REVIEW THAT), AND IF YOU'D HAD THE FORESIGHT TO TIE THE PROPER TIPPET ON THE LEADER IN ADVANCE, YOU COULD CHANGE YOUR LEADER/TIPPET IN LESS THAN A MINUTE WITHOUT HAVING TO CUT ANY LINE OR TIE ANY KNOTS.

THIS IS DONE AS FOLLOWS (SEE Ⓐ ABOVE): PASS THE PERFECTION KNOT ON THE LEADER OVER THE ONE ON THE LEADER BUTT, PUT THE END OF THE TIPPET THROUGH THE PERFECTION KNOT ON THE LEADER BUTT AND PULL TIPPET AND ALL OF THE LEADER THROUGH. IT'S DONE (SEE ILLUSTRATION Ⓑ FOR ANTICIPATED RESULTS). NOW JUST TIE ON A FLY.

YOU MIGHT OBJECT THAT WITH THE LEADER BUTT THERE ARE TWO RATHER CONSPICUOUS PERFECTION KNOTS WHICH MIGHT WELL INCREASE THE CHANCE THAT THE FISH WILL BE FOREWARNED. AND I WOULD FEEL GRATIFIED, YOU HAVE ABSORBED THAT CRITICAL POINT, FRIGHTENED FISH CAN'T BE CAUGHT, BUTT (SIC.), THOSE KNOTS WILL ONLY BE 4 TO 6 INCHES FROM YOUR BULKY AND COLORFUL FLY LINE AND THE FISH WOULD CERTAINLY SEE THAT FIRST. IN ADDITION I MUST HOPE THAT BY THE TIME YOU FINISH READING THIS MANUAL YOU WILL HAVE LEARNED THAT YOU NEVER LET THAT FLY LINE OR LEADER BUTT GET ANYWHERE NEAR THE FISH !

IT'S THE LOCALS, WHO LIKE TO KEEP THEIR FREEZER STOCKED, WHO HATE CATCH AND RELEASE LAWS.

HAY BUD, GOT A MATCH?

ALL I SAID WAS I THOUGHT THE CATCH—N—RELEASE LAW WAS A GREAT IDEA

UP AND ACROSS

WHILE YOU SHOULD USUALLY FISH UPSTREAM, NOT ONLY BECAUSE IT ALLOWS YOU TO SNEAK UP BEHIND THE FISH BUT ALSO BECAUSE YOU CAN BETTER CONTROL THE DRIFT OF YOUR FLY, YOU **DON'T CAST DIRECTLY UP**. IF YOU DO THIS YOUR FLY LINE, FOLLOWED BY YOUR LEADER AND TIPPET, DRIFT DIRECTLY OVER THE FISH JUST BEFORE YOUR LURE ARRIVES. THIS IS NOT THE WAY TO CONVINCE THESE VERY TIMID CARNIVORES THAT THEY HAVE NOTHING TO FEAR. INSTEAD YOU CAST "UP AND ACROSS" THUS REVEALING A MINIMUM OF YOUR RIG TO THE ADVERSARIES. AND REMEMBER, LATER IN THE SEASON, WHEN THE WATER IS VERY LOW AND CLEAR, YOU MAY HAVE TO SWITCH TO A LONGER AND THINNER LEADER AND TIPPET.

IN EXTREME CASES YOU MIGHT EVEN HAVE TO CAST DOWNSTREAM EMPLOYING THE "SHORT CAST" SO THAT THE FLY GETS TO THE FISH FIRST. IN SUCH AN EXTREMITY YOU MUST BE EITHER VERY FURTIVE OR VERY LUCKY. REMEMBER,

FRIGHTENED FISH CAN'T BE CAUGHT!

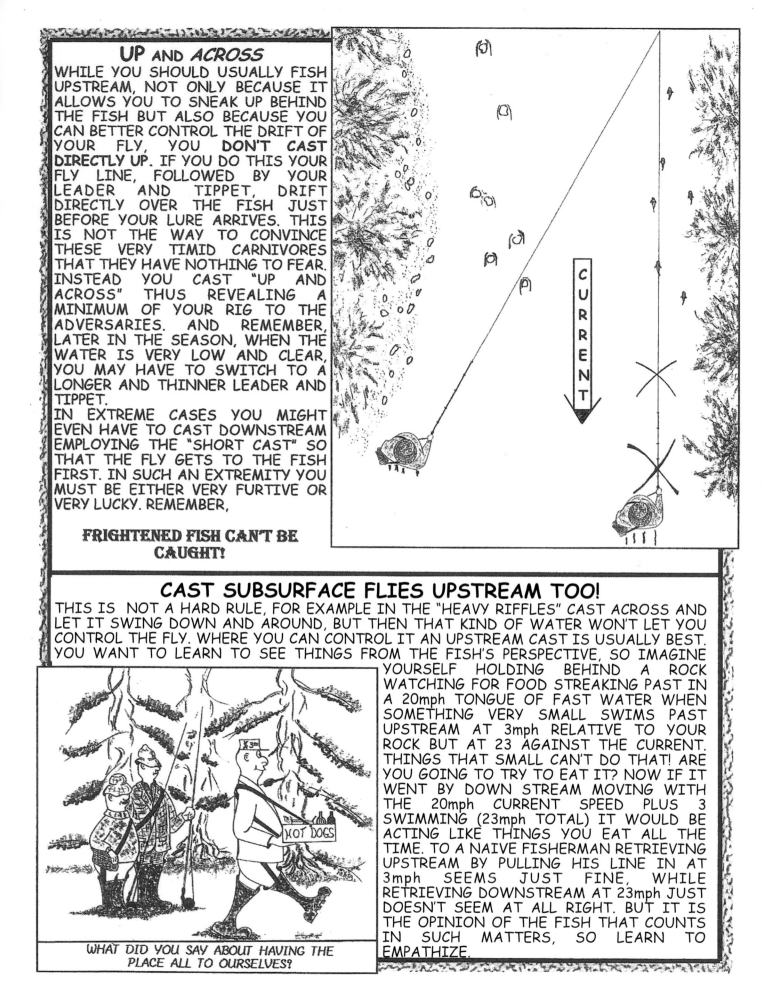

CAST SUBSURFACE FLIES UPSTREAM TOO!

THIS IS NOT A HARD RULE, FOR EXAMPLE IN THE "HEAVY RIFFLES" CAST ACROSS AND LET IT SWING DOWN AND AROUND, BUT THEN THAT KIND OF WATER WON'T LET YOU CONTROL THE FLY. WHERE YOU CAN CONTROL IT AN UPSTREAM CAST IS USUALLY BEST. YOU WANT TO LEARN TO SEE THINGS FROM THE FISH'S PERSPECTIVE, SO IMAGINE YOURSELF HOLDING BEHIND A ROCK WATCHING FOR FOOD STREAKING PAST IN A 20mph TONGUE OF FAST WATER WHEN SOMETHING VERY SMALL SWIMS PAST UPSTREAM AT 3mph RELATIVE TO YOUR ROCK BUT AT 23 AGAINST THE CURRENT. THINGS THAT SMALL CAN'T DO THAT! ARE YOU GOING TO TRY TO EAT IT? NOW IF IT WENT BY DOWN STREAM MOVING WITH THE 20mph CURRENT SPEED PLUS 3 SWIMMING (23mph TOTAL) IT WOULD BE ACTING LIKE THINGS YOU EAT ALL THE TIME. TO A NAIVE FISHERMAN RETRIEVING UPSTREAM BY PULLING HIS LINE IN AT 3mph SEEMS JUST FINE, WHILE RETRIEVING DOWNSTREAM AT 23mph JUST DOESN'T SEEM AT ALL RIGHT. BUT IT IS THE OPINION OF THE FISH THAT COUNTS IN SUCH MATTERS, SO LEARN TO EMPATHIZE.

WHAT DID YOU SAY ABOUT HAVING THE PLACE ALL TO OURSELVES?

STILL, A **DOWN** AND *ACROSS* CAST IS SOMETIMES CALLED FOR. THIS ONE SHOULD BE DONE WITH A FLY THAT SIMULATES SOMETHING THAT SWIMS, LIKE A "SOFT HACKLE" WET FLY TO IMITATE A SWIMMING NYMPH, OR A "STREAMER" FOR A SMALL FISH. THE FLY SHOULD BE HEAVILY WEIGHTED TO KEEP IT DEEP (USE SPLIT SHOTS IF YOU MUST).
A TONGUE OF FAST WATER HAS BEEN ADDED TO THE ILLUSTRATION (CENTER STREAM) SO THAT A COUPLE THINGS YOU SHOULD HAVE LEARNED CAN BE REINFORCED.

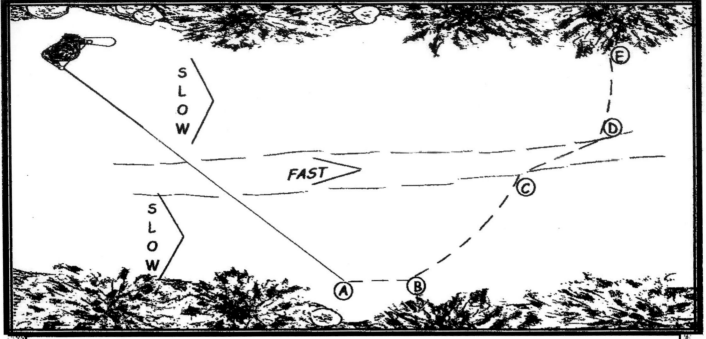

YOU STAND NEAR ONE SHORE AND CAST TOWARD THE OTHER, ANGLING DOWN STREAM. FIRST STRIP SOME EXTRA LINE FROM THE REEL AND LET IT DANGLE TO THE WATER, YOU'LL BE NEEDING IT. AS SOON AS THE FLY LINE SETTLES ON THE TONGUE OF FAST WATER IT WILL BEGIN TO BOW DOWN STREAM, SO YOU SHOULD TOSS AN UPSTREAM "MEND" IMMEDIATELY (NOT ILLUSTRATED). THE FLY LANDS AT POINT *A* AND THE TASK NOW IS TO GET IT DOWN DEEP. IF THE LINE DOES BEGIN TO BOW DOWN STREAM AGAIN THE FLY WILL BE DRAGGED BACK TOWARD YOUR SHORE INSTEAD OF SETTLING. TO GET IT DOWN YOU MUST LET IT "DEAD DRIFT", WHICH MEANS GIVE IT SLACK, BUT IN THIS CASE YOU TOSSED THAT "MEND" AND THE FASTER CURRENT IS ALREADY DRAGGING THE LINE DOWN STREAM AGAIN, CREATING SLACK BETWEEN YOU AND YOUR LURE, SO JUST LET IT SETTLE. SHOULD ALL THE SLACK COME OUT OF THE LINE BEFORE YOU FEEL THE FLY IS DEEP ENOUGH FEED OUT SOME MORE OF THAT EXTRA DANGLING LINE.
WHEN YOU JUDGE THAT THE THING IS DOWN THERE (THIS IS AT POINT *B*), GET THE SLACK OUT OF YOUR LINE AND THE CURRENT WILL START SWINGING (SWIMMING) IT ACROSS TO YOUR SIDE.
WHEN IT REACHES THE FAST WATER (AT *C*) IF YOU JUST LET IT CONTINUE TO SWING THROUGH THE SWIFTER CURRENT IT WILL APPEAR TO THE FISH TO BE SWIMMING FAR TO FAST AND THEY WILL PROBABLY "REFUSE" IT. IN ADDITION IT WILL BE PUSHED TOWARD THE SURFACE WHILE YOU WANT IT DEEP, SO GIVE IT MORE OF THAT EXTRA SLACK. BUT DON'T LET IT "DEAD DRIFT", JUST LET IT FALL DOWN STREAM AS YOU ALLOW IT TO PULL OUT EXTRA LINE THROUGH THE GUIDES ON THE ROD SO THAT IT APPEARS TO THE FISH TO BE TRYING VAINLY TO SWIM UPSTREAM. DONE THIS WAY YOU'LL BE ABLE TO FEEL A "TAKE".
WHEN THE FLY REACHES *D* HOLD THE LINE AGAIN AND IT WILL SWING NATURALLY TO YOUR SIDE OF THE STREAM (POINT *E*).
YOU RECOGNIZE THAT AT POINTS *C* AND *D* YOUR IMITATION IS CROSSING A "MARGIN". NO GUARANTEES, BUT IF THERE ARE FISH THEY'RE LIKELY TO BE THERE ABOUTS.
REMEMBER WHEN FISHING DOWN STREAM: 1. THE FISH ARE LOOKING YOUR WAY, TRY NOT TO BE SEEN. 2. DON'T GRIND THE ROOKS BENEATH YOUR FEET, SOUND TRAVELS MUCH BETTER IN WATER. 3. IF YOU KICK UP SAND IT MAY DRIFT RIGHT IN THEIR FACE.

(FRIGHTENED FISH CAN'T BE CAUGHT)

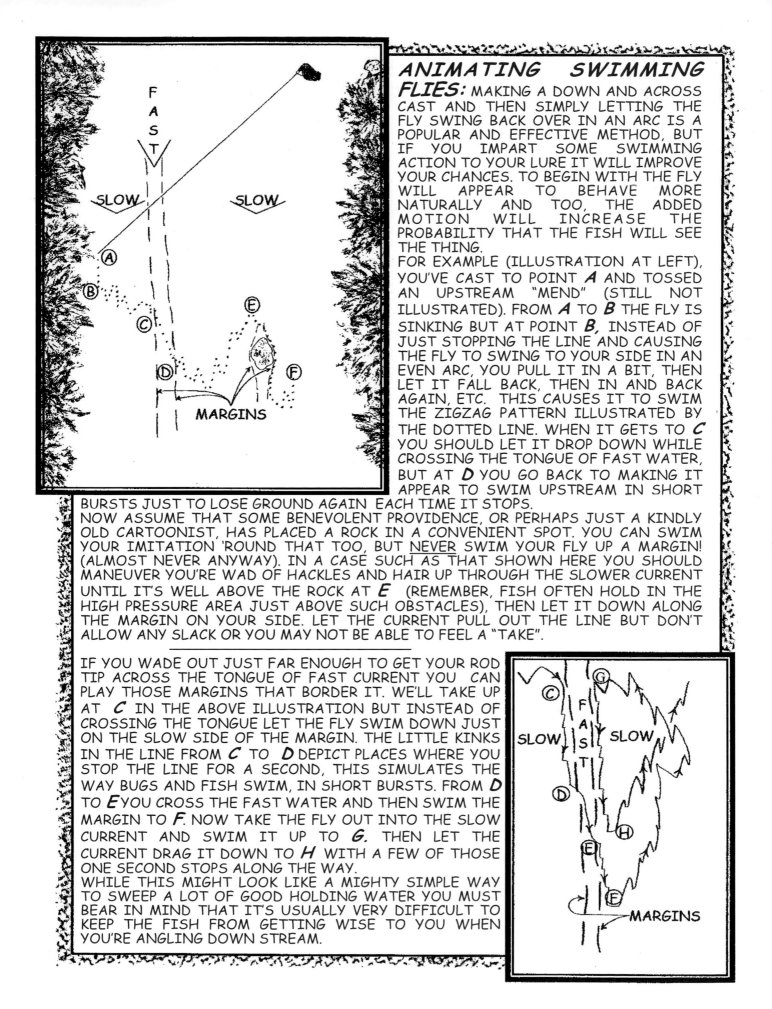

ANIMATING SWIMMING FLIES:

MAKING A DOWN AND ACROSS CAST AND THEN SIMPLY LETTING THE FLY SWING BACK OVER IN AN ARC IS A POPULAR AND EFFECTIVE METHOD, BUT IF YOU IMPART SOME SWIMMING ACTION TO YOUR LURE IT WILL IMPROVE YOUR CHANCES. TO BEGIN WITH THE FLY WILL APPEAR TO BEHAVE MORE NATURALLY AND TOO, THE ADDED MOTION WILL INCREASE THE PROBABILITY THAT THE FISH WILL SEE THE THING.

FOR EXAMPLE (ILLUSTRATION AT LEFT), YOU'VE CAST TO POINT *A* AND TOSSED AN UPSTREAM "MEND" (STILL NOT ILLUSTRATED). FROM *A* TO *B* THE FLY IS SINKING BUT AT POINT *B*, INSTEAD OF JUST STOPPING THE LINE AND CAUSING THE FLY TO SWING TO YOUR SIDE IN AN EVEN ARC, YOU PULL IT IN A BIT, THEN LET IT FALL BACK, THEN IN AND BACK AGAIN, ETC. THIS CAUSES IT TO SWIM THE ZIGZAG PATTERN ILLUSTRATED BY THE DOTTED LINE. WHEN IT GETS TO *C* YOU SHOULD LET IT DROP DOWN WHILE CROSSING THE TONGUE OF FAST WATER, BUT AT *D* YOU GO BACK TO MAKING IT APPEAR TO SWIM UPSTREAM IN SHORT BURSTS JUST TO LOSE GROUND AGAIN EACH TIME IT STOPS.

NOW ASSUME THAT SOME BENEVOLENT PROVIDENCE, OR PERHAPS JUST A KINDLY OLD CARTOONIST, HAS PLACED A ROCK IN A CONVENIENT SPOT. YOU CAN SWIM YOUR IMITATION 'ROUND THAT TOO, BUT NEVER SWIM YOUR FLY UP A MARGIN! (ALMOST NEVER ANYWAY). IN A CASE SUCH AS THAT SHOWN HERE YOU SHOULD MANEUVER YOU'RE WAD OF HACKLES AND HAIR UP THROUGH THE SLOWER CURRENT UNTIL IT'S WELL ABOVE THE ROCK AT *E* (REMEMBER, FISH OFTEN HOLD IN THE HIGH PRESSURE AREA JUST ABOVE SUCH OBSTACLES), THEN LET IT DOWN ALONG THE MARGIN ON YOUR SIDE. LET THE CURRENT PULL OUT THE LINE BUT DON'T ALLOW ANY SLACK OR YOU MAY NOT BE ABLE TO FEEL A "TAKE".

IF YOU WADE OUT JUST FAR ENOUGH TO GET YOUR ROD TIP ACROSS THE TONGUE OF FAST CURRENT YOU CAN PLAY THOSE MARGINS THAT BORDER IT. WE'LL TAKE UP AT *C* IN THE ABOVE ILLUSTRATION BUT INSTEAD OF CROSSING THE TONGUE LET THE FLY SWIM DOWN JUST ON THE SLOW SIDE OF THE MARGIN. THE LITTLE KINKS IN THE LINE FROM *C* TO *D* DEPICT PLACES WHERE YOU STOP THE LINE FOR A SECOND, THIS SIMULATES THE WAY BUGS AND FISH SWIM, IN SHORT BURSTS. FROM *D* TO *E* YOU CROSS THE FAST WATER AND THEN SWIM THE MARGIN TO *F*. NOW TAKE THE FLY OUT INTO THE SLOW CURRENT AND SWIM IT UP TO *G*. THEN LET THE CURRENT DRAG IT DOWN TO *H* WITH A FEW OF THOSE ONE SECOND STOPS ALONG THE WAY.

WHILE THIS MIGHT LOOK LIKE A MIGHTY SIMPLE WAY TO SWEEP A LOT OF GOOD HOLDING WATER YOU MUST BEAR IN MIND THAT IT'S USUALLY VERY DIFFICULT TO KEEP THE FISH FROM GETTING WISE TO YOU WHEN YOU'RE ANGLING DOWN STREAM.

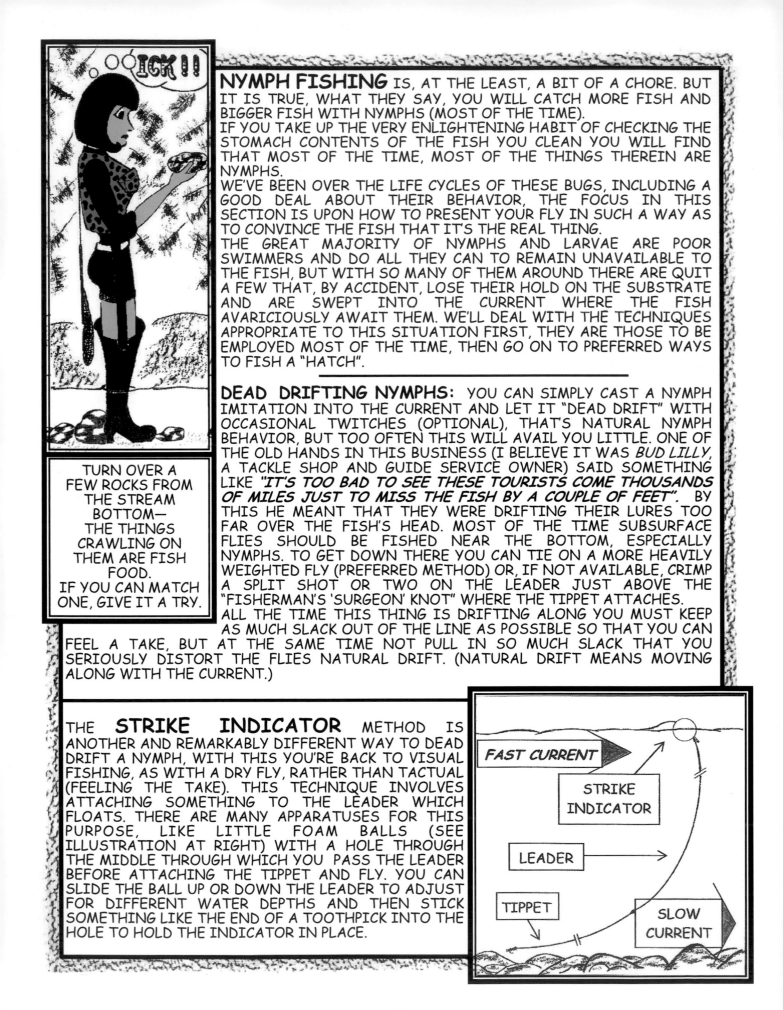

NYMPH FISHING

NYMPH FISHING IS, AT THE LEAST, A BIT OF A CHORE. BUT IT IS TRUE, WHAT THEY SAY, YOU WILL CATCH MORE FISH AND BIGGER FISH WITH NYMPHS (MOST OF THE TIME).

IF YOU TAKE UP THE VERY ENLIGHTENING HABIT OF CHECKING THE STOMACH CONTENTS OF THE FISH YOU CLEAN YOU WILL FIND THAT MOST OF THE TIME, MOST OF THE THINGS THEREIN ARE NYMPHS.

WE'VE BEEN OVER THE LIFE CYCLES OF THESE BUGS, INCLUDING A GOOD DEAL ABOUT THEIR BEHAVIOR, THE FOCUS IN THIS SECTION IS UPON HOW TO PRESENT YOUR FLY IN SUCH A WAY AS TO CONVINCE THE FISH THAT IT'S THE REAL THING.

THE GREAT MAJORITY OF NYMPHS AND LARVAE ARE POOR SWIMMERS AND DO ALL THEY CAN TO REMAIN UNAVAILABLE TO THE FISH, BUT WITH SO MANY OF THEM AROUND THERE ARE QUIT A FEW THAT, BY ACCIDENT, LOSE THEIR HOLD ON THE SUBSTRATE AND ARE SWEPT INTO THE CURRENT WHERE THE FISH AVARICIOUSLY AWAIT THEM. WE'LL DEAL WITH THE TECHNIQUES APPROPRIATE TO THIS SITUATION FIRST, THEY ARE THOSE TO BE EMPLOYED MOST OF THE TIME, THEN GO ON TO PREFERRED WAYS TO FISH A "HATCH".

TURN OVER A FEW ROCKS FROM THE STREAM BOTTOM—
THE THINGS CRAWLING ON THEM ARE FISH FOOD.
IF YOU CAN MATCH ONE, GIVE IT A TRY.

DEAD DRIFTING NYMPHS: YOU CAN SIMPLY CAST A NYMPH IMITATION INTO THE CURRENT AND LET IT "DEAD DRIFT" WITH OCCASIONAL TWITCHES (OPTIONAL), THAT'S NATURAL NYMPH BEHAVIOR, BUT TOO OFTEN THIS WILL AVAIL YOU LITTLE. ONE OF THE OLD HANDS IN THIS BUSINESS (I BELIEVE IT WAS *BUD LILLY*, A TACKLE SHOP AND GUIDE SERVICE OWNER) SAID SOMETHING LIKE *"IT'S TOO BAD TO SEE THESE TOURISTS COME THOUSANDS OF MILES JUST TO MISS THE FISH BY A COUPLE OF FEET"*. BY THIS HE MEANT THAT THEY WERE DRIFTING THEIR LURES TOO FAR OVER THE FISH'S HEAD. MOST OF THE TIME SUBSURFACE FLIES SHOULD BE FISHED NEAR THE BOTTOM, ESPECIALLY NYMPHS. TO GET DOWN THERE YOU CAN TIE ON A MORE HEAVILY WEIGHTED FLY (PREFERRED METHOD) OR, IF NOT AVAILABLE, CRIMP A SPLIT SHOT OR TWO ON THE LEADER JUST ABOVE THE "FISHERMAN'S 'SURGEON' KNOT" WHERE THE TIPPET ATTACHES.

ALL THE TIME THIS THING IS DRIFTING ALONG YOU MUST KEEP AS MUCH SLACK OUT OF THE LINE AS POSSIBLE SO THAT YOU CAN FEEL A TAKE, BUT AT THE SAME TIME NOT PULL IN SO MUCH SLACK THAT YOU SERIOUSLY DISTORT THE FLIES NATURAL DRIFT. (NATURAL DRIFT MEANS MOVING ALONG WITH THE CURRENT.)

THE **STRIKE INDICATOR** METHOD IS ANOTHER AND REMARKABLY DIFFERENT WAY TO DEAD DRIFT A NYMPH, WITH THIS YOU'RE BACK TO VISUAL FISHING, AS WITH A DRY FLY, RATHER THAN TACTUAL (FEELING THE TAKE). THIS TECHNIQUE INVOLVES ATTACHING SOMETHING TO THE LEADER WHICH FLOATS. THERE ARE MANY APPARATUSES FOR THIS PURPOSE, LIKE LITTLE FOAM BALLS (SEE ILLUSTRATION AT RIGHT) WITH A HOLE THROUGH THE MIDDLE THROUGH WHICH YOU PASS THE LEADER BEFORE ATTACHING THE TIPPET AND FLY. YOU CAN SLIDE THE BALL UP OR DOWN THE LEADER TO ADJUST FOR DIFFERENT WATER DEPTHS AND THEN STICK SOMETHING LIKE THE END OF A TOOTHPICK INTO THE HOLE TO HOLD THE INDICATOR IN PLACE.

FAST CURRENT

STRIKE INDICATOR

LEADER

TIPPET

SLOW CURRENT

THE **BOWTIE** IS A POPULAR TYPE OF STRIKE INDICATOR BECAUSE YOU CAN INSTALL OR REMOVE IT WITHOUT CUTTING OFF YOUR FLY. ON THE OTHER HAND, THE YARN FROM WHICH IT IS FASHIONED WON'T FLOAT AS WELL AS MANY OF THE ALTERNATIVES. IT'S UP TO YOU. YOU TIE YOUR OWN BOWTIES, JUST CUT SEVERAL PIECES OF SYNTHETIC YARN ABOUT AS LONG AS THE MAXIMUM YOU THINK YOU MIGHT NEED (2 INCHES SHOULD DO), STACK THEM TOGETHER AND TIE THEM AROUND THE MIDDLE USING A STURDY THREAD. THEN COMB THE STRANDS IN THE YARN APART WITH SOMETHING LIKE THE SAFETY PIN YOU WERE ADVISED TO CARRY. IT IS BEST TO USE YARN OF A COLOR THE FISH ARE ACCUSTOMED TO SEEING ON THE SURFACE, WHITE OR A PALE YELLOW OR GREEN DO WELL. YOU'LL BE TRIMMING THESE TO THE SIZE YOU NEED ON THE STREAM (THAT SIZE DEPENDS ON THE SURFACE ROUGHNESS AND ESPECIALLY THE WEIGHT OF THE FLY AND SINKERS YOU HAVE ADDED). CUT THEM DOWN AS MUCH AS POSSIBLE.

TO ADD ONE TO YOUR RIG SIMPLY PUT AN OVERHAND KNOT IN YOUR LEADER (SEE BELOW) ABOUT TWICE AS FAR ABOVE THE FLY AS YOU ESTIMATE THE WATER TO BE DEEP, THEN PUSH THE BOWTIE HALFWAY THROUGH AND TIGHTEN THE KNOT.

BECAUSE THE SURFACE CURRENT IS USUALLY FASTER THAN THE CURRENT NEAR THE BOTTOM, WHERE YOUR FLY SHOULD BE, THE DISTANCE FROM STRIKE INDICATOR TO FLY MUST BE GREATER THAN THE WATER DEPTH AND MAKING IT ONLY TWICE AS LONG OFTEN WILL NOT SUFFICE. THE FASTER THE CURRENT THE GREATER THAT DISTANCE MUST BE.

THE TEST? YOUR FLY SHOULD OCCASIONALLY DRAG BOTTOM WHICH WILL CAUSE YOUR STRIKE INDICATOR TO HESITATE IN ITS DRIFT. IF THIS HAPPENS CONTINUALLY THE FLY'S TOO DEEP, IF NEVER, THE FLY'S TOO SHALLOW, ADJUST ACCORDINGLY.

APPLY FLY FLOATANT TO THE BOWTIE WHEN NEEDED. IF YOU MUST USE A SINKER SQUEEZE IT ON JUST ABOVE THE SURGEON'S KNOT CONNECTING THE LEADER AND TIPPET.

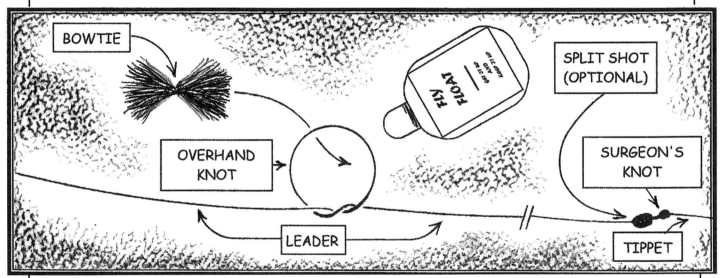

THE MAJOR PROBLEM WITH THIS RIG, WHATEVER TYPE STRIKE INDICATOR YOU USE, IS THAT IT'S VERY DIFFICULT TO CAST. EVEN THE EXPERTS ADMIT TO SPENDING A GOOD DEAL OF TIME UNTYING THE SNARLS THAT SO OFTEN ENSUE. MOST OF THEM WOULD AGREE THAT WHENEVER POSSIBLE YOU SHOULD USE A "ROLL CAST", OR BETTER, A "WATER LOADED CAST". WE SHOULD STEP THROUGH THIS WATER LOADED CAST IN SOME DETAIL, BUT FIRST, AS A PREREQUISITE, GO THROUGH THE CHANGES TO THE OVERHEAD CAST REQUIRED TO DELIVER SUCH A CUMBERSOME LOAD.

WHEN PERFORMING THE **OVERHEAD CAST** WITH A **HEAVY RIG** YOU SHOULD MAKE A FEW MODIFICATIONS:

FIRST THE TIGHT, CONTROLLED LOOP YOU GOT FROM CASTING 11 O'CLOCK—1 O'CLOCK MUST GIVE WAY TO A MORE OPEN LOOP, THIS YOU DO BY EXTENDING THE CASTING STROKE TO 45 DEGREES FORE AND AFT OF VERTICAL (ON THE CLOCK THAT WOULD BE 10:30 TO 1:30).

SECOND, WHILE THE FORECAST IS STILL DONE WITH AS MUCH POWER, IT IS NO LONGER A "WHACK", BACK IT OFF TO A HEAVE.

FINALLY, WHEN "LOADING" THE LINE ON FORE AND BACKCAST, YOU MUST ALLOW IT TO STRAIGHTEN COMPLETELY, START THE NEXT STROKE BEFORE THEN AND THAT HEAVY FLY MAY SLINGSHOT AROUND AND CATCH YOUR LEADER (PROBABLY THE MOST COMMON WAY TO CREATE A SNARL WITH A HEAVY RIG).

THE **WATER LOADED CAST** CAN BE USED WITH ANY TYPE OF FLY BUT IS REALLY DESIRABLE WITH AN UNUSUALLY HEAVY ONE, OR WHEN YOU'VE ADDED A STRIKE INDICATOR.

FIRST IDENTIFY THE LINE ALONG WHICH YOU WISH YOUR FLY TO DRIFT, THIS WILL USUALLY BE THE STRIP OF STREAM WHERE THE CURRENT HAS CUT THE DEEPEST CHANNEL (IT IS SIMULATED IN THE ILLUSTRATION BY THE HEAVY DASHED VERTICAL LINE WITH CURRENT DIRECTION SHOWN BY THE ARROW HEADS). WADE OUT UNTIL YOU'RE ABOUT TWO ROD LENGTHS FROM A POINT HALF WAY DOWN THIS LINE OF DRIFT (THAT'S THE POINT LABELED **A**). NEXT JUST FLIP THE FLY AND INDICATOR OUT TO POINT **A** AND BEGIN TO STRIP LINE FROM THE REEL AND FEED IT OUT TOWARD THE LOWER ROD GUIDE. AIM THE ROD TIP STRAIGHT DOWN THE FLY LINE, BOTH HORIZONTALLY AND VERTICALLY, TOWARD THE INDICATOR (YOU DO THIS TO MINIMIZE THE DRAG AS THE LINE SLIPS OUT THROUGH THE GUIDES SO THAT THE INDICATOR AND FLY WILL DRIFT AS NATURALLY AS POSSIBLE). (THIS IS A TIME WHEN A CLEAN FLY LINE REALLY MAKES A DIFFERENCE.) WATCH THE INDICATOR CLOSELY, IT IS NOT UNUSUAL TO HOOK A FISH ON THIS DOWN STREAM PART OF THE DRIFT, AND MEND THE LINE IF NECESSARY.

WHEN THE FLY GETS AS FAR DOWN STREAM (POINT **B**) AS YOU WISH TO CAST UPSTREAM (POINT **C**), STOP THE LINE, WAIT TILL IT STRAIGHTENS, THEN WAIT A FEW MORE SECONDS WHILE THE CURRENT PUSHES THE FLY TOWARD THE SURFACE (THIS TOO MAY EXCITE THE FISH, SO BE READY FOR A TAKE, BUT THIS TIME, WITH THE SLACK OUT OF THE LINE, YOU'LL MORE LIKELY FEEL IT THAN SEE IT).

NEXT TURN UPSTREAM AND "HEAVE" THE CAST POINTING THE ROD TIP WHERE YOU HOPE THE FLY WILL GO (POINT **C**), STOP HIGH ENOUGH (SAY 10:30) TO SET THE LOOP. ONCE THE LOOP IS SET LET THE ROD TIP DOWN (MY SECOND FAVORITE WAY TO CREATE A SNARL IS TO LET THE JUNK I'M CASTING STRIKE THE ROD, IF YOU DROP THE TIP <u>AFTER SETTING THE LOOP</u> THIS IS LESS LIKELY). WHEN YOUR RIG HITS THE WATER START STRIPPING IN LINE JUST AS YOU WOULD WITH A DRY FLY AND, JUST AS WITH A DRY, GO TO "MINDING AND MENDING". WHEN THE INDICATOR GETS BACK TO POINT **A** FOLLOW THE INSTRUCTIONS ABOVE FOR THE DOWN STREAM PART OF THE DRIFT (POINT **A** TO POINT **B**).

SIR ISAAC NEWTON COULD HAVE, IN A WAY DID, WARN YOU OF THE DIFFICULTY IN THIS CAST, YOU ARE LIMITED IN THE EXTENT TO WHICH THE FORWARD THRUST OF THE LINE CAN BE REDIRECTED TO EITHER SIDE. IF YOU WANT THE THING TO GO WIDER THAN IT'S WILLING, YOU CAN EITHER LET THE FLY DRIFT TO POINT **B** AND LEAVE IT DANGLING UNTIL YOU WADE TO A NEW POSITION, OR RISK AN OVERHEAD CAST OR TWO TO REALIGN YOUR TRAJECTORY.

ONE OF THE DIFFICULT THINGS ABOUT USING A STRIKE INDICATOR IS RECOGNIZING THE VERY SUBTLE DIFFERENCE BETWEEN THE **_HESITATION_** IN THE MOTION OF THE INDICATOR WHICH OCCURS WHEN YOUR FLY, OR SPLIT SHOT, DRAGS BOTTOM, AND THE SLIGHT **_TUG_** OR **_JERK_** YOU SEE WHEN A FISH TAKES THE FLY. WITH ENOUGH EXPERIENCE YOU'LL GET BETTER AT IT BUT, IN ANY CASE, I SUGGEST THAT **_WHEN IN DOUBT, SET THE HOOK!_** YOU HAVE LITTLE TO LOSE, IF NO FISH, JUST GO BACK TO FISHING OUT THE DRIFT.

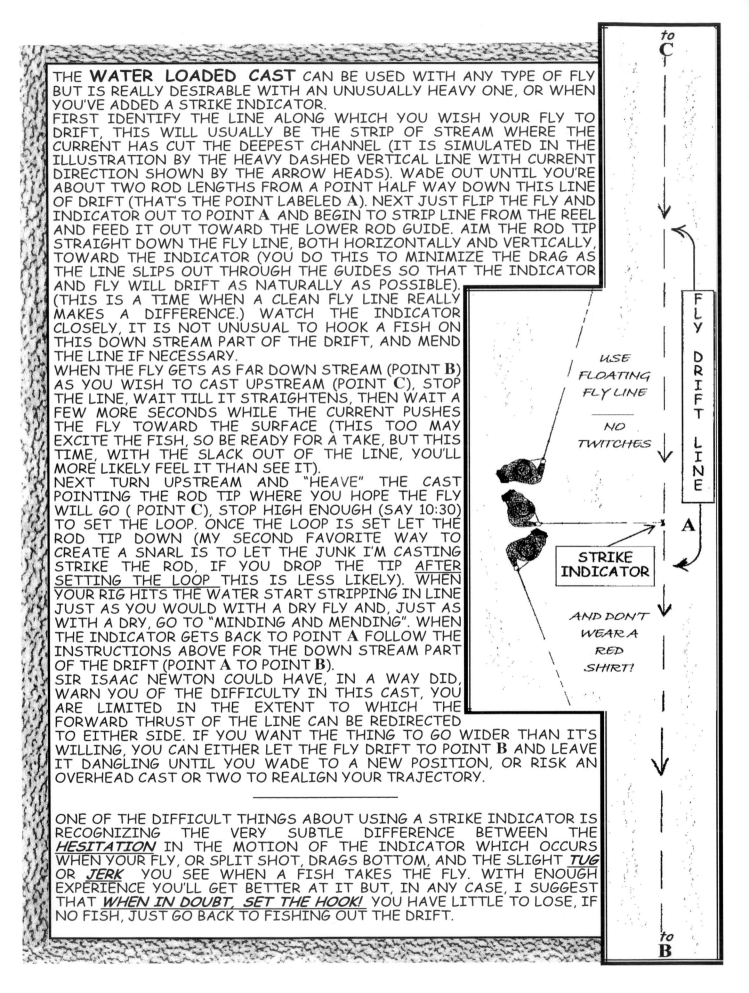

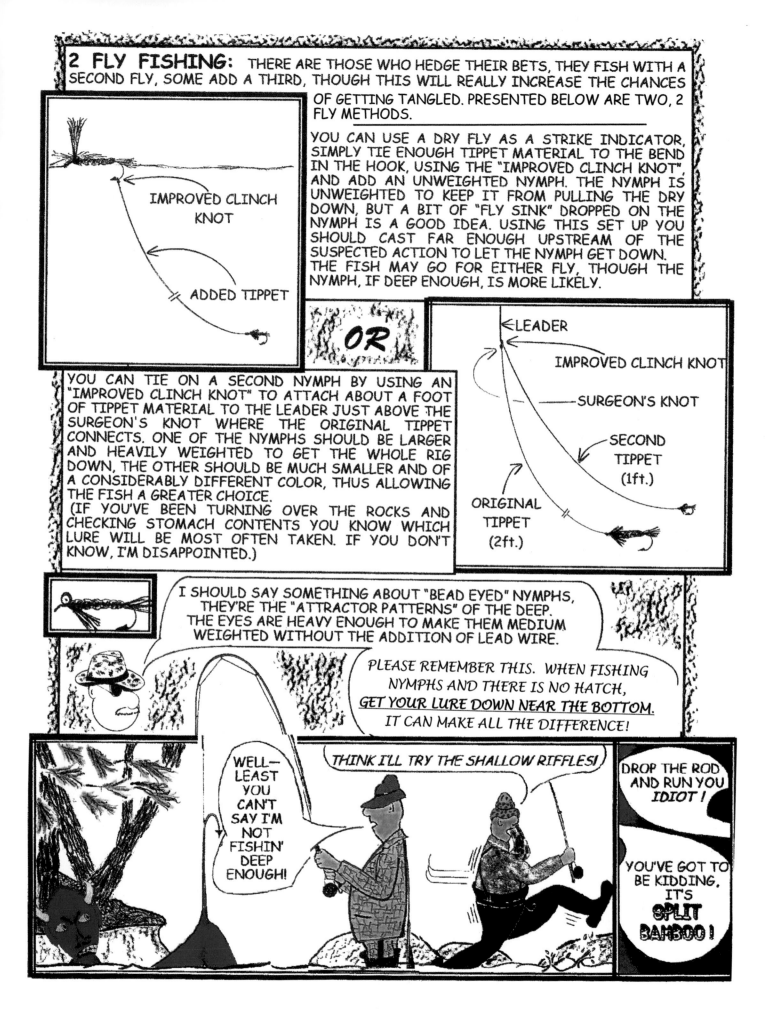

STILL WATER NYMPHING

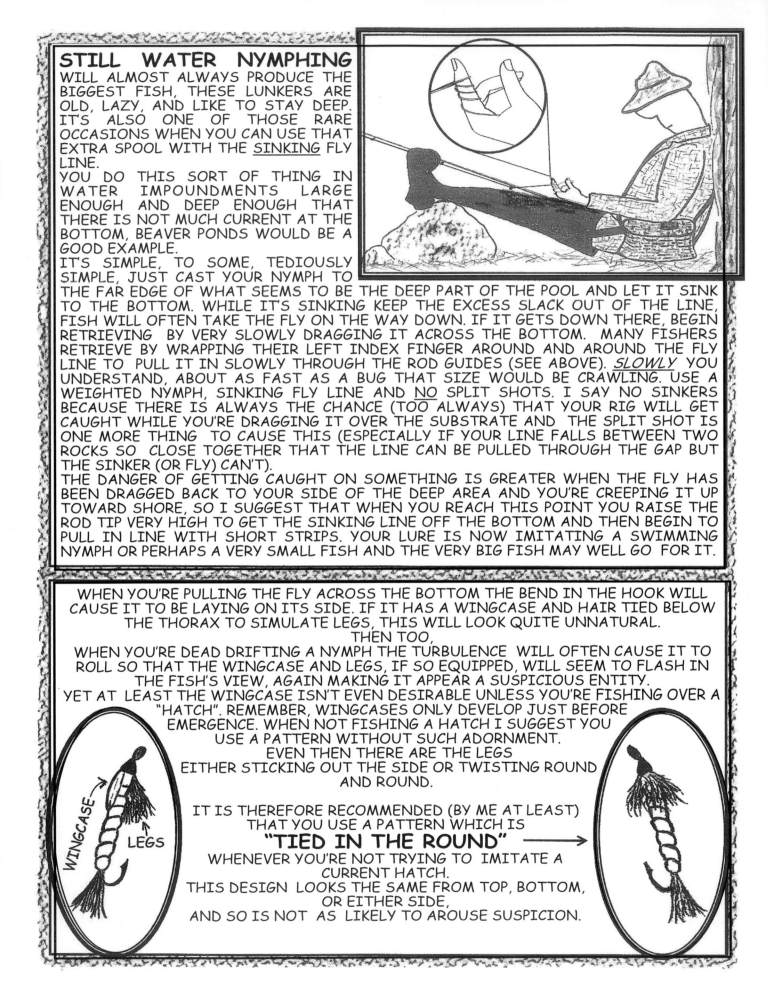

WILL ALMOST ALWAYS PRODUCE THE BIGGEST FISH, THESE LUNKERS ARE OLD, LAZY, AND LIKE TO STAY DEEP. IT'S ALSO ONE OF THOSE RARE OCCASIONS WHEN YOU CAN USE THAT EXTRA SPOOL WITH THE <u>SINKING</u> FLY LINE.

YOU DO THIS SORT OF THING IN WATER IMPOUNDMENTS LARGE ENOUGH AND DEEP ENOUGH THAT THERE IS NOT MUCH CURRENT AT THE BOTTOM, BEAVER PONDS WOULD BE A GOOD EXAMPLE.

IT'S SIMPLE, TO SOME, TEDIOUSLY SIMPLE, JUST CAST YOUR NYMPH TO THE FAR EDGE OF WHAT SEEMS TO BE THE DEEP PART OF THE POOL AND LET IT SINK TO THE BOTTOM. WHILE IT'S SINKING KEEP THE EXCESS SLACK OUT OF THE LINE, FISH WILL OFTEN TAKE THE FLY ON THE WAY DOWN. IF IT GETS DOWN THERE, BEGIN RETRIEVING BY VERY SLOWLY DRAGGING IT ACROSS THE BOTTOM. MANY FISHERS RETRIEVE BY WRAPPING THEIR LEFT INDEX FINGER AROUND AND AROUND THE FLY LINE TO PULL IT IN SLOWLY THROUGH THE ROD GUIDES (SEE ABOVE). *SLOWLY* YOU UNDERSTAND, ABOUT AS FAST AS A BUG THAT SIZE WOULD BE CRAWLING. USE A WEIGHTED NYMPH, SINKING FLY LINE AND <u>NO</u> SPLIT SHOTS. I SAY NO SINKERS BECAUSE THERE IS ALWAYS THE CHANCE (TOO ALWAYS) THAT YOUR RIG WILL GET CAUGHT WHILE YOU'RE DRAGGING IT OVER THE SUBSTRATE AND THE SPLIT SHOT IS ONE MORE THING TO CAUSE THIS (ESPECIALLY IF YOUR LINE FALLS BETWEEN TWO ROCKS SO CLOSE TOGETHER THAT THE LINE CAN BE PULLED THROUGH THE GAP BUT THE SINKER (OR FLY) CAN'T).

THE DANGER OF GETTING CAUGHT ON SOMETHING IS GREATER WHEN THE FLY HAS BEEN DRAGGED BACK TO YOUR SIDE OF THE DEEP AREA AND YOU'RE CREEPING IT UP TOWARD SHORE, SO I SUGGEST THAT WHEN YOU REACH THIS POINT YOU RAISE THE ROD TIP VERY HIGH TO GET THE SINKING LINE OFF THE BOTTOM AND THEN BEGIN TO PULL IN LINE WITH SHORT STRIPS. YOUR LURE IS NOW IMITATING A SWIMMING NYMPH OR PERHAPS A VERY SMALL FISH AND THE VERY BIG FISH MAY WELL GO FOR IT.

WHEN YOU'RE PULLING THE FLY ACROSS THE BOTTOM THE BEND IN THE HOOK WILL CAUSE IT TO BE LAYING ON ITS SIDE. IF IT HAS A WINGCASE AND HAIR TIED BELOW THE THORAX TO SIMULATE LEGS, THIS WILL LOOK QUITE UNNATURAL.
THEN TOO,
WHEN YOU'RE DEAD DRIFTING A NYMPH THE TURBULENCE WILL OFTEN CAUSE IT TO ROLL SO THAT THE WINGCASE AND LEGS, IF SO EQUIPPED, WILL SEEM TO FLASH IN THE FISH'S VIEW, AGAIN MAKING IT APPEAR A SUSPICIOUS ENTITY.
YET AT LEAST THE WINGCASE ISN'T EVEN DESIRABLE UNLESS YOU'RE FISHING OVER A "HATCH". REMEMBER, WINGCASES ONLY DEVELOP JUST BEFORE EMERGENCE. WHEN NOT FISHING A HATCH I SUGGEST YOU USE A PATTERN WITHOUT SUCH ADORNMENT.
EVEN THEN THERE ARE THE LEGS EITHER STICKING OUT THE SIDE OR TWISTING ROUND AND ROUND.

IT IS THEREFORE RECOMMENDED (BY ME AT LEAST) THAT YOU USE A PATTERN WHICH IS
"TIED IN THE ROUND" ⟶
WHENEVER YOU'RE NOT TRYING TO IMITATE A CURRENT HATCH.
THIS DESIGN LOOKS THE SAME FROM TOP, BOTTOM, OR EITHER SIDE,
AND SO IS NOT AS LIKELY TO AROUSE SUSPICION.

WINGCASE

LEGS

NYMPHING A HATCH:

IN THE SECTION HEADED EMPIRICIST, IN THE CHAPTER COVERING FLY SELECTION, THERE IS A CONSIDERABLE DISCOURSE ON INSECT EMERGENCE BEHAVIOR. IF YOU HAVEN'T READ THAT RECENTLY I WOULD SUGGEST YOU REVIEW IT (IT'S ONLY EIGHT PAGES, WITH LOTS OF PICTURES). THIS SECTION PRESENTS A SUMMERY OF THE THREE BASIC PATTERNS OF EMERGENCE BEHAVIOR ALONG WITH SUGGESTIONS ON HOW TO FISH EACH. BUT BEFORE COVERING THESE A BIT SHOULD BE SAID ABOUT THE PECULIARITIES OF THE FISH'S BEHAVIOR DURING A "HATCH".

THE FISH WILL GATHER TO THE HATCH AREA IN UNUSUALLY LARGE NUMBERS AND, RATHER THAN LURKING IN "HOLDING WATER", WILL BE ON THE MOVE, TWISTING EVERY WAY AND PICKING OFF NYMPHS WITH WHAT SOMETIMES SEEMS ABANDON. WHAT IS IMPORTANT TO YOU (OTHER THAN MOST LIKELY CATCHING A LOT MORE FISH) IS THAT THEY ARE CONCENTRATING ON SWALLOWING EVERYTHING OF THE SIZE AND COLOR, AND WHICH BEHAVES IN GENERALLY THE SAME WAY AS, THE HATCHING INSECT. THEY ARE THEREFORE NOT NEARLY AS CAUTIOUS AND SO YOU CAN MAKE A CLOSER APPROACH (THOUGH YOU SHOULD STILL BE STEALTHFULL IN THIS APPROACH).

THE THREE GENERAL PATTERNS OF **EMERGENCE BEHAVIOR:**

1) THERE ARE THOSE SPECIES WHICH CRAWL ASHORE OR UP SOMETHING WHICH STICKS ABOVE THE SURFACE. THEY MOLT OUT OF THE FISH'S REACH AND FLY OFF. WHEN FISHING SUCH A HATCH YOU'RE STUCK WITH THE OLD "DEAD DRIFTING", THOUGH A WING CASE ON THE FLY WOULD NOW BE APPROPRIATE. YOUR ADVANTAGE IS THAT THERE ARE PROBABLY A LOT MORE FISH AND THEY ARE BEING RATHER CARELESS.

2) SOME RISE TO THE SURFACE FILM AND BREAK OUT OF THE EXOSKELETON (MOLT) IN OR JUST BENEATH IT. HERE THE "RISING METHOD" CAN BE EFFECTIVE (THIS WILL BE DESCRIBED ON THE NEXT PAGE), BUT YOU HAVE THE ALTERNATIVE OF DEAD DRIFTING A NYMPH IMITATION JUST BELOW THE SURFACE FILM. FOR THIS YOU NEED AN UNWEIGHTED FLY AND SHOULD APPLY FLY FLOATANT TO THE LEADER AND TIPPET DOWN TO ABOUT 8 INCHES ABOVE THE LURE.

3) FINALLY THERE ARE THOSE WHICH RISE TO THE SURFACE MOLTING SOMEWHERE ALONG THE WAY. THAT WHICH FINISHES THE ASSENT AND CLIMBS OUT ONTO THE SURFACE FILM IS AN ADULT, THOUGH ITS WINGS ARE ONLY PARTLY UNFOLDED (IT'S CALLED AN "EMERGER", ILLUSTRATED BELOW. SUGGESTIONS FOR FISHING EMERGERS FOLLOW SHORTLY).

UNFORTUNATELY

(YOU KNEW THAT WAS COMING, DIDN'T YOU?)
THERE ARE MANY SPECIES WHICH EMPLOY SOME VARIATION OF THE ABOVE RATHER SIMPLIFIED EMERGENCE PATTERNS.

STUNTED WING ↘

EMERGER

TAKE THE *GREEN DRAKE* (THE ONE THAT HATCHES IN EARLY SEASON ON NORTH FORK), THIS ONE BEGINS BY CRAWLING TOWARD SHORE, BUT WHEN CALMER, AND USUALLY SHALLOWER WATER IS REACHED, THE MIGRATION ENDS. (DURING THIS PHASE YOU COULD FISH AN IMITATION "DEAD DRIFT".) NOW IT ASCENDS TO THE SURFACE MOLTING THE EXOSKELETON ON THE WAY. (HERE, IF WATER CONDITIONS ALLOW, THE "RISING METHOD" MIGHT WORK.) BY THE TIME IT REACHES THE SURFACE IT'S A "DUN" (FIRST STAGE MAYFLY ADULT) BUT ITS WINGS AREN'T FULLY EXTENDED, INSTEAD THEY'RE FOLDED OVER THE BACK AND LESS THAN HALF THEIR ACTUAL LENGTH. (YOU CAN IMITATE THIS WITH AN "EMERGER" PATTERN FISHED NOT TOO FAR BELOW THE SURFACE.) FINALLY THEY CRAWL OUT ON THE SURFACE FILM, EXTEND THEIR WINGS, WAIT FOR THEM TO DRY AND TAKE FLIGHT.

THEN THERE'S THE *RED QUILL*, THE IMPORTANT LATE SEASON HATCH ON NORTH FORK. THE QUILLS BEGIN MOVING TO CALMER AND SHALLOWER WATER AS THEY APPROACH MATURITY, THERE IS NO REAL MIGRATION. WHEN THE HATCH STARTS THEY CLIMB UP SOMETHING UNTIL THEY'RE ABOVE THE WATER TO MOLT. HOWEVER SOME WILL MOLT A FEW INCHES BELOW THE SURFACE. THESE THEN LET GO AND RISE THE FEW INCHES TO THE TOP AS "EMERGERS". SO YOU CAN FISH SUCH PATTERNS, THOUGH HERE THEY ARE BEST FISHED JUST UNDER THE SURFACE FILM. IT IS ONLY A FEW SECONDS BEFORE THEY CLIMB OUT, DRY THEIR WINGS AND FLY OFF.

THE **RISING METHOD** IS USED TO SIMULATE THE NYMPH'S BEHAVIOR DURING THAT BRIEF BUT CRITICAL TIME WHEN THEY ASCEND FROM STREAM BOTTOM TO THE SURFACE (EMERGENCE).
USE A WEIGHTED NYMPH (PREFERABLY WITH WINGCASE) OR WET FLY WHICH "MATCHES THE HATCH", A LEADER/TIPPET AT LEAST THREE TIMES AS LONG AS THE DEPTH OF THE WATER, FLOATING FLY LINE AND <u>NO</u> SINKERS.
YOU WILL BE FISHING DOWN STREAM SO MIND YOUR STEALTH!
THE PROCEDURE IS SIMPLE, JUST WADE OUT TO A POSITION DIRECTLY UP CURRENT OF THE LINE ALONG WHICH THE FLY IS TO DRIFT AND PLACE THE FLY IN THE WATER DOWN STREAM. HOLD THE LINE UNTIL THE LEADER STRAIGHTENS OUT BELOW AND THEN POINT THE ROD TIP DOWN AT THE FLY. NOW BEGIN TO STRIP LINE FROM THE REEL AND FEED IT THROUGH THE ROD GUIDES. WHEN THE END OF THE FLOATING LINE IS AS FAR UPSTREAM OF THE POINT WHERE YOU WANT THE FLY TO RISE AS THE LEADER AND TIPPET ARE LONG, STOP THE LINE (POINT **A** IN THE ILLUSTRATION) AND HOLD IT THERE. NOW YOU WAIT BECAUSE THE FLY IS MAKING ITS WAY DOWN FROM WELL UPSTREAM (IT'S AT POINT **B**). IT WILL BE TRAILING SO FAR BEHIND NOT ONLY BECAUSE THE CURRENT IS SLOWER DOWN THERE BUT MORE SO BECAUSE IT'S DRAGGING AND TUMBLING ALONG THE BOTTOM (THE DASHED LINE BETWEEN **B** AND **C** IS MEANT TO ILLUSTRATE ITS TORTURED COURSE). WHEN THE FLY GETS DOWN STREAM FAR ENOUGH THAT THE LEADER/TIPPET STRAIGHTENS (POINT **C**) THE CURRENT WILL FORCE IT TO THE SURFACE (AT **D**). IT IS DURING THIS **"RISE"** THAT YOU EXPECT THE ACTION.

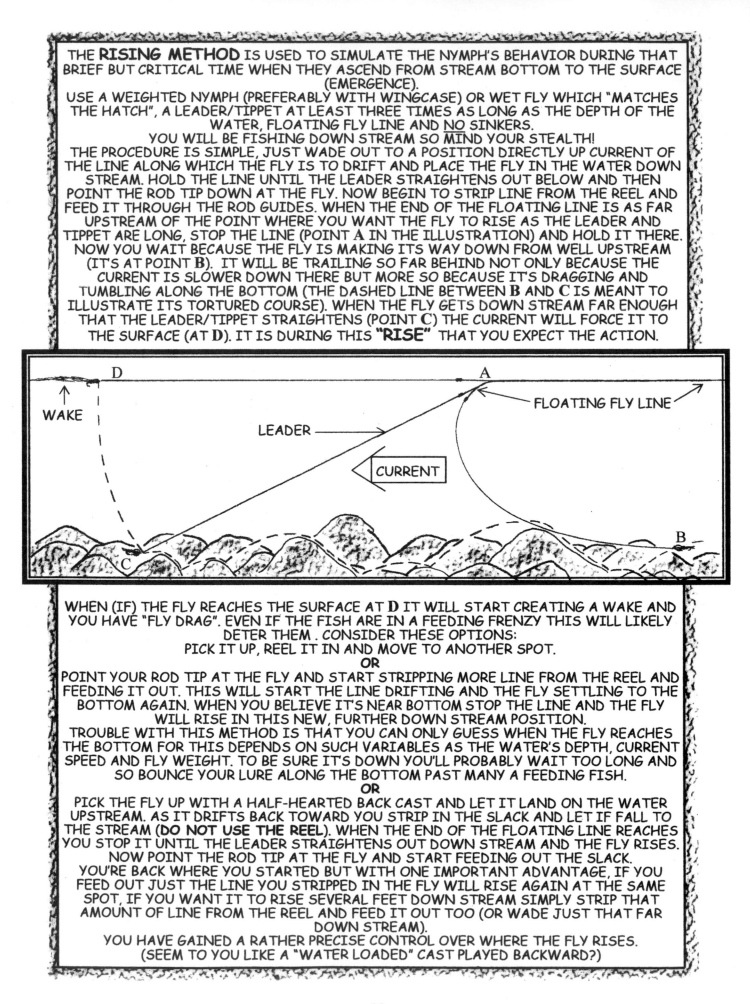

WHEN (IF) THE FLY REACHES THE SURFACE AT **D** IT WILL START CREATING A WAKE AND YOU HAVE "FLY DRAG". EVEN IF THE FISH ARE IN A FEEDING FRENZY THIS WILL LIKELY DETER THEM. CONSIDER THESE OPTIONS:
PICK IT UP, REEL IT IN AND MOVE TO ANOTHER SPOT.
OR
POINT YOUR ROD TIP AT THE FLY AND START STRIPPING MORE LINE FROM THE REEL AND FEEDING IT OUT. THIS WILL START THE LINE DRIFTING AND THE FLY SETTLING TO THE BOTTOM AGAIN. WHEN YOU BELIEVE IT'S NEAR BOTTOM STOP THE LINE AND THE FLY WILL RISE IN THIS NEW, FURTHER DOWN STREAM POSITION.
TROUBLE WITH THIS METHOD IS THAT YOU CAN ONLY GUESS WHEN THE FLY REACHES THE BOTTOM FOR THIS DEPENDS ON SUCH VARIABLES AS THE WATER'S DEPTH, CURRENT SPEED AND FLY WEIGHT. TO BE SURE IT'S DOWN YOU'LL PROBABLY WAIT TOO LONG AND SO BOUNCE YOUR LURE ALONG THE BOTTOM PAST MANY A FEEDING FISH.
OR
PICK THE FLY UP WITH A HALF-HEARTED BACK CAST AND LET IT LAND ON THE WATER UPSTREAM. AS IT DRIFTS BACK TOWARD YOU STRIP IN THE SLACK AND LET IF FALL TO THE STREAM (**DO NOT USE THE REEL**). WHEN THE END OF THE FLOATING LINE REACHES YOU STOP IT UNTIL THE LEADER STRAIGHTENS OUT DOWN STREAM AND THE FLY RISES.
NOW POINT THE ROD TIP AT THE FLY AND START FEEDING OUT THE SLACK.
YOU'RE BACK WHERE YOU STARTED BUT WITH ONE IMPORTANT ADVANTAGE, IF YOU FEED OUT JUST THE LINE YOU STRIPPED IN THE FLY WILL RISE AGAIN AT THE SAME SPOT, IF YOU WANT IT TO RISE SEVERAL FEET DOWN STREAM SIMPLY STRIP THAT AMOUNT OF LINE FROM THE REEL AND FEED IT OUT TOO (OR WADE JUST THAT FAR DOWN STREAM).
YOU HAVE GAINED A RATHER PRECISE CONTROL OVER WHERE THE FLY RISES.
(SEEM TO YOU LIKE A "WATER LOADED" CAST PLAYED BACKWARD?)

FISHING AN **EMERGENCE** WITH **DRY FLIES** : DURING THE "EMERGENCE" PHASE OF A HATCH MOST SPECIES RISE TO THE TOP AND CLIMB OUT ON THE SURFACE FILM. WHENEVER THIS IS THE CASE YOU CAN FISH AN IMITATION OF THE ADULT FLY DRY. REMEMBER YOU MUST "MATCH THE HATCH", SAME SIZE AND COLOR AT LEAST. BUT THERE IS THE QUESTION OF HOW LONG THE BUG WILL REMAIN ON THE WATER. AS ALWAYS, THIS VARIES WITH SPECIES.
THE BAETIS, FOR EXAMPLE, WILL MOLT IN THE SURFACE FILM AND THEN BE AIR BORN ALMOST IMMEDIATELY. HERE, WHILE AN "EMERGER" PATTERN MIGHT BE BEST, A DRY (DUN) WILL SOMETIMES WORK.
THE RED QUILL, THAT IS THOSE THAT DON'T CRAWL UP OUT OF THE WATER BEFORE MOLTING, WILL REMAIN ON THE SURFACE LONGER (A FEW SECONDS), MAKING A DRY FLY A BETTER BET BY FAR.
BUT THE GREEN DRAKE IS A DRY FLY FISHER'S DREAM. THEY TAKE QUITE A FEW SECONDS TO DRY THEIR WINGS AND SO MAY FLOAT SOME DISTANCE.

NOTE: HAFELE AND HUGHES, IN THE COMPLETE BOOK OF WESTERN HATCHES, TELL OF FISHING A GREEN DRAKE EMERGENCE USING IMITATIONS OF DUNS THEY HAD FOUND IN THE BUSHES. THEY WEREN'T WORKING. THEN THEY MANAGED TO CATCH A DUN WHICH HAD JUST EMERGED AND FOUND THAT ITS BODY WAS QUITE A BIT LIGHTER IN COLOR. WHEN THEY TRIED AN IMITATION OF THAT COLOR THEY BEGAN CATCHING FISH. UNDERSTAND THAT THE BUGS IN THE BUSH WERE THE SAME SPECIES, AND STILL DUNS, BUT WITHIN AN HOUR OR TWO THEIR COLOR HAD CHANGED ENOUGH THAT THE FISH REFUSED IT.
STILL WONDER WHY SOME FLY FISHERS ARE A BIT SNOBBISH? (PLEASE BELIEVE THAT THIS IS NOT TRUE OF YOUR AUTHOR, I PREFER TO ADOPT AN AIR OF SAD EYED AND SILENT CONDESCENSION.)

WE CAN COVER THE REST OF WHAT NEEDS TO BE SAID ABOUT TECHNIQUE BY **"WADING" THROUGH** A FISHING EPISODE. I WILL ENDEAVOR TO MINIMIZE REPEATING WHAT HAS PREVIOUSLY BEEN SAID, BUT THEN, THAT'S WHAT I SAID LAST TIME. FIRST, ***DON'T SELECT YOUR FLY IN CAMP***, WAIT UNTIL YOU'RE AT STREAM SIDE AND HAVE HAD A CHANCE TO LOOK THINGS OVER. TROUBLE IS, WHEN YOU GET THERE YOU MAY DECIDE YOU SHOULD USE SOMETHING ELSE, BUT IT'S TOO MUCH TROUBLE TO MAKE THE CHANGE, AND BESIDES, IT WILL COST YOU A COUPLE INCHES OF TIPPET. SO YOU STICK WITH WHAT YOU TIED ON AND, ASSUMING YOUR NEW JUDGMENT WAS CORRECT, YOU BEGIN AT A DISADVANTAGE. IN ADDITION, YOU'LL LEARN MORE QUICKLY IF YOU TRUST THESE STREAM SIDE CONCLUSIONS, BASED ON CAREFUL OBSERVATION, AND THEN TEST THEM.

I FEAR, MY DEAR, WE BEST FORE**GO** THE FORE**PLAY**

IF YOU'RE FAR ENOUGH FROM THE STREAM TO HAVE A VISTA, DO YOU SEE SMALL **BIRDS** (IN MY EXPERIENCE BARN SWALLOWS OR NIGHTHAWKS) DIVING, REELING, SOARING JUST TO DIVE AGAIN? AS IF TRYING TO RECREATE THE *BATTLE OF BRITAIN*? AND ALL OF THIS IN A RATHER CONFINED AREA JUST ABOVE THE STREAM? THIS ALMOST CERTAINLY MEANS THAT THERE ARE MAYFLIES MATING AND THE BIRDS ARE PICKING THEM OUT OF THE AIR. THE SURVIVING FEMALES WILL BE DIPPING TO THE WATER TO LAY THEIR EGGS (IF THAT IS THE MANNER OF THEIR SPECIES) AND IF YOU CAN COME UP WITH A FLY TO MATCH THEM YOU SHOULD HAVE VERY GOOD FISHING.

EVEN WHEN AT SOME DISTANCE FROM THE STREAM YOU SHOULD BEGIN LOOKING FOR INSECTS, PARTICULARLY **GRASSHOPPERS**. THESE THINGS COVER A LOT OF TERRITORY AND THEIR FLYING LEAPS OFTEN TERMINATE IN THE WATER WHERE THEY JERK AROUND FUTILELY TRYING TO GET AIRBORNE AGAIN ("TWITCHES" ARE RECOMMENDED WHEN IMITATING GRASSHOPPERS). IF THEY'RE AROUND TRY TO DETERMINE THE RIGHT SIZE AND COLOR (USUALLY TAN OR YELLOW). YOU MIGHT CHOOSE TO START FISHING WITH AN IMITATION OF SOMETHING ELSE, BUT BEAR THE HOPPERS IN MIND IF ALL ELSE FAILS.

AS YOU NEAR THE STREAM WATCH FOR THE AQUATIC BUGS (MAY, CADDIS AND STONEFLIES). WHEN AT STREAM SIDE ARE THERE SIGNS OF **SURFACE FEEDING?** IF SO, CAN YOU TELL WHAT THE FISH ARE TAKING?
THE ABSENCE OF SURFACE FEEDING DOESN'T MEAN THAT DRY FLIES WON'T WORK, THOUGH IT DOESN'T BODE TOO WELL FOR THEM. STILL, IF YOU'RE SET ON IT, TRY ONE. THEN TOO, WHAT ABOUT **ANTS** CRAWLING OUT ON THE BRANCHES OVER THE WATER?

NOW, AFTER YOU'VE LOOKED IT ALL OVER, IS THE TIME TO DECIDE WHAT TO TIE ON.

THE TAKE

WE'LL ASSUME THAT YOU'VE TIED ON A DRY FLY, IDENTIFIED WHAT LOOKS LIKE GOOD HOLDING WATER AND PLACED YOU'RE OFFERING DELICATELY ON THE WATER ABOUT SIX FEET UPSTREAM THEREOF **(WATCHING YOUR BACKSIDE AS YOU CAST)**. AS THE FLY FLOATS DOWN YOU'RE STRIPPING IN LINE TO KEEP OUT EXCESS SLACK, "MENDING" IF NECESSARY AND, ABOVE ALL, **KEEPING YOUR EYE ON THE FLY!** (IF YOU LOSE SIGHT OF THE THING YOU'LL BE AT A CONSIDERABLE DISADVANTAGE.) YET DESPITE YOUR DILIGENCE, EVEN YOUR CERTAINTY THAT YOU DIDN'T LOSE IT, STILL THE FLY'S GONE AND THERE IS NOTHING THERE BUT AN EXPANDING CIRCLE OF RIPPLES, AS IF SOMEONE HAD TOSSED IN A PEBBLE,

SET THE HOOK!!

WHEN A FISH TAKES A BUG ON THE SURFACE IT IS USUALLY DONE IN THIS WAY:

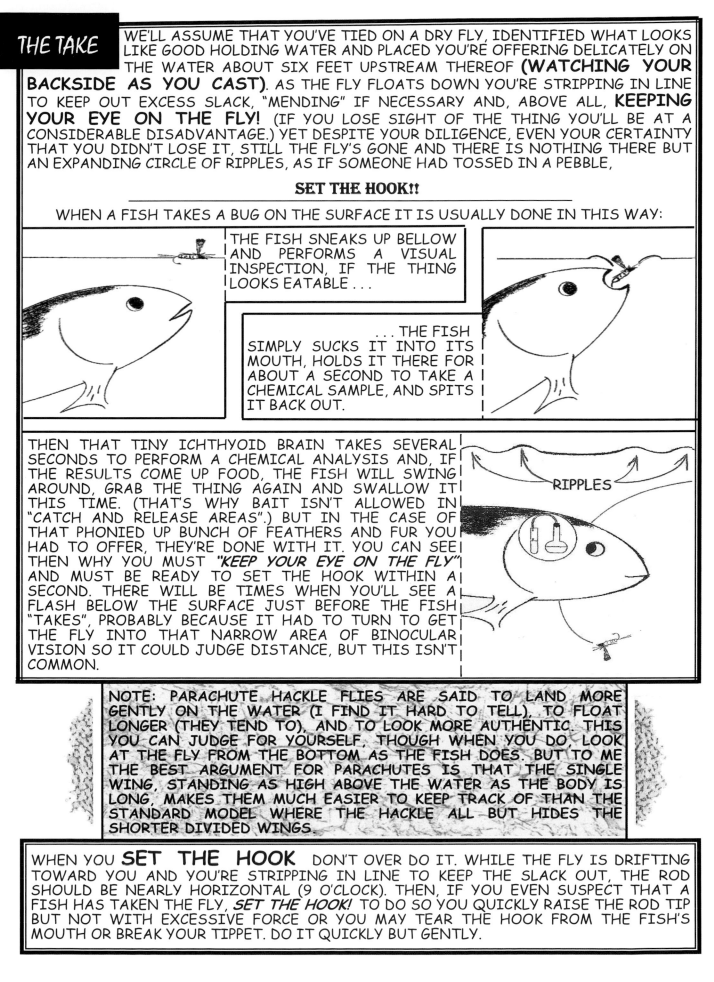

THE FISH SNEAKS UP BELLOW AND PERFORMS A VISUAL INSPECTION, IF THE THING LOOKS EATABLE . . .

. . . THE FISH SIMPLY SUCKS IT INTO ITS MOUTH, HOLDS IT THERE FOR ABOUT A SECOND TO TAKE A CHEMICAL SAMPLE, AND SPITS IT BACK OUT.

THEN THAT TINY ICHTHYOID BRAIN TAKES SEVERAL SECONDS TO PERFORM A CHEMICAL ANALYSIS AND, IF THE RESULTS COME UP FOOD, THE FISH WILL SWING AROUND, GRAB THE THING AGAIN AND SWALLOW IT THIS TIME. (THAT'S WHY BAIT ISN'T ALLOWED IN "CATCH AND RELEASE AREAS".) BUT IN THE CASE OF THAT PHONIED UP BUNCH OF FEATHERS AND FUR YOU HAD TO OFFER, THEY'RE DONE WITH IT. YOU CAN SEE THEN WHY YOU MUST *"KEEP YOUR EYE ON THE FLY"* AND MUST BE READY TO SET THE HOOK WITHIN A SECOND. THERE WILL BE TIMES WHEN YOU'LL SEE A FLASH BELOW THE SURFACE JUST BEFORE THE FISH "TAKES", PROBABLY BECAUSE IT HAD TO TURN TO GET THE FLY INTO THAT NARROW AREA OF BINOCULAR VISION SO IT COULD JUDGE DISTANCE, BUT THIS ISN'T COMMON.

RIPPLES

NOTE: PARACHUTE HACKLE FLIES ARE SAID TO LAND MORE GENTLY ON THE WATER (I FIND IT HARD TO TELL), TO FLOAT LONGER (THEY TEND TO), AND TO LOOK MORE AUTHENTIC. THIS YOU CAN JUDGE FOR YOURSELF, THOUGH WHEN YOU DO, LOOK AT THE FLY FROM THE BOTTOM AS THE FISH DOES. BUT TO ME THE BEST ARGUMENT FOR PARACHUTES IS THAT THE SINGLE WING, STANDING AS HIGH ABOVE THE WATER AS THE BODY IS LONG, MAKES THEM MUCH EASIER TO KEEP TRACK OF THAN THE STANDARD MODEL WHERE THE HACKLE ALL BUT HIDES THE SHORTER DIVIDED WINGS.

WHEN YOU **SET THE HOOK** DON'T OVER DO IT. WHILE THE FLY IS DRIFTING TOWARD YOU AND YOU'RE STRIPPING IN LINE TO KEEP THE SLACK OUT, THE ROD SHOULD BE NEARLY HORIZONTAL (9 O'CLOCK). THEN, IF YOU EVEN SUSPECT THAT A FISH HAS TAKEN THE FLY, *SET THE HOOK!* TO DO SO YOU QUICKLY RAISE THE ROD TIP BUT NOT WITH EXCESSIVE FORCE OR YOU MAY TEAR THE HOOK FROM THE FISH'S MOUTH OR BREAK YOUR TIPPET. DO IT QUICKLY BUT GENTLY.

"PLAYING" A FISH: ONCE THE HOOK IS SET THINGS BECOME HECTIC. OFTEN YOU'LL FIND THAT THE FIRST THING THE FISH DOES IS TO CHARGE YOU, AND DO SO MOST ENERGETICALLY. AT THIS POINT YOUR PROBLEM IS TO (ATTEMPT TO) KEEP THE SLACK OUT OF THE LINE, SO YOU STRIP IT IN AS FAST AS POSSIBLE, PROBABLY PULLING THE ROD TIP STRAIGHT UP OVER YOUR HEAD WITH ARMS EXTENDED AND SOMETIMES EVEN GOING UP ON YOUR TOES. THIS ONLY GOES ON FOR A FEW SECONDS, BUT THEY'RE LONG ONES.

FACT IS THE FISH NEVER INTENDED TO COME YOUR WAY, BUT WHEN YOU SET THE HOOK YOU JERKED ITS HEAD IN YOUR DIRECTION AND A FISH CAN ONLY SWIM THE WAY HE'S POINTED. HE'LL SOON CATCH ON AND WILL THEN MAKE AN IMPRESSIVE EFFORT TO RECTIFY THE ERROR. AT THIS POINT YOUR NEW MANTRA IS:

"DON'T BUST YOUR TIPPET".

YOU'LL PROBABLY HAVE TO GIVE THE FISH SOME LINE, BUT MAKE HIM WORK FOR IT. JUST RELAX THAT RIGHT INDEX FINGER AND LET THE LINE BE PULLED THROUGH, THOUGH JUST ENOUGH TO PROTECT THE TIPPET.

NEXT PROBLEM IS THE CURRENT, IF THE FISH HEADS DOWN STREAM THE FORCE OF THAT CURRENT WILL ADD TO HIS STRENGTH, PUTTING A POTENTIALLY OVERWHELMING STRAIN ON THAT WISPY LITTLE STRAND OF MONOFILAMENT. THEN THERE ARE THINGS LIKE ROOTS EXPOSED BY EROSION, BRANCHES DANGLING IN THE WATER, ALL KINDS OF STUFF THE FISH CAN GET YOUR LINE TANGLED AROUND.

THE TRICK HERE IS TO **"TURN"** HIM AWAY FROM SUCH THINGS. THIS IS DONE BY POINTING THE ROD TOWARD THE FISH (THOUGH YOU KEEP THE TIP UP) AND THEN SWEEPING THE ROD IN A WIDE ARCH IN THE DIRECTION YOU WANT THE FISH TO GO. YOU'RE NOT DRAGGING HIM AROUND BUT SIMPLY POINTING HIS NOSE TOWARD SAFER WATER, HE CAN ONLY FOLLOW THAT NOSE..

I FORGET, HOW DO YOU TIE A SURGEON'S KNOT?

(UNFORTUNATELY THIS IS ONE OF THOSE THINGS THAT JUST SOUNDS EASY.)

DURING THE EARLY PART OF THIS STRUGGLE YOU SHOULD NOT USE THE REEL, YOU HAVE BETTER CONTROL WHEN STRIPPING. HOWEVER, WHEN THE FISH IS IN CLOSE ENOUGH TO LAND IT COULD BECOME ENTANGLED IN ALL THAT FLY LINE ON THE WATER, SO WHEN YOU THINK YOU HAVE ADEQUATE CONTROL REEL THE STUFF IN.

NOTE: ACCORDING TO THE ICHTHYOLOGISTS, WHEN A FISH IS INVOLVED IN A LIFE OR DEATH STRUGGLE TOXIC CHEMICALS BUILD UP IN ITS SYSTEM WHICH MAY RESULT IN ITS DEATH SOON AFTER RELEASE. THE LONGER THE BUSINESS OF LANDING THE THING TAKES, THE GREATER THE CHANCE THAT IT WILL NOT SURVIVE. SO PLEASE DON'T PLAY AROUND WHEN YOU'RE "PLAYING" A FISH

THROUGHOUT ALL OF THIS YOU NEED THE FLEXIBILITY OF THE ROD, WHEN THE FISH VEERS YOUR WAY THE ROD STRAIGHTENS TO TAKE UP THE SLACK, WHEN THE FISH LUNGES AWAY IT BENDS TO PROTECT YOUR TIPPET, SO KEEP IT WELL ELEVATED.

AND THEN YOU MUST **"LAND"** THE LITTLE BEAST. YOU CAN, OF COURSE, **"BEACH"** IT, THAT IS DRAG IT ASHORE, ASSUMING THAT YOU'RE CLOSE TO SHORE AND THERE IS A SUITABLE PATCH OF DRY LAND. BUT THIS YOU SHOULD *NOT* DO IF YOU PLAN TO RELEASE IT. FISH EVOLVED IN AN AQUATIC ENVIRONMENT WHERE THERE IS AN EVEN PRESSURE ON THEIR BODIES ALL AROUND, SO NATURE HAS NOT EQUIPPED THEM WITH THE MUCH STRONGER RIB CAGE FOUND IN TERRESTRIAL ANIMALS. WHEN THEY FLOP AROUND ON THE BEACH THEY ARE DAMAGING VITAL ORGANS, SO PLEASE DON'T "BEACH" THEM UNLESS YOU PLAN TO KEEP THEM.

THE PREFERRED METHOD IS TO **"NET"** THEM. TO DO SO YOU SHOULD BE STANDING IN AT LEAST A FOOT OF WATER, THOUGH IT WOULD BE BETTER IF YOU WADE IN A BIT DEEPER SO THAT YOU DON'T HAVE TO BEND OVER AS FAR. THE PRIMARY PROBLEM IN NETTING IS THAT EVERY TIME YOU GET THE FISH CLOSE TO THE NET IT FINDS SOME RESERVE OF ENERGY AND CHARGES AWAY. THIS YOU PREVENT BY BOTH OVERWHELMING AND OVERPOWERING YOUR VICTIM. FIRST GET THE FISH IN CLOSE ENOUGH THAT YOU WON'T HAVE TO STRIP OR REEL IN ANYMORE LINE FOR , OF COURSE, YOUR LEFT HAND WILL BE OTHERWISE OCCUPIED. THEN GRIP THE NET IN YOUR LEFT HAND AND EXTEND IT OUT IN FRONT DOWN NEAR WATER LEVEL. NEXT, WHEN HE IS NEAR THE SURFACE, BEGIN PULLING THE FISH IN BY RAISING THE ROD UP AND OVER YOUR HEAD. YOU SHOULD KEEP THE FISH UP AND PLOWING THROUGH THE SURFACE FILM SO THAT HE IS LESS CAPABLE OF MAKING ANY EVASIVE MANEUVER AND MOVING QUICKLY ENOUGH THAT HE HAS NO CHANCE TO CONSIDER HIS PREDICAMENT. BECAUSE THE NET IS IN YOUR LEFT HAND THE ROD MUST BE CROSSED TO THAT SIDE CAUSING THE ROD TIP TO PASS OVER YOUR LEFT SHOULDER. WHEN THE FISH NEARS THE NET DIP IT INTO THE WATER, DRAW THE FISH OVER IT AND THEN RAISE IT QUICKLY. I MUST EMPHASIZE THAT ALL OF THIS IS DONE IN ONE EXPEDITIOUS FLOW OF MOVEMENTS, ANY HESITATION AFTER YOU BEGIN AND YOU MAY HAVE TO BEGIN AGAIN.

A WICKED WITCH CAST A SPELL ON ME, FOR A KISS YOU COULD HAVE YOUR VERY OWN PRINCESS

DID I FORGET TO MENTION THAT IT'S A CATCH AND RELEASE AREA ? SEE YOU AROUND CHUMP

BEFORE YOU **REMOVE** THE **HOOK** FROM THE FISH'S MOUTH PULL A LITTLE BIT OF SLACK FROM THE REEL, FOR IF THE LINE IS TAUT AND THE HOOK COMES FREE BEFORE YOU GET A PROPER GRIP ON THE FLY, YOU COULD FIND THE THING STUCK IN YOUR THUMB OR FINGER.
(SHOULD THIS HAPPEN YOU'LL BE POINTEDLY MADE AWARE OF ANOTHER ARGUMENT FOR BARBLESS HOOKS.)
FOR THE UNINITIATED I SHOULD ADD THAT TROUT HAVE NO TEETH, JUST A ROUGHNESS THAT FEELS LIKE 80 GRIT SAND PAPER ON THE UPPER AND LOWER LIP. THEY CANNOT BITE SO THE ONLY THING THAT MIGHT DRAW BLOOD IN THIS OPERATION IS YOUR HOOK,
KEEP YOUR MIND ON THAT.

IF YOU WISH TO **RELEASE** THE **FISH** YOU SHOULD FIRST WET YOUR HAND AND THEN CRADLE THE ANIMAL AS ILLUSTRATED—**_DO NOT SQUEEZE_ !**
OBVIOUSLY WHEN HOLDING IT LIKE THIS YOU HAVE NO GRIP, SO IF IT MOVES YOU'LL LIKELY LOSE IT,
BUT THAT'S THE IDEA ANYWAY.
ACTUALLY THE FISH USUALLY SEEM TO BE EXHAUSTED AND STUNNED AT THIS POINT AND WILL BE SO DOCILE THAT THE REAL CONCERN IS FOR THEIR SURVIVAL.
WHEN YOU HAVE THE FISH CRADLED LOWER IT INTO THE WATER WITH THE HEAD POINTED INTO THE CURRENT SO THAT WATER FLOWS INTO ITS MOUTH, ACROSS THE GILLER MEMBRANES AND OUT THROUGH THE GILLS (ARTIFICIAL RESPIRATION). USUALLY IN LESS THAN FIVE SECONDS, RARELY MORE THAN TEN, THE FISH WILL SWIM NORMALLY OUT OF YOUR HAND.
ALL OF THIS CAN BE DONE WITHOUT REMOVING THE FISH FROM THE NET IF YOU SIMPLY HOLD IT FROM OUTSIDE THE NET AND GET ITS HEAD POINTED OUT THE OPENING.

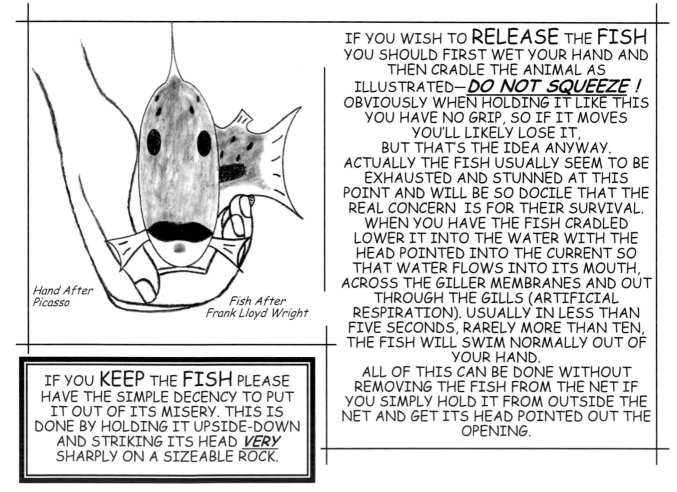

Hand After Picasso

Fish After Frank Lloyd Wright

IF YOU **KEEP** THE **FISH** PLEASE HAVE THE SIMPLE DECENCY TO PUT IT OUT OF ITS MISERY. THIS IS DONE BY HOLDING IT UPSIDE-DOWN AND STRIKING ITS HEAD _VERY_ SHARPLY ON A SIZEABLE ROCK.

CLEANING TROUT

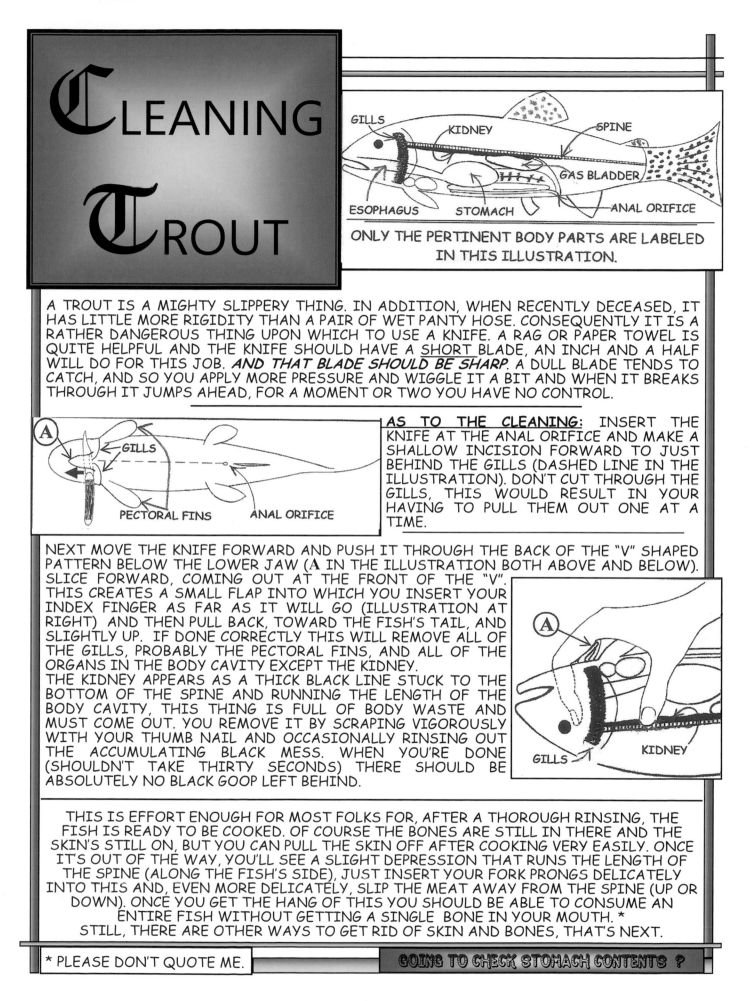

GILLS
KIDNEY
SPINE
GAS BLADDER
ESOPHAGUS
STOMACH
ANAL ORIFICE

ONLY THE PERTINENT BODY PARTS ARE LABELED IN THIS ILLUSTRATION.

A TROUT IS A MIGHTY SLIPPERY THING. IN ADDITION, WHEN RECENTLY DECEASED, IT HAS LITTLE MORE RIGIDITY THAN A PAIR OF WET PANTY HOSE. CONSEQUENTLY IT IS A RATHER DANGEROUS THING UPON WHICH TO USE A KNIFE. A RAG OR PAPER TOWEL IS QUITE HELPFUL AND THE KNIFE SHOULD HAVE A <u>SHORT</u> BLADE, AN INCH AND A HALF WILL DO FOR THIS JOB. *AND THAT BLADE SHOULD BE SHARP.* A DULL BLADE TENDS TO CATCH, AND SO YOU APPLY MORE PRESSURE AND WIGGLE IT A BIT AND WHEN IT BREAKS THROUGH IT JUMPS AHEAD, FOR A MOMENT OR TWO YOU HAVE NO CONTROL.

A
GILLS
PECTORAL FINS
ANAL ORIFICE

AS TO THE CLEANING: INSERT THE KNIFE AT THE ANAL ORIFICE AND MAKE A SHALLOW INCISION FORWARD TO JUST BEHIND THE GILLS (DASHED LINE IN THE ILLUSTRATION). DON'T CUT THROUGH THE GILLS, THIS WOULD RESULT IN YOUR HAVING TO PULL THEM OUT ONE AT A TIME.

NEXT MOVE THE KNIFE FORWARD AND PUSH IT THROUGH THE BACK OF THE "V" SHAPED PATTERN BELOW THE LOWER JAW (**A** IN THE ILLUSTRATION BOTH ABOVE AND BELOW). SLICE FORWARD, COMING OUT AT THE FRONT OF THE "V". THIS CREATES A SMALL FLAP INTO WHICH YOU INSERT YOUR INDEX FINGER AS FAR AS IT WILL GO (ILLUSTRATION AT RIGHT) AND THEN PULL BACK, TOWARD THE FISH'S TAIL, AND SLIGHTLY UP. IF DONE CORRECTLY THIS WILL REMOVE ALL OF THE GILLS, PROBABLY THE PECTORAL FINS, AND ALL OF THE ORGANS IN THE BODY CAVITY EXCEPT THE KIDNEY.
THE KIDNEY APPEARS AS A THICK BLACK LINE STUCK TO THE BOTTOM OF THE SPINE AND RUNNING THE LENGTH OF THE BODY CAVITY, THIS THING IS FULL OF BODY WASTE AND MUST COME OUT. YOU REMOVE IT BY SCRAPING VIGOROUSLY WITH YOUR THUMB NAIL AND OCCASIONALLY RINSING OUT THE ACCUMULATING BLACK MESS. WHEN YOU'RE DONE (SHOULDN'T TAKE THIRTY SECONDS) THERE SHOULD BE ABSOLUTELY NO BLACK GOOP LEFT BEHIND.

A
GILLS
KIDNEY

THIS IS EFFORT ENOUGH FOR MOST FOLKS FOR, AFTER A THOROUGH RINSING, THE FISH IS READY TO BE COOKED. OF COURSE THE BONES ARE STILL IN THERE AND THE SKIN'S STILL ON, BUT YOU CAN PULL THE SKIN OFF AFTER COOKING VERY EASILY. ONCE IT'S OUT OF THE WAY, YOU'LL SEE A SLIGHT DEPRESSION THAT RUNS THE LENGTH OF THE SPINE (ALONG THE FISH'S SIDE), JUST INSERT YOUR FORK PRONGS DELICATELY INTO THIS AND, EVEN MORE DELICATELY, SLIP THE MEAT AWAY FROM THE SPINE (UP OR DOWN). ONCE YOU GET THE HANG OF THIS YOU SHOULD BE ABLE TO CONSUME AN ENTIRE FISH WITHOUT GETTING A SINGLE BONE IN YOUR MOUTH. *
STILL, THERE ARE OTHER WAYS TO GET RID OF SKIN AND BONES, THAT'S NEXT.

* PLEASE DON'T QUOTE ME.

GOING TO CHECK STOMACH CONTENTS ?

SKINNING:
THERE ARE THOSE WHO EAT THE SKIN, SCALES AND ALL, FOR DESPITE THEIR BEING ALMOST INVISIBLE, THE SCALES ARE THERE. IN FACT, BECAUSE THEY'RE SO SMALL, THERE ARE A LOT MORE OF THEM. THESE YOU CAN REMOVE, ALONG WITH THE SKIN, AS FOLLOWS:

1. FIRST CLEAN (EVISCERATE) THE FISH AS DESCRIBED ON THE PRIOR PAGE.
2. NEXT REMOVE ALL OF THE FINS (YOU MAY LEAVE THE TAIL). THIS CAN BE DONE WITH A POCKET KNIFE, BUT IS MORE SAFELY AND EASILY ACCOMPLISHED WITH A PAIR OF DIKES.
   (IF YOU'VE COMPLETELY REMOVED THE FIN THERE WILL BE A LITTLE WHITE AREA WHERE THE MEAT SHOWS THROUGH THE FISH'S SKIN.)
3. YOU THEN TURN THE HEAD OVER THE BACK TO POSITION **A**, AS SHOWN HERE. DO NOT TEAR THE HEAD FREE, BUT YOU WILL SNAP THE SPINE AS YOU ROTATE IT.

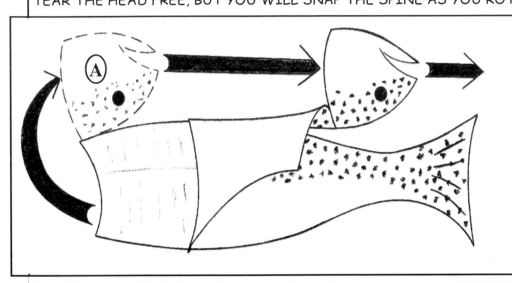

4. NOW GRIP THE FISH'S BODY AFT OF THE CENTER WITH THE LEFT HAND (A RAG OR PAPER TOWEL IS VERY USEFUL HERE) AND PULL THE HEAD STRAIGHT BACK WITH THE RIGHT. THE SKIN WILL PEAL OFF AS YOU PULL. WHEN IT GETS BACK TO YOUR LEFT HAND MOVE SAID FORWARD, GRIP THE EXPOSED MEAT AND THEN CONTINUE PULLING THE HEAD BACK UNTIL THE SKIN SEPARATES FROM THE FISH AT THE TAIL.

YOU WILL SOMETIMES FIND THAT THE MEAT STICKS TO THE SKIN AND PULLS OFF IN LITTLE CHUNKS AND STRIPS. THIS IS BECAUSE IT HAS BECOME TOO WARM AND SO HAS SOFTENED. IF IT'S A WARM DAY AND THE FISH HAVE BEEN OUT OF THE WATER FOR A WHILE I WOULD SUGGEST THAT YOU CLEAN THEM, PUT THEM BACK ON THE STRINGER, THEN DUNK THEM BACK IN THE STREAM FOR A SHORT TIME. IN MY EXPERIENCE THE WATER TEMPERATURES UP IN THE MOUNTAINS WILL FIRM THE MEAT BACK UP IN ABOUT HALF AN HOUR (MAYBE LONGER, MAYBE NOT AT ALL IN LATE SUMMER).

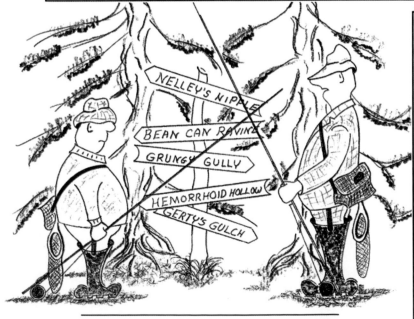

I LIKE IT BETTER WHEN THEY USE INDIAN NAMES, LEAST YOU DON'T KNOW WHAT THEY MEAN

NOTE: MANY STATES REQUIRE THAT YOU DISPOSE OF THE FISH'S ENTRAILS IN A TRASH RECEPTACLE, THOUGH IN SOME YOU'RE ALLOWED TO THROW THEM IN THE STREAM. HOWEVER, WHERE THIS IS PERMITTED, YOU'RE SUPPOSED TO PUNCTURE THE "GAS BLADDER". THIS ORGAN (WHICH IS LABELED IN THE FIRST ILLUSTRATION IN THIS CHAPTER) ENABLES THE FISH TO ADJUST ITS BUOYANCY SO THAT IT CAN REMAIN EFFORTLESSLY AT THE DEPTH IT CHOOSES. IF THE BLADDER IS GASSED UP THE WASTE YOU THROW IN THE CREEK WILL FLOAT, IF YOU PUNCTURE THE THING THE VISCERA WILL SINK AS IT SHOULD.

FILLETING:

TO KNOW JUST A BIT ABOUT THE FISH'S SKELETAL STRUCTURE IS HELPFUL IN THIS UNDERTAKING. WHILE IT IS SIMPLE ENOUGH THAT EVEN I CAN ILLUSTRATE IT, I HAVE STILL TAKEN LIBERTIES. REALLY IT IS ONLY IN THIS, THAT THE FISH ACTUALLY HAS JUST MORE THAN TWICE AS MANY OF EACH TYPE OF BONE AS I HAVE BOTHERED TO PORTRAY. AND ONE OTHER THING, NOT BEING AN ICHTHYORTHOPEDIST*, I'VE NAMED A COUPLE THINGS HERE MYSELF. FORGIVE ME.

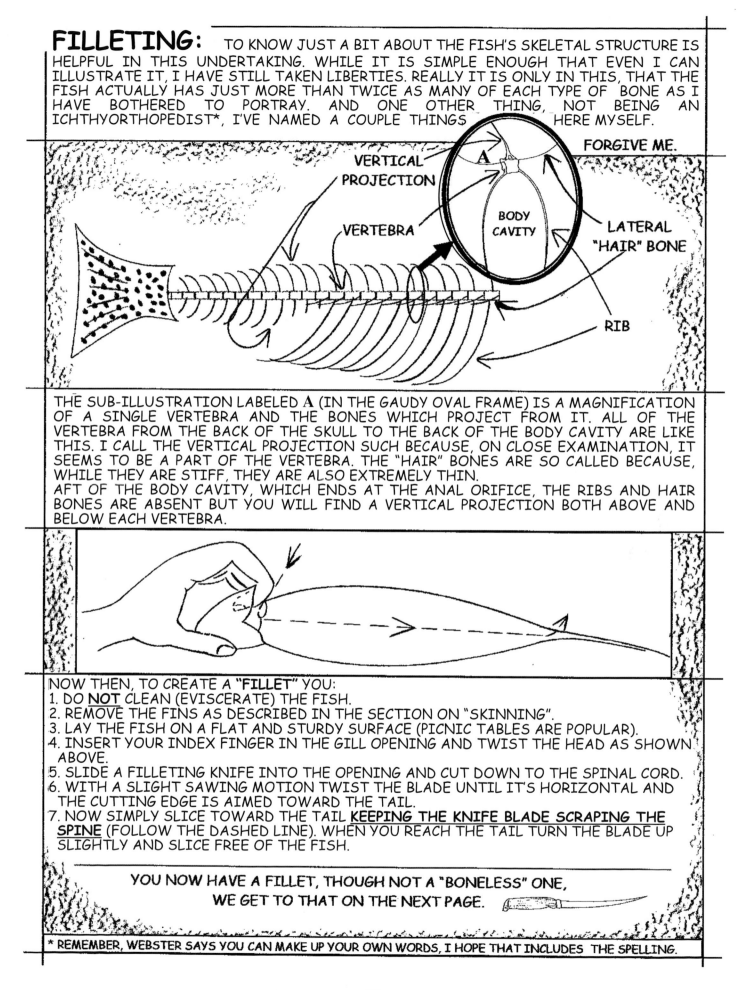

THE SUB-ILLUSTRATION LABELED **A** (IN THE GAUDY OVAL FRAME) IS A MAGNIFICATION OF A SINGLE VERTEBRA AND THE BONES WHICH PROJECT FROM IT. ALL OF THE VERTEBRA FROM THE BACK OF THE SKULL TO THE BACK OF THE BODY CAVITY ARE LIKE THIS. I CALL THE VERTICAL PROJECTION SUCH BECAUSE, ON CLOSE EXAMINATION, IT SEEMS TO BE A PART OF THE VERTEBRA. THE "HAIR" BONES ARE SO CALLED BECAUSE, WHILE THEY ARE STIFF, THEY ARE ALSO EXTREMELY THIN.
AFT OF THE BODY CAVITY, WHICH ENDS AT THE ANAL ORIFICE, THE RIBS AND HAIR BONES ARE ABSENT BUT YOU WILL FIND A VERTICAL PROJECTION BOTH ABOVE AND BELOW EACH VERTEBRA.

NOW THEN, TO CREATE A "FILLET" YOU:
1. DO **NOT** CLEAN (EVISCERATE) THE FISH.
2. REMOVE THE FINS AS DESCRIBED IN THE SECTION ON "SKINNING".
3. LAY THE FISH ON A FLAT AND STURDY SURFACE (PICNIC TABLES ARE POPULAR).
4. INSERT YOUR INDEX FINGER IN THE GILL OPENING AND TWIST THE HEAD AS SHOWN ABOVE.
5. SLIDE A FILLETING KNIFE INTO THE OPENING AND CUT DOWN TO THE SPINAL CORD.
6. WITH A SLIGHT SAWING MOTION TWIST THE BLADE UNTIL IT'S HORIZONTAL AND THE CUTTING EDGE IS AIMED TOWARD THE TAIL.
7. NOW SIMPLY SLICE TOWARD THE TAIL **KEEPING THE KNIFE BLADE SCRAPING THE SPINE** (FOLLOW THE DASHED LINE). WHEN YOU REACH THE TAIL TURN THE BLADE UP SLIGHTLY AND SLICE FREE OF THE FISH.

YOU NOW HAVE A FILLET, THOUGH NOT A "BONELESS" ONE,
WE GET TO THAT ON THE NEXT PAGE.

* REMEMBER, WEBSTER SAYS YOU CAN MAKE UP YOUR OWN WORDS, I HOPE THAT INCLUDES THE SPELLING.

BONING A FILLET:

WHEN YOU SLICED THE MEAT FROM THE FISH BY RUNNING THE KNIFE RIGHT ALONG THE SPINE YOU CUT THROUGH THE RIBS AND "HAIR" BONES, SO THEY ARE NOW PART OF THE FILLET.

TO GET RID OF THE RIBS:

1. FIRST RINSE THE MEAT THOROUGHLY AND THEN TURN IT OVER (INSIDE UP), YOU'LL FIND THE RIBS RIGHT ON THE SURFACE IN THE LOWER FRONT QUADRANT (SEE ILLUSTRATION).

2. NEXT YOU SIMPLY SLICE THROUGH JUST BARELY BELOW THE RIB BONES (OBVIOUSLY THE FURTHER BELOW YOU CUT THE MORE MEAT YOU'LL WASTE).

3. **BUT DO NOT HOLD THE RIBS AS DRAWN HERE, WITH YOUR FINGER AND THUMB IN FRONT OF THE KNIFE** ! INSTEAD HOLD THE FILLET BEHIND (TO THE RIGHT IN THIS ILLUSTRATION) THE RIBS AND BEGIN THE CUT, WHEN THE KNIFE IS FAR ENOUGH UNDER THAT YOU CAN PINCH THE LAST RIB FROM BEHIND THE BLADE, DO SO AND CONTINUE THE OPERATION. ALL OF THE RIBS SHOULD COME FREE AS A UNIT BECAUSE THEY WILL BE CONNECTED BY MEAT AND TISSUE.

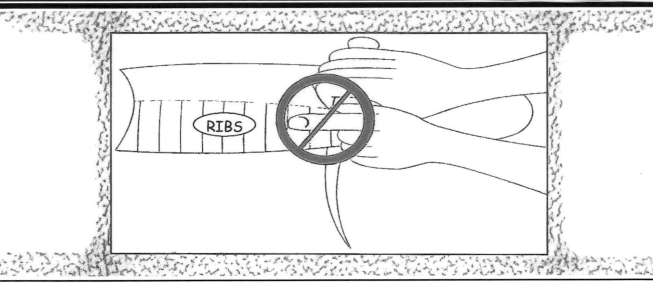

HAVING COMPLETED THE ABOVE YOUR FILLET IS FREE OF THE RIBS, BUT THOSE THINGS I CALLED THE "HAIR" BONES ARE STILL IN THERE. IF YOU RUN YOUR FINGERS ALONG THE LINE WHERE THE SPINE WAS YOU CAN FEEL THEIR TIPS. THERE IS NO PRACTICAL WAY TO GET THESE OUT (THERE ARE ABOUT THIRTY OF THEM) BUT, AS IT HAPPENS, NO NEED EITHER. IF YOU THOROUGHLY COOK THE FISH THEY APPARENTLY SIMPLY DISSOLVE, OR AT LEAST BECOME SO SOFT THAT YOU CAN'T DISTINGUISH THEM FROM THE MEAT
(RECALL THAT THEY ARE EXTREMELY THIN, THOUGH QUITE STIFF, BEFORE COOKING).

AND HOW CAN YOU COMPLAIN ABOUT WINDING UP WITH A CALCIUM FORTIFIED "BONELESS" FILLET?

THE BIG PROBLEM WITH THIS METHOD OF PREPARATION IS THE LOSS OF MEAT. IT'S THE SPINE THAT CAUSES THE DIFFICULTY. YOU REMOVE A FILLET FROM BOTH SIDES, BUT YOU CAN'T CUT IN 'ROUND THE SPINE.
IF YOU PRESS DOWN ON THE FISH'S SIDE YOU SOMEWHAT FLATTEN ITS SHAPE AND LOSE LESS MEAT WHEN YOU CUT, BUT THIS IS DANGEROUS AND CERTAINLY NOT RECOMMENDED UNLESS YOU WEAR SOMETHING TO PROTECT YOUR LEFT HAND. FORTUNATELY THERE ARE FILLETING GLOVES MADE OF METAL LIKE "KEVLAR" WHICH, ACCORDING TO ONE MANUFACTURER, "RESISTS EVEN THE SHARPEST EDGES" (I WISH THEY'D USE A MORE ENCOURAGING WORD THAN RESISTS).

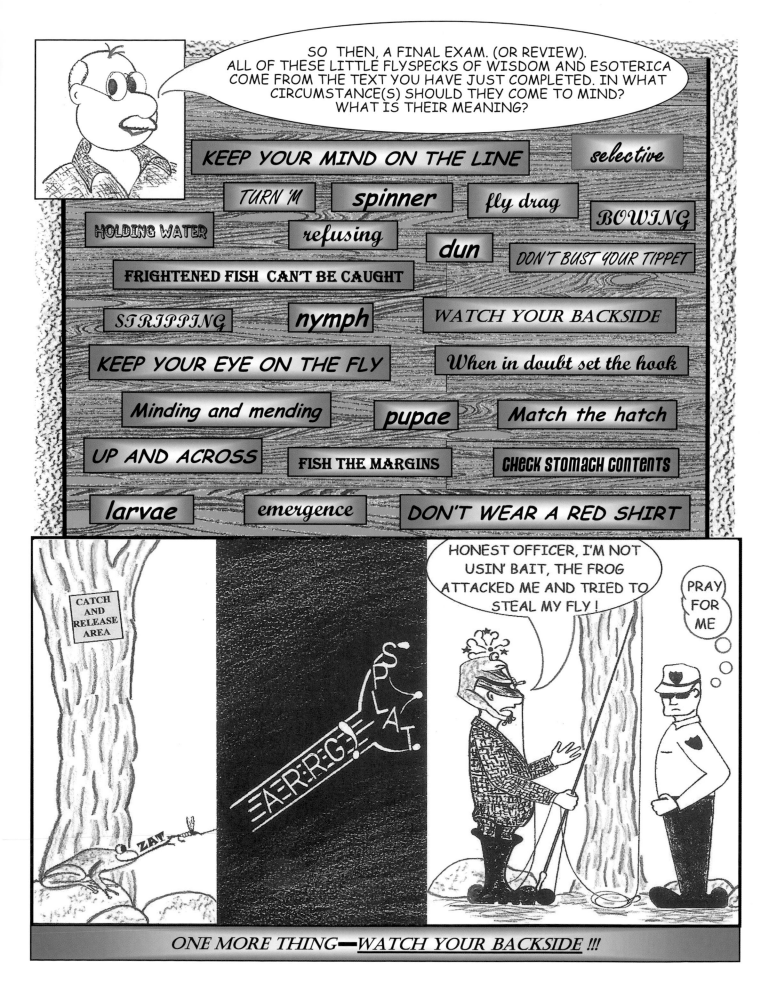

ABOUT MR. RAHTZ

AS AN ARMY BRAT, MIKE GREW UP EVERYWHERE—FROM THE ISLAND OF GUAM TO FALLS CHURCH, VA. HE NEVER LIVED AT THE SAME ADDRESS FOR MORE THAN A YEAR UNTIL HE WAS IN HIGH SCHOOL.

AFTER SCHOOL HE JOINED THE AIR FORCE, GOT A RATHER GOOD JOB FOR SOMEONE YOUNG AND SINGLE, A LOADMASTER (THAT'S A CREW MEMBER ON A CARGO PLANE), AND THE TRAVELLING REALLY STARTED. MIKE'S BEEN FROM KUALA LUMPUR TO VENICE TO FAIRBANKS (HE WAS THERE ONCE WHEN IT WAS 75° BELOW ZERO, INCLUDING THE CHILL FACTOR). A FREQUENT STOP WAS ONE OF THE LAST ICE-BOUND ROCKS IN THE ALEUTIAN ISLANDS (IT WAS A RADAR STATION AND THEY HELPED TO SUPPLY IT). HE SPENT HIS LAST YEAR IN THE SERVICE IN VIETNAM, INTERESTING JOB FLYING AROUND IN A CARGO PLANE IN A COMBAT ZONE. THEY CAN SHOOT AT YOU, YOU CAN'T SHOOT BACK.

ONCE OUT OF THE SERVICE MIKE BECAME A FLIGHT INSTRUCTOR, EVEN AN INSTRUMENT INSTRUCTOR, BUT THERE WAS NO FUTURE IN THAT SO HE WENT BACK TO COLLEGE AND COMPLETED A MASTER'S DEGREE IN PSYCHOLOGY.

HE THEN SET TO WORK DOING "HUMAN FACTORS" RESEARCH, THAT WENT WELL UNTIL THEY MADE HIM THE BOSS. AFTER HALF A DOZEN YEARS OF IT MIKE QUIT AND STARTED TRAVELLING AGAIN. HE'S BEEN AT THAT FOR MORE THAN 20 YEARS NOW, WITH OVER A QUARTER MILLION MILES TOURING ON MOTORCYCLES.

WASN'T IT MARK TWAIN WHO SAID, "YOU CAN NEVER GO HOME"? EVEN IF HE COULD, HE'D NEVER FIND IT.